D1163740

2.50

Pearlman Memorial Library
Central Bible College
Springfield, Missouri

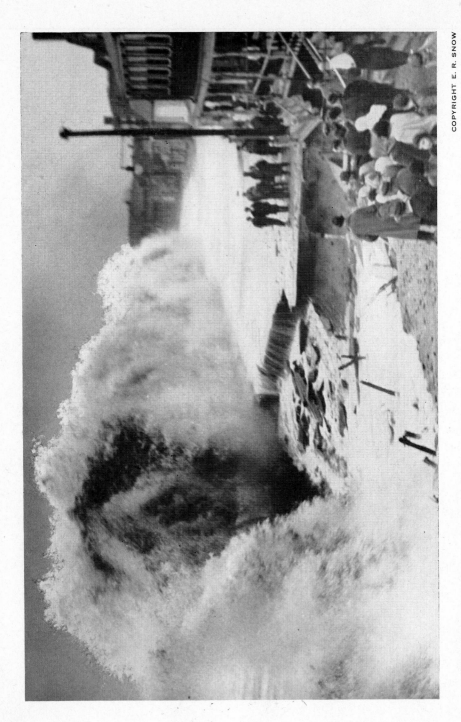

COPYRIGHT E. R. SNOW

RECORD BREAKING WAVES CRASHING AGAINST THE WINTHROP SEA-WALL NOVEMBER 22, 1944

GREAT STORMS

AND

FAMOUS SHIPWRECKS

OF THE

NEW ENGLAND COAST

BY

EDWARD ROWE SNOW

AUTHOR OF

*The Islands of Boston Harbor; The Story of Minot's Light;
Castle Island; Historic Fort Warren;
Sailing Down Boston Bay*

❦

25728

THE YANKEE PUBLISHING COMPANY

72 BROAD STREET

BOSTON, MASSACHUSETTS

Pearlman Memorial Library
Central Bible College
Springfield, Missouri

Copyright, 1943
By Edward Rowe Snow

—————

No part of this book may be used or quoted without the written permission of the author.

SECOND EDITION
DECEMBER 1944

BOSTON PRINTING COMPANY
BOSTON, MASSACHUSETTS

PRINTED IN THE UNITED STATES OF AMERICA

IN MEMORY OF

ANN FARLEY JOHNSON

WHO LOVED THE OCEAN IN ALL ITS MOODS

PREFACE

THIS volume on storms and shipwrecks would never have been finished if it were not for the faithful and untiring work which my wife, Anna-Myrle, so willingly carried out. She has proved a bulwark against which the vicissitudes of constant personal trials and discouragements have stormed in vain. My mother, Alice Rowe Snow, has also given unselfishly of her time and energy.

Dr. Robert Earle Moody has been of vital assistance from time to time, his expert knowledge of Maine history proving of great value. Carlo Vacca has made outstanding contributions with chosen bits from the literary store at his command. The practical suggestions of Nathan R. Krock guided the writer across several uncharted seas. I am grateful to those who helped in former years, Edwin T. Ramsdell and Dino Valz.

There are probably some whose help was of importance whose names are not recorded here, but I have tried to be faithful in my acknowledgements. In addition to those included in the text, I am grateful to the following:

William Alcott, William Sumner Appleton, Dorothy Blanchard, James L. Bruce, Clarence S. Brigham, John Joseph Collins, Madeleine Connors, Elizabeth Darling, W. Sidney Davey, Mrs. Joost De Haan, Thomas Harrison Eames, the late Alfred Ela, Elsie Eastman, Edward Felton, Dr. William Flynn, Kathleen S. Fuller, Laura Gibbs, Julia B. Gullage, Raymond Hanson, George J. Hanton, Francis

F. Haskell, Frank O. Hilt, Theodore Hebert, Cornelius F. Hurley, Marie J. Hession, Marion Haskell, the late William C. Ham, M. C. M. Hatch, Vern J. Haegg, Channing Howard, Vincent Holmes, Mary Hodgess, Paul George Lambert, Fred Lindsey, Honor McCusker, Thomas Jay Manning, Eleanor Gregory Metcalf, Charles Roscoe Magee, Alba Mann, Sherwood Mowry, Harold Orne, Liam O'Sullivan, John O'Connell, John M. Richardson, John C. Poland, John Rosenthal, Joseph W. Sears, John R. Smith, Irwin Smith, Philip J. Smith, Annabel Snow, Donald Burnham Snow, Edward Donald Snow, the late Edward Sumpter Snow, Eunice T. Snow, John I. Snow, Robert A. Snow, Willis Snow, Winthrop J. Snow, William U. Swan, Harriet Swift, Ruth B. Swift, John Sylvia, James S. Thomas, Ernest D. Sproul, Benjamin E. Stewart, William P. Sawyer, Sarah E. Walsh, John G. Weld, and Dorothy G. Wayman.

Generous assistance was furnished by the following institutions: The Bostonian Society, the Boston Public Library, the Marine Museum, the Massachusetts Historical Society, the United States Coast Guard, the Society for the Preservation of New England Antiquities, the Massachusetts Archives, the Suffolk Court House, the Boston Marine Society, the Harvard College Library, the Boston Athenaeum, the Peabody Museum and Essex Institute, both of Salem, the National Archives, and the American Antiquarian Society.

I shall not forget the kindness of those who assisted me.

E. R. S.

Winthrop, Mass.
December 7, 1943.

TABLE OF CONTENTS

ILLUSTRATIONS

INTRODUCTION

WHEN wintry gales are stirring up the mighty Atlantic until the surf thunders with awe-inspiring fury upon the New England shores, when white, biting flakes of a violent blizzard hit in from the northeast in ever increasing tempo to make you realize that a great storm is in the making, or when driving sleet rattles against the windows with such ferocity that the strongest mansion shudders and creaks from the efforts of the tempest, I offer you this volume.

After settling back in your easy chair, with a roaring blaze crackling and sparkling in the fire-place at your side, you can feel that nature reigns supreme, and that man is indeed a puny being in contrast. With your thoughts in proper perspective, then is the time to peruse the pages of this book.

The volume contains the story of the constant struggle between man and the elements, nature against what civilization has built to oppose her. And here in New England is a proving ground of all efforts to conquer the storms and gales as they sweep in from the sea, for northeastern United States gets far more than its share. So crowded are the archives of New England history with tales of not hundreds, but thousands of shipwrecks that I know some of you will look in vain for a wreck which you in particular recall. It was physically impossible to include every storm or wreck of interest, but all the important disasters form a part of this volume.

There is an average of three outstanding storms a

year. About every five years, according to my research which includes from 1630 to 1942, there is what might be called a "snorter," while each quarter century has its terrific gale. Once a century a storm of gigantic proportions sweeps across the New England area, leaving death and desolation in its wake.

The book follows either a chronological or geographical pattern with two exceptions, the *Somerset* and the *Portland* Gale. In addition to the major storms and wrecks, which are arranged chronologically, there are others which are grouped together by geographical or state classifications.

Slightly under 9200 wrecks and over 650 storms were examined as to their importance; only a relatively few had the outstanding characteristics to allow inclusion. In spite of the research work I realize that many shipwrecks have eluded my notice, but if they are important enough to be included in a future edition, you must let me know about them.

As the volume nears completion, Byron's lines about the ocean come to mind:

Ten thousand fleets sweep over thee in vain;
  Man marks the earth with ruin—his control
Stops with the shore.

"The reading of a storm is not so bad as the feeling of it."

COTTON MATHER

THE STORY OF THE SOMERSET

DURING the height of the American Revolution a powerful enemy warship was caught in that graveyard of shipping, the Peaked Hill Bars, and wrecked on the white sands of Cape Cod. The complete account of what happened to the ship, its supplies, and crew form an intriguing part of American history. Paul Revere, as well as Lord Byron's uncle, and Henry Wadsworth Longfellow are connected one way or another with the tale, which includes the ship's capture by an enterprising Provincetown blacksmith and a 120-mile hike of the prisoners from Cape Cod to Boston. Although many Cape Cod narrators mention the shipwreck, the entire account of the *Somerset* has never been told as a separate story.

The huge British 64-gun man-of-war *Somerset* was launched at Chatham, England, on July 18, 1746, as a guard ship of the British fleet. Not until after the Boston Tea Party were conditions in North America considered serious enough for the Earl of Dartmouth to take action. Writing from England on October 17, 1774, to Governor Gage in Boston, Dartmouth told the governor that he had ordered three guard ships to proceed to Boston with British marines, under command of the noted Major Pitcairn. The names of the vessels were the *Asia*, the *Boyne*, and the *Somerset*.[1]

The frigate *Somerset* sailed by Boston Light December 19, 1774, and headed for the inner harbor. Commanded by Captain George Ourry, with more than 500 sailors and marines aboard and her guns plainly visible to the onlookers ashore, the great battleship presented itself as a formidable opponent to scions of liberty. Four years later she was defeated by a greater antagonist—the sea.

The following spring the *Somerset* dropped anchor between Boston and Charlestown. In the evening of April 18, 1775, an alert watcher from the ship could have detected two signal lamps flashing their warning messages from the Old North Church. On the Boston shore three men[2] climbed into a skiff and started across the harbor. Their leader was Paul Revere, on his way to warn the patriots that the British were planning to march to Lexington and Concord. Revere was apprehensive lest the guard on the *Somerset* should halt them as they rowed by, but he escaped by five minutes the restraining order which reached the *Somerset* from shore. Years later Revere wrote of the incident as follows:

"Two friends rowed me across Charles
River, a little to the eastward where the *Somerset*
man-of-war lay. It was then young flood, the
ship was winding, & the moon was Rising."

In his well-known poem about Paul Revere's ride, the poet Henry Wadsworth Longfellow also mentions the British frigate *Somerset:*

Then he said, "Good night!" and with muffled roar
Silently rowed to the Charlestown shore,
Just as the moon rose over the bay,
Where swinging wide at her moorings lay
The Somerset, British man-of-war;
A phantom ship, with each mast and spar
Across the moon like a prison bar,
And a huge black hulk, that was magnified
By its own reflection in the tide.

Paul Revere went on to arouse the Middlesex farmers until he was captured between Lexington and Concord. The *Somerset* lay in Boston Harbor until May 28, when during the battle of Chelsea Creek the *Somerset* kept up a continuous fire on the Americans defending the Chelsea shore.[3]

The *Somerset* also played an important role at Bunker Hill. During the peaceful hours in the early morning of June 17, 1775, the sentry on the deck heard the rattle of picks and shovels coming from the nearby Charlestown shore. With the arrival of dawn Captain Ourry noticed there were breastworks thrown up on Breed's Hill and weighed anchor at once, maneuvering for a position to command Charlestown Neck.

The *Somerset's* captain watched the two unsuccessful attempts upon Breed's Hill by the British soldiers. His men assisted Clinton's reinforcements by rowing them over in the *Somerset's* longboats in time for the third and successful assault on what the British called Bunker Hill. Thus the *Somerset* and Captain Ourry had a vital part in the eventual British victory in the Battle of Bunker Hill.

After the battle, the *Somerset* remained near Boston for some months, later receiving orders to report back to England. By the spring of 1777 the frigate was again off the New England coast, capturing and sinking many American privateers and supply ships.

On Friday, May 30, 1777, the frigate *Boston* was cruising near the Banks when she sighted an English convoy. She immediately gave chase, but fled the scene on falling in with a large English man-of-war, which Captain Hector McNeill of the *Boston* wrote down in his journal as the "Sumner Set of 64 guns."[4]

After keeping free of the *Somerset* for several days the *Boston* completely eluded the British warship one stormy night, forcing Captain Ourry to abandon his plans for the capture of the American frigate.

During these raids up and down the New England coast Captain Ourry found that Provincetown Harbor was admirably suited to his purposes, and he and his vessel were frequent visitors at the tip of the Cape. Helpless to offer resistance, the men of the Cape gradually grew to hate the tall spars and majestic sails of the British man-of-war as they spied the *Somerset* beating her way into the Cape's best harbor.

With the ladies it seems that a different story can be told. The girls of Provincetown were just as pretty and attractive then as they are now, and it was not long before many feminine hearts were made to beat faster when the *Somerset* came back into the harbor from a voyage. With several hundred of the sturdiest British marines and sailors aboard, perhaps it was only natural that the ladies of Provincetown responded to the admiration of the British navy.

With the men of Provincetown it was another matter, naturally. The marines and sailors were sent ashore on countless occasions to gather whatever supplies of eggs, butter, and meat they could obtain, and tradition suggests the only pay the people ever received was a sermon the ship's chaplain preached in Provincetown. During this period Captain Ourry, probably a pleasant Englishman, was pictured as a blackhearted pirate, whom the mothers of the Cape conveniently adopted as a symbol of what would happen to bad little boys and girls if they did not behave, threatening the youngsters with the appearance of the black-whiskered Captain Ourry.[5]

There is no reason to doubt that the British officers and men made considerable progress with the young Cape Cod girls, the war evidently causing little difference in the ardor of the courtship. For tangible evidence, E. A. Grozier, late editor of the *Boston Post,* is authority for the statement that the surgeon on a British ship, Dr. William Thayer, and Miss Lucy Rich of North Truro were married, with Dr. Thayer later leaving the British navy and becoming an American citizen. Descendants of this happy union are still living on Cape Cod.

But the days of the *Somerset* were numbered. One morning in the fall of 1778 reports came that the French fleet was near, headed for Boston, so all English sail quickly left the Provincetown Harbor in pursuit. There were around 550 men aboard the *Somerset* at this time.

When the fleet was at sea, on November 1, an easterly storm began to lash the entire coast with unusual fury. The *Somerset,* far out in the Bay, tried to make Provincetown Harbor, but the gale increased. Captain Ourry found himself caught in the dangerous triangle of the Highlands, Chatham, and Pollock Rip Shoals. Soon the dreaded stretches of the Peaked Hill Bars could be seen. Captain Ourry maneuvered the *Somerset* to escape, but the breaking waves of the great reef soon had the mighty frigate in their grasp. The treacherous currents swung her around until she was in the trough of the sea, the ship plunged her keel into the sands of the outer bar, and the sailing days of the *Somerset* were over.

Back in Provincetown the inhabitants had gathered on High Pole Hill. Jubilant or depressed, as the case may have been, the men and women of the Cape realized that the

Somerset was doomed. What a cry of satisfaction must have gone up from all except a few of the crowd on the hill when the *Somerset* struck the bar!

One of the men on the sand dune that day organized a small band of husky citizens to capture the crippled vessel should she come ashore. He was William Spenser, a young blacksmith, who took his force across the dunes to the beach, there establishing a watch over the shipwreck.[6] The tide was coming in and Spenser believed the ship would be delivered to him at high water.

Out on the doomed frigate, exciting events were taking place as spar after spar crashed down on the deck. Many men were soon lost overboard in the great billows which swept over the *Somerset*. Captain Ourry now ordered the abandonment of the ship. The first longboat was manned and launched. With about fifty men aboard, the journey of the longboat through the breakers began. But the surf-man's terror, a breaking wave with a giant crest, came riding toward the longboat, crashed into it, and engulfed the sailors. All were lost.

The tide was now coming in rapidly. Captain Ourry ordered every gun thrown through the ports, with all available merchandise put over the side to lighten the ship. Just before the tide reached its height a giant wave swept in, lifting the *Somerset* off the bar. Another and another followed, carrying the battleship toward shore. Blacksmith William Spenser and his men were waiting, however, and when the *Somerset* grated on the beach, he rushed down with his men and placed an armed guard around the ship. Two hours later the tide had receded enough to allow Spenser to go aboard with a small detail. He demanded the surrender of Captain Ourry.

Captain Ourry had already realized the impossible situation he was in. Perhaps to Spenser's surprise, he unbuckled his sword, surrendering it along with the *Somerset* to the Provincetown blacksmith. Spenser now organized the men of Cape Cod for the task of handling the British prisoners. Of the marines and sailors on the *Somerset*, 480 had landed safely on the beach; probably from fifty to seventy perished in the surf. The beach was crowded with people, anxious to turn the tables on the Britishers who had visited them under slightly different circumstances a few days before. At low water the populace began to salvage articles of every description from the sea. An unbelievable amount of material actually was saved from the ocean, making the wreck of the *Somerset* one of the most valuable enterprises in Cape history.

Before long utter confusion reigned at the scene of the wreck. Men appeared on the beach from almost every hamlet and village within twenty-five miles, plunging at once into discussions and arguments as to the disposition of the rich spoils from the ship. But as Captain Ourry had surrendered to William Spenser, the Provincetown blacksmith decided to go up the coast to Plymouth and libel the vessel. Brigadier Joseph Otis, at home with his dying father, describes the events at the wreck as "very Riotous doings" and feared that "Wicked work" had been carried out. His letter[7] to the Council in Boston follows:

Barnstable November 4 1778

Kind Sir

I have just received express from the Commanding Officer of the Millitia Truro, informing Me that the Somersett a British Ship is Wreckt about four miles East of the Race, and bilged,

that they had gott out yesterday about 60 men
the Capts of the Ship and marriners included.
The Sea is running high they lost one boatload
of them. how many was alive aboard the wreck
they could not tell.

There was some American Prisoners aboard
who say they parted in the storm with 15 Sail of
the line bound for Boston. Have ordered an
officer from here to go down and assist the officers
below in conducting the prisoners along. Who
shall march without delay for Boston. But what
to do for bread for them I know not as there is
none to be had where they are and their own
being all wett. Any Orders from the Hon.
Councill. if my conduct is not approved of.
Please to tell me by word and they shall be
Pursued.

I send this by express whose bill I hope
will be paid which he will give in.

I am yr Honours Humble
Servt   Joseph Otis.

An immediate reply was sent to Brigadier Otis from
the Council in Boston. The Massachusetts Board of War
approved the actions of the brigadier, and only in the
matter of feeding the prisoners were the members unable
to find a solution. Their only comment[8] regarding food
borders on the classic:

"If you have not bread for the prisoners
let them live without as many better
men have done before them."

Before the message arrived much had happened.
Brigadier Otis had sent Major Hamblin and Colonel Hal-

lett to take charge of the goods at the wreck, but ran into
the organized band of blacksmith Spenser, who prevented
the officers from "Interfering with what was saved."

Spenser had told Colonel Doane of Wellfleet to take
charge in his absence while he went to Plymouth to libel
the *Somerset*. This action greatly upset Brigadier Otis,
who wrote the Council that "I have meet with nothing
more Chimerical," adding that Spenser was quite haughty
in his demeanor. "I look on him a poor being and his
abettors," were Otis's words.

The tremendous task of moving the 480 prisoners
began. The officers were allowed to sail to Boston, but the
450 men had to traverse the great wastes of the Cape land
on foot. This enormous, ragged horde, with little food and
in winter time, began their 120-mile journey from the tip
of Cape Cod to Boston. Several of the sailors, bruised and
bleeding from their encounter with the storm, were forced
to march along with the rest.

The 450 prisoners, together with their captors, started
their strange journey. One of the unwritten sagas of
Revolutionary history was the march of the 500 across the
sands of Cape Cod during the winter of 1778. Naturally,
they had to be fed. From the beginning of their walk
until they passed through the limits of Eastham they cost
the inhabitants a total of over two thousand dollars.[9]

After the outskirts of Sandwich had been passed the
residents of Cape Cod decided their part of the march was
over. Many of them left and returned to their homes. The
450 British marines and sailors now broke up into smaller
bands, some of them without guards. Apparently able to
choose their own destination, some of the *Somerset's* sailors
never reached Boston at all, appearing in Abington, Bridge-

water, and other nearby towns.

When the authorities heard what was happening, sheriffs were dispatched to round up as many of the prisoners as could be found. Most of the trouble developed after Plymouth had been left behind, so traffic sentinels for the prisoners were set up along the way to guide the men. By this time every Cape Cod man seems to have departed for home, with no other guards to take their place. Gradually the prisoners were found and collected into groups by the sheriffs, but it is not clear who led the bands into Boston town. We do know that special guards had to be placed near Boston Neck to round up the men when they arrived. Evidence points to the date of November 13 as the time when the majority finished their 120-mile journey. Probably half a hundred escaped before Boston was reached. The men were placed aboard the old French snow *Penet*.[10] This decrepit old hulk was admittedly unseaworthy, and proved a poor vessel for the quartering of prisoners.

One pitiful case was that of the purser, Edward Cyron. An old and tired man, he had been injured in the shipwreck. Forced to march on with the others, he collapsed on the road, where he lay several days, before the guard found him. Finally he reached Boston, and was confined with others aboard the *Penet*. On December 5 he petitioned for his release, signing his request in the feeble, quivering signature of a old man. By arrangement with Admiral Byron, uncle of the poet, Edward Cyron finally was released and sent to Rhode Island.[11]

Five vessels were needed to transport the entire cargo of the *Somerset* to Boston. Captain Hedge of the sloop *Sally* brought 16 cannon, mostly eighteen pounders, while the sloop *Cumberland* under Captain Rider landed 18 can-

non at Boston. Captain Ingraham's vessel made two trips
between the Cape and Boston loaded with cannon each trip.
On April 7, 1779, Colonel Paul Revere announced that he
had been able to mount several of the *Somerset's* guns on
platforms at Castle Island, and would soon have all of the
21 cannon which had been landed there in place.[12]

Returning to the officers who had been sailed across to
Boston, we find that it was suggested they be placed ashore
on Noddle's Island, where Henry H. Williams then lived.
Williams reminded the billeting officers that his houses had
been burned shortly before the battle of Chelsea Creek, the
same engagement in which the *Somerset* had shelled the
Chelsea shore. Samuel Sewall's old farm house on Hog
Island, now Orient Heights, was finally agreed upon as the
logical quarters for the officers of the British navy. After
a few weeks spent in Sewall's old residence, Captain Ourry
of the *Somerset* presented a petition[13] to the gentlemen of
the Massachusetts Council requesting his inclusion in an
exchange of officers. The letter follows:

State of Massachusetts Bay
Council Chambers
Jan. 28, 1779

Ordered that this Commissary of Prisoners
of War for this State be and he hereby is directed
to convey without loss of time from this State to
Providence in the State of Rhode Island Captain
Ourry and the other Officers late Belonging to the
Sommersett and there cause them to be sent to
Newport on Rhode Island first taking Captain
Ourry's Parole that he will cause Colonel Joseph
Ward now Prisoner at New York & Capt Burke
now on Parole here to be liberated and dis-

charged from Parole for his the said Ourry & one Lieutenant arriving there or to return himself and the other officers late belonging to the Somersett to be given in exchange for Officers of ours of equal rank . . . . And first causing the said Ourry & other Officers at Hog Island to settle their accounts which they have contracted since their captivity.

Attest—John Avery Deputy.

In a few days the exchange was agreed upon, and Captain Ourry left Hog Island for Providence, taking with him one of his lieutenants. A short time later a mate and thirteen sailors escaped from the prison snow *Penet*, presenting themselves to the captain of one of the American naval ships then in the harbor. After considerable discussion they were all admitted into the service of this country, and, as far as is known, never returned to England. The remaining officers and men were gradually exchanged in cartels landing them at Providence and Newport. Other events crowded into the Revolutionary picture, with the story of the *Somerset* fading into the background.

More than one hundred years after the wreck the bones of the British man-of-war pushed their huge bulk up through the sands of Cape Cod. Shortly after she was exposed, in the winter of 1885-1886, E. A. Grozier of the *Boston Post* visited the wreck on the beach. He found the *Somerset* in Dead Man's Hollow, often referred to as Aunt Sukie's Hollow. In the early months of 1941 the late Levi Kelly, veteran life saver, visited the scene where in 1886 he had last noticed the frigate. In the presence of First Class Boatswain's Mate Manuel Henrique the ancient life saver estimated that the massive hulk of the *Somerset* is about fifty to seventy-five yards east of the present location of the Halfway House of the Race Point Coast Guard beach patrol.[14]

When she was exposed in the year 1886 several fine photographs of her ancient timbers were made by Province-town cameramen. The writer has talked with four different men who believe that they know where the *Somerset* lies buried at the present time. Not one of them agrees on the location. It is no wonder, however, that confusion may exist as to the location of the British man-of-war. The sands of the Cape can shift a tremendous amount in one tide, and it is almost unbelieveable what a windstorm can do on a winter's night above the high tide mark. With these two forces at work together over a period of years, entire contours disappear and new identifications have to be made. Possibly an easterly gale in the next few years will again uncover this patriach among Cape Cod ship-wrecks, or she may lie undiscovered indefinitely. Perhaps it would be wisest in any case to let the bones of the mighty *Somerset* rest in the white sands which have shared her secret for so many years, for what more fitting end to the saga of the *Somerset* than that it should lie buried forever in its sandy grave on the great beach of Cape Cod?

THE 1635 TEMPEST

A MAJORITY of the readers will remember the great hurricane of 1938, but relatively few are aware that history tells of one of equal if not superior force which swept along the New England coast over three centuries ago, during the month of August 1635. There are not many sources to which we can refer in covering this epic storm of the days of the Pilgrims and Puritans, but those who did record their experiences in that terrific gale were exact in their statements and concise in their accounts.

Anthony Thacher, John Winthrop, William Bradford, and Richard Mather have all left references to the tempest in their writings, but there were countless others whose stories of that terrible August hurricane will never be known.

Thacher's Island itself is named because of the shipwreck of Anthony Thacher during that wild gale along the New England shores. It was on this island off Gloucester, Massachusetts, that the tiny pinnace, *Watch and Wait*, was hurled during the first great storm for which we have records. Shortly after the wreck, Thacher wrote to his brother, Peter, telling the complete story of this early shipping disaster. The pinnace, which ran regularly up and down the coast, was owned by Isaac Allerton,[1] and stopped at many settlements between Piscataqua and Boston. This was the vessel on which Thacher planned to take passage. Reverend John Avery and Anthony Thacher

were cousins, and had sworn "a league of perpetual friendship" which included an agreement never to foresake each
other.   Avery, formerly a preacher of Wiltshire, England,
came to Newbury in 1634.   The residents of Marblehead
were anxious that he assume leadership of their church,
so Avery made plans to move there with his family and
Anthony Thacher's household.[2]

The pinnace, *Watch and Wait*, on its trip down the
coast stopped at Ipswich, August 11, 1635, to pick up the
eleven members of the Avery family, the seven members
of the Thacher clan, and a William Eliot, "sometimes of
New Sarum."   Four mariners manned the boat.   After
proper religious observances, the pinnace was soon on the
high seas bound for Marblehead.   Nothing of importance
occurred until the night of August 14, when a gale hit the
vessel, ripping apart the sails.   The crew refused to go
aloft in the darkness of that August night, as the wind and
waves had created an angry sea, so the captain dropped
anchor until morning.

Before the sun came up, the tempest had increased
until it blew a veritable gale.   Thacher says that even the
Indians could not recall a fiercer blow than the storm
which caught the pinnace off Cape Ann.   Possibly it was
the worst hurricane in all New England history.   The
anchors on the *Watch and Wait* began to drag, then snapped
completely.   The horrified crew and passengers were helpless to act.   Anthony Thacher tells us[3] in his own words
what followed:

> "My cousin and I perceived our danger,
> solemnly recommended ourselves to God, the
> Lord both of earth and seas, expecting with
> every wave to be swallowed up and drenched in

the deeps. And as my cousin, his wife, and my
tender babes, sat comforting and cheering one
the other in the Lord against ghastly death, which
every moment stared us in the face, and sat
triumphing upon each one's forehead, we were
by the violence of the waves and fury of the
winds (by the Lord's permission) lifted up upon
a rock between two high rocks, yet all was one
rock, but it raged with the stroke which came
into the pinnace, so as we were presently up to
our middle in water as we sat. The waves came
furiously and violently over us, and against us;
but by reason of the rock's proportion could not
lift us off, but beat her all to pieces. Now look
with me upon our distress, and consider of my
misery, who beheld the ship broken, the water
in her, and violently overwhelming us, my goods
and provisions swimming in the seas, my friends
almost drowned, and mine own poor children so
untimely (if I may so term it without offense),
before my eyes drowned, and ready to be
swallowed up, and dashed to pieces against the
rocks by the merciless waves, and myself ready
to accompany them."

The captain resigned himself to the elements. The
foremast went by the boards, the mainmast snapped into
three pieces, and the pinnace began to break up. When
the waves smashed into the cabin, the children started to
cry frantically, while the older people knelt in prayer.
One of the sailors was washed overboard and then into
the cabin, striking against Thacher. Aroused by the im-
pact, Thacher looked out of the cabin to see trees on a

THE 1635 TEMPEST   37

nearby island. The captain, determined to find out what the land was, went out on deck, but never was seen again. The sailor who had hit Thacher went out, jumped into the water, and started to swim to land. He, too, was never seen again.

Commending themselves to the Lord, the two families awaited the end of their sufferings. The children wept silently now, as all seemed resigned to their fate, whatever it might be. Suddenly a gigantic wave, much higher than any other, struck the weakened craft, sweeping Thacher, his daughter Mary, his cousin Avery, and Avery's eldest son away. Anthony Thacher continues:

"All the rest that were in the bark were drowned by the merciless seas. We four by that wave were swept clean away from off the rock also into the sea; the Lord, in one instant of time, disposing of fifteen souls of us according to his good pleasure and will . . . God in his mercy caused me to fall by the stroke of the wave, flat on my face, for my face was toward the sea, insomuch that as I was sliding off the rock into the sea the Lord directed my toes into a joint in the rock's side, as also the tops of some of my fingers with my right hand, by means whereof, the waves leaving me, I remained so, having on the rock only my head above the water . . . I stood bolt upright as if I had stood upon my feet, but I felt no bottom, nor had any footing for to stand upon, but the waters."

Thacher grabbed at a fragment of the ship's mast, but missed it, and was washed along by the waves until he was beached on the island.[4] His wife, caught in some

of the wreckage, was also hurled up on the shore, and
they discovered each other, alone of all the passengers
and crew still alive. They thought of their five children,
now gone from them, and Thacher blamed himself for
taking them on the voyage. But Thacher tells us that
they soon made plans for the future, whatever it might
bring:

"I found a knapsack cast on the shore, in
which I had a steel, flint, and powderhorn. Going further I found a drowned goat, then I found
a hat, and my son William's coat, both of which
I put on. My wife found one of her petticoats,
which she put on. I found also two cheeses,
and some butter, driven ashore. . . . So taking a
piece of my wife's neckcloth which I dried in
the sun, I struck fire, and so dried and warmed
our wet bodies; and then skinned the goat, and
having found a small brass pot, we boiled some
of her. Our drink was brackish water; bread
we had none.

"There we remained until the Monday following; when, about three of the clock in the
afternoon, in a boat that came that way, we went
off that desolate island, which I named after
my name, Thacher's Woe, and the rock, Avery
his Fall, to the end that their fall and loss, and
mine own, might be had in perpetual remem-
brance. In the isle lieth the body of my cousin's
eldest daughter, whom I found dead on the
shore."

The next day Thacher and his wife reached Marblehead. Later their plans took them to Yarmouth, on Cape

Cod, where their three children, born after the disaster, continued the family traditions. As a memorial to their ancestors, the Thacher family have preserved a fragment of the cloth saved from that wreck by Thacher.

John Greenleaf Whittier describes the shipwreck off the coast of Cape Ann in his *Swan Song of Parson Avery.*[5]

> *There was wailing in the shallop, woman's wail*
> *   and man's despair,*
> *A crash of breaking timbers on the rocks so*
> *   sharp and bare,*
> *And, through it all, the murmur of Father*
> *   Avery's prayer.*
>
> *There a comrade heard him praying, in the*
> *   pause of wave and wind,*
> *'All my own have gone before me, and I linger*
> *   just behind;*
> *Not for life I ask, but only, for the rest thy*
> *   ransomed find!'*
>
> *The ear of God was open to his servant's last*
> *   request;*
> *As the strong wave swept him downward, the*
> *   sweet hymn upward pressed,*
> *And the soul of Father Avery went singing to*
> *   his rest.*

Elsewhere along the coast there were other terrible disasters and occurrences. The tide rose to a height of twenty feet in the neighborhood of Buzzard's Bay and Providence. William Bradford, in his story[6] of the *Plimoth Plantation*, tells of the great cyclone:

"This year the 14. or 15. of August (being Saturday) was such a mighty storm of wind and raine as none living in these parts, either English or Indians, ever saw. Being like (for the time it continued) to those Hurricanes and Tuffoons that writers make mention in the Indies. It began in the morning, a little before day, and grue not be degrees, but came with a violence in the beginning, to the great amasmente of many.

.   .   .   .

It continued not (in the extremities) above 5. or 6. hours, but the violence began to abate. The signes and marks of it will remaine this 100. years in these parts wher it was sorest."

The storm also showed its violence off the coast of Maine. Reverend Richard Mather and his family, later important in Boston and New England history, were aboard the ship *James*. They were off the Isles of Shoals when the gale hit the Bristol ship. The master ran the vessel into a strait between the islands, trusting that he had reached a protecting harbor, but the *James* was soon in trouble. Three anchors were lowered and lost, whereupon the *James* sailed away from the questionable advantage of the Isles of Shoals, running before the wind until near the mainland. Soon the captain found himself on a lee shore off Piscataqua, with no hope of rescue. When the ship was less than a cable's length from the rocks, the wind swung around to the northwest, and the *James* was saved. All around the vessel could be seen the wreckage from other less fortunate ships which had foundered. The Mather family, together with about one hundred others from Lancashire, England, reached Boston the next

PHOTO JOHN ROSENTHAL

TIMBERS OF THE BRITISH FRIGATE SOMERSET, WRECKED IN 1778
HER BONES ARE PICTURED AS THEY SHOWED THROUGH
THE CAPE COD SANDS IN 1886.

COURTESY NEW BEDFORD STANDARD AND GEORGE REYNOLDS

VINEYARD SOUND LIGHTSHIP
LOST WITH ALL HANDS DURING SEPTEMBER 1944 HURRICANE

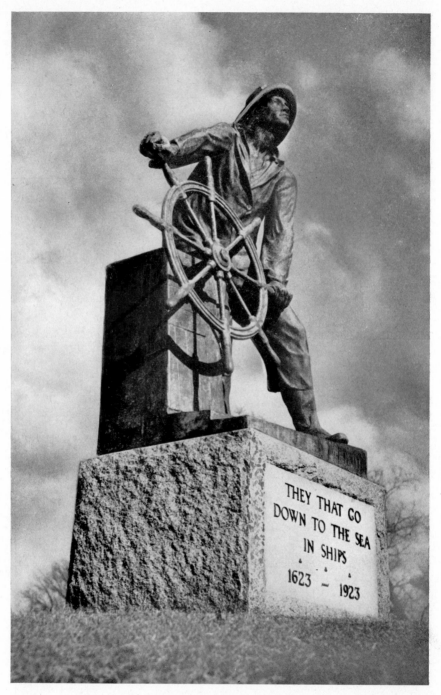

COURTESY GLOUCESTER CHAMBER OF COMMERCE

THE GLOUCESTER FISHERMAN
BY LEONARD CRASKE
DEDICATED TO THOSE WHO HAVE PERISHED AT SEA
OVER 8,000 MEN HAVE BEEN LOST FROM GLOUCESTER ALONE.

THE CITY OF SALISBURY
WRECKED OFF GRAVES LIGHT APRIL 22, 1938.

THE LAST HOURS OF THE "ZOO" SHIP CITY OF SALISBURY
EARLY IN OCTOBER 1938.

SURFMAN ELLIS AND HIS HEROIC RESCUER, ELMER MAYO
THE ACCOUNT OF THE DISASTER SO AFFECTED THE PEOPLE OF AND AROUND
NEW ENGLAND THAT $36,583.52 WAS RAISED FOR THE
FAMILIES OF THOSE DROWNED.

A CAPE COD WRECKER AT WORK ON THE TUNNEL RIDGE

day, but they had narrowly escaped death in that August
hurricane of 1635.

The *Angel Gabriel,* also from Bristol, England, left
the old world in company with the *James* on June 22,
1635.[7] Passengers claimed to notice many indications
of approaching disaster as the days passed, so that when
the storm actually hit, it confirmed the worst fears of the
superstitious ones aboard. Monhegan Island was land-
marked and passed, with the great ship approaching the
iron shores of Pemaquid Point, Maine. The anchors
failed to hold when the ship reached a point directly off
the shore, and the *Angel Gabriel* crashed high on the rocks
where now stands Pemaquid Point Light. Johnston tells
us that there were only five drowned in the disaster, but
that all the possessions of the one hundred passengers were
lost.

A story that has reached us concerning the wreck of
the *Angel Gabriel* is about a Mr. Bailey. When the ship
sailed, Bailey said farewell to his wife, planning to send
for her as soon as he was established in New England.
After he was wrecked on Pemaquid Point, he wrote a long
letter back home telling of the fury of the great storm.
The letter was so vivid and realistic in its portrayal of
the terrible shipwreck that when his wife read the communication, she was afraid to make the journey across the
Atlantic as had been planned. He, in turn, had been so
impressed with the shipwreck's terrors that he did not
dare to brave the Atlantic again, staying on in America
without returning to her. And so the years went by, she
in England, he in America, each hoping and praying that
the other would make the journey across the water.

Neither ever did, however, and they never saw each other again.

Perley tells us[8] of an old man, living in Ipswich, who sailed often with his dog which he had taught to steer the boat. When the storm threatened, it was believed the old man would not sail, but he started down the river just the same, the dog at the wheel. Having been warned of the hurricane, he remarked he would sail out even though the devil awaited him on the high seas. Neither the old man nor his steering dog was ever seen again.

Governor John Winthrop of Massachusetts, writing in his journal of August 16, tells that a southwest wind had been blowing the previous week, changing at midnight to a northeast gale, which blew with much violence and was accompanied by heavy rain. Many hundreds of trees all around Boston were blown down, some houses were destroyed, and several ships parted their cables in the harbor. The tempest continued fiercely all that night until dawn. John Winthrop tells us that it then changed to northwest:

"About eight of the clock the wind came about to N. W. very strong, and it being then about high water, by nine the tide was fallen about 3 feet. Then it began to flow again about one hour, and rose about two or three feet, which was conceived to be, that the sea was grown so high abroad with the N. E. wind, that, meeting with the ebb, it forced it back again."

Thus the northeast wind gave Boston two tides in twelve hours, which has never happened again. Governor Winthrop says that the tempest was felt as far away as Cape Sable[9] but was more violent to the south of Boston.

CANNIBALISM IN MAINE

THE observant traveler who makes his way along the southern coast of Maine near York Beach notices far off the shore a lighthouse rising high into the sky. This tall, slender beacon seems to come sheer out of the ocean but a keen eye can clearly see a narrow ledge at the base. On this ledge, which the surf submerges in the severe winter storms, one of the most harrowing tragedies of New England maritime history was located more than two hundred years ago.

On the 25th of September, 1710, Captain John Deane sailed from London on his ship the *Nottingham Galley*. After loading stores in Ireland, he began the long journey to America.[1] Prevailing weather so hindered his progress that for over eighty days he did not sight land. Then thick weather shut in. Another two weeks went by before the ship reached a point near Boon Island, where the lighthouse stands today. Without warning, the *Nottingham Galley* crashed against the ragged ledges and quickly went to pieces.

Although the night was dark all the crew landed safely. When morning came they saw that they were far from the mainland. In spite of their unhappy situation Captain Deane tells us in his original narrative (which he recommends "to the serious perusal of all, but especially sea-faring men") that they were joyful to be alive and thanked Providence for their deliverance.

Several miles to the southeast they could see vessels

entering and leaving Portsmouth Harbor, but there was no response to the shipwrecked men's frantic signals. A tent made from a torn remnant of the sail was their only shelter. Through it the bitter winds of late December whistled and blew, swirling the snow across the icy ledges. Fire they had none, nor were they able to kindle one in all the time they were forced to spend on the ledge.

Food was scarce — three cheeses and some beef bones that had washed ashore and this little supply was soon gone. The mariners made plans to leave the desolate rock since the only chance of being rescued was the slight possibility of a sailing vessel's coming within hailing distance. So the hungry men built a crude boat only to have the pounding surf break it before it had hardly been launched. A short time later three sailing vessels passed the island on their way down the coast but there was no response to the sailors' frantic attempts to attract attention.

In spite of the handicap of frostbitten feet, a Swedish sailor directed the building of a small raft. On it they stepped a mast and hoisted a sail made of two canvas hammocks. The Swede and another sailor launched the craft into the breakers which immediately overturned the raft. The two sailors barely escaped with their lives. Again the determined Scandinavian set out, this time with another sailor, the first man having been weakened by immersion. Off toward the mainland the raft floated, with the two men waving their farewells to the hopeful crew. But misfortune struck, for later in the week the body of the sailor was found frozen on the mainland; the Swede was never again seen.

Let Captain Deane[2] continue the story:

"About the latter end of December the Car-

penter, a fat Man, naturally of a dull, heavy,
phlegmatick Constitution, and aged about 47,
always very ill from his first coming on Shore.
. . . soon grew speechless, tho' retaining his
Senses. . . . Dying that night, his Body remain'd
in the Tent till the Morning, when the Master,
as usual, going out in Quest of Provisions,
order'd the People to remove the Corps to some
Distance."

The marooned men's hunger became intense. Starving, they discussed means of preserving their existence.
Inevitably, the body of the dead carpenter engaged their
attention. At last a vote was taken and a majority was for
eating the dead body. Did the captain tell the truth when
he wrote that he, at first, would have no part in it and only
yielded when he found himself overruled? In any event
the carpenter's remains were at once cut up.

"A few thin Slices, wash'd in Salt-water,
were brought into the Tent, and given to every
one, with a good Quantity of Rockweed to supply the Place of Bread. The first Piece the
Master eat, was Part of the Gristles that com-
pose the Breast, having the Flesh scrap'd clean
off, for his Stomach, as yet, abominated the
loathsome Diet, tho' his importunate Appetite
had, more than once, led him to survey with a
longing Eye the Extremities of his fore Fingers.
. . . The Mate, and two other Opposers refus'd
to partake of the Flesh that Night, but were the
first next Morning to beg an equal Share in the
common Allowance."

But better times were in store for the men at Boon

Island. The unfortunate men who had braved the seas on the raft had not died in vain, for they were the means of the eventual rescue of their comrades at Boon Island. Some men from Portsmouth, their curiosity excited by the finding of the dead sailor and the raft on the shore, sailed in a shallop to explore the rocks of Boon Island. When they arrived, they found the survivors and took them to the mainland.

So runs the captain's story. But although the account of Captain Deane has seldom been challenged by modern writers there exists another version of the tale.[3] Written by the mate, the boatswain, and one of the crew, the book was printed in London in 1711 and differs in many respects from the captain's narrative.

The authors charge that early in the voyage Captain Deane beat several of the crew so severely as to cripple them. From then on matters went from bad to worse. The captain had intended to betray the vessel to the French, but never could get close enough to a French ship to give himself up. When Cape Sable was sighted, the captain seemed purposely to delay the voyage. Noting the proximity of land, the mate appealed to the captain to haul off. Whereupon the captain answered "That he wou'd not take his Advise though the Ship should go to the Bottom, threatened to shoot the Mate with a Pistol." That night, the eleventh of December, 1710, the *Nottingham Galley* struck on Boon Island. The wreck, declared the captain's accusers, was deliberately planned in order to get the ship's high insurance money. Other items in the captain's account were challenged by his subordinates, but regardless of motives, the two narratives agree in the essential facts.[4]

THE PIRATE SHIP WHIDAH

ONE of the outstanding marine calamities in New England during the eighteenth century was the wreck of the pirate ship *Whidah* at Cape Cod in April 1717. This disaster terminated the career of the infamous Captain Samuel Bellamy, as notorious a pirate as ever sailed the Spanish main. A rich treasure was lost when the ship crashed off the shores of the Cape, and the white sands of the beach still conceal the pirate's booty from Bellamy's wrecked flagship.

Captain Bellamy, who hailed from the west of England, journeyed in 1716 to the West Indies to raise a sunken vessel. As the venture proved a failure, he hoisted the Jolly Roger and sailed away in search of ships to plunder and treasures to steal. After cruising and looting for several months, the pirate captured the *Saint Michael*, out of Bristol, and brought her into the harbor at Blanco. Four men from the seized vessel were forced by Bellamy to sign papers with the pirate band. One of them, Thomas Davis, figured prominently in the shipwreck which occurred the following year.[1]

In February 1717 the London galley *Whidah* was sailing through the Windward Passage between Porto Rico and Cuba. Having just finished a successful slaving voyage, the *Whidah* carried a rich cargo, which included gold, ivory, and silver. Captain Lawrence Prince commanded the crew of fifty men, and his subsequent behavior indicated that he was an extremely timid man.

Pearlman Memorial Library
Central Bible College
Springfield, Missouri

Cruising through the same waters, pirate Bellamy sighted the heavily laden *Whidah* far ahead of him and gave chase. Three long days and nights he followed the ship, and at the end of the third day sailed close enough to fire a shot at the galley. To the amazement of Bellamy this single shot ended the chase, for the *Whidah* hauled down her flag in surrender. Somewhat taken back by the speed of Captain Prince's capitulation, Captain Bellamy rewarded the Englishman for giving up so easily by presenting him with the *Sultana* of the Bellamy fleet. Captain Lawrence Prince was then allowed to sail for England with ten members of his original crew. It is possible that some of Bellamy's good nature was caused by the discovery aboard the *Whidah* of £20,000 in gold and silver treasure.

Captain Bellamy was still in good spirits a few weeks later when he ran in with a sloop in charge of Captain Beer of Newport. After capturing the sloop and removing the cargo, Bellamy wished to let Beer sail away with his ship, but the other pirates objected so strenuously that Bellamy finally gave in. Part of the conversation between the two men has been preserved by Johnson in his *History of the Pirates*.[2]

"I am sorry they won't let you have your sloop again," said Bellamy. "Damn the sloop, we must sink her, and she might be of use to you. Though damn you, you are a sneaking puppy." Bellamy then suggested that Captain Beer would be a welcome addition to the pirate band, but the Newport man declined the doubtful compliment.

"You are a devilish conscience rascal, damn ye," answered Bellamy. "I am a free prince, and I have as much authority to make war on the whole world as he who has a hundred sail of ships . . . This my conscience tells me." But at the end of his speech, Bellamy agreed to set Captain Beer ashore at Block Island, and before the end of the month Beer reached his home in Newport.

A few days after the above incident the *Whidah* fell in with the pinky[3] *Mary Anne,* loaded with wine. Captain Andrew Crumpstey, master of the pinky, was placed aboard the *Whidah,* with a pirate crew taking charge of the *Mary Anne.* Four vessels now made up the Bellamy fleet, and orders were hoisted to set sail on a northwest by north course. On the afternoon of April 26, 1717, a heavy fog shut in, followed by a severe thunderstorm about ten that evening.

By this time most of the pirates aboard the wine pinky *Mary Anne* had drunk to excess, and as a result their navigation suffered. The fleet was off Cape Cod, although the sailors aboard the *Mary Anne* probably did not realize it. It was not until the vessel was wallowing in the trough of the sea just outside the breakers on the beach that the pirates realized their position. Before they could claw off, the *Mary Anne* grounded amidst the breakers off what is now Orleans, Massachusetts. The masts were quickly cut down and the pinky drove high on the beach. When morning came, the pirates found themselves near Slutts-Bush at the back of Stage Harbor. In the distance, safely anchored beyond the surf, were two other vessels of the fleet, but the *Whidah* was nowhere in sight.

Ten miles to the northward, Captain Bellamy was having his own troubles. Losing sight of the remainder of his fleet, he continued to shape his course to the northward, but finding breakers ahead, he anchored. The anchors failed to hold, and the *Whidah* crashed against a sand bar off the shore with terrific force, capsizing almost at once.

Soon the 146 persons were struggling in the raging surf.
One by one they gave up the fight and sank to their death.
Of the pirate crew, only two were tossed by the ocean's
waves above the edge of the receding tide, Thomas Davis
and John Julian, a Cape Cod Indian. This tragedy, which
cost the lives of 144 men, was Cape Cod's first great shipwreck.[4]

Although the Boston *News-Letter* of April 29, 1717,
gives Captain Crumpstey credit for purposely steering the
Whidah aground when the pirates were intoxicated, there
is no testimony to substantiate the newspaper report.
Davis, the only white survivor of the *Whidah*, makes no
mention of this theory in his sworn testimony, so that the
reader is left to form his own conclusions.

The two survivors walked to the residence of Samuel
Harding, two miles away, where they asked the Cape Cod
man to go over to the vessel with them. By noon more
than a score of persons were removing supplies from the
wreck. Meanwhile, Justice Doane, the local magistrate,
arrived and arrested the two survivors of the pirate ship.
Seven others from the *Mary Anne* had already been appre-
hended at the Eastham Tavern, and the nine men were taken
to the Boston jail, where they languished in irons until the
following October.

When Governor Samuel Shute heard of the treasure
ship ashore at Cape Cod, he decided to take definite action
in the matter. Issuing a proclamation taking possession
of everything of value from the wreck, the governor sent
his most trusted mariner, Captain Cyprian Southack, to
the scene of the disaster.

Captain Southack seems to have been a most colorful
individual. Before 1700 he had already made a map of

the Boston shoreline, and by 1734 his chart of Massachusetts Bay was completed. His sketch of Boston Light of
that period is still preserved. Master of the Province
Galley for at least twenty years, Southack without question knew more about our treacherous coastline than any
other mariner of his generation. In spite of his many
interests, it is safe to say that he never forgot his experiences at the scene of the pirate shipwreck on Cape Cod.

Leaving Boston May 1 on the sloop *Nathaniel,* he
sailed into what is now Provincetown Harbor the following afternoon. At this time a narrow though shallow
channel called Jeremy's Dream by some, and Jeremiah's
Gutter by others cut Cape Cod in two between Orleans and
Eastham, and Captain Southack came through this natural
canal in his whaleboat.

The people were not willing to give up their spoils
from the wreck of the *Whidah.* Caleb Hopkins of Freetown
and Samuel Harding, to whose house Davis went the morning of his escape, were especially eager to keep their goods.
Arriving at Eastham, Southack posted notices to the effect
that the governor had authorized him to go into any house
or cellar and open any chests or trunks to look for plunder
belonging to the pirate ship.

Captain Southack now decided to salvage the treasure
from the *Whidah.* He could see the anchor of the vessel
at low water out on the bar, but the sea was too rough for a
trip in the whale boat. Southack waited for a week before
the sea quieted enough for a visit to the scene of the wreck.
Rowing out to the remains of the vessel the master of the
Province Galley was unable to find any treasure. Discouraged by his failure, Southack loaded what goods he
could find aboard a sloop sailing for Boston. This sloop

in turn was captured by pirates.

The following October the pirates from the Bellamy fleet were tried in Boston, and seven condemned to death. Thomas South, and Thomas Davis were freed, while evidently the Cape Cod Indian, Julian, had died in jail. The other six pirates were sentenced to be executed at Charlestown Ferry, November 15, 1717. A large and fascinated crowd witnessed the hanging of the six buccaneers, whose bodies were later cut down and thrown into open boats to be taken out to one of the harbor islands.[5]

What had happened to the treasure? There have been many conflicting stories told of the wreck and subsequent events. Henry David Thoreau was informed by John Newcomb, the Wellfleet oysterman, that he had seen the iron caboose of the *Whidah* during an extremely low run of tides. Around 1863, according to Perley, the wreck was exposed again, but the treasure still eluded the searchers. Thoreau and his companion, William De-Costa, found some of the coins on the bar near the wreck during the middle of the last century.

The usual legend is told of the pirate who returned to the scene of the disaster. Year after year he hovered nearby, refusing companionship and operating alone at night on the beach. His last days were spent near the wreck, and when he died a belt with considerable gold was found on his body. There are those who say that this returned pirate had located the treasure, but the writer is among those who think the tale should be doubted.

THE GALE OF 1723

ALMOST a century elapsed after the 1635 storm swept the New England coast when the great February hurricane of 1723 descended on the inhabitants. If we are able to believe the chroniclers of the period, it was the highest tide ever seen in Boston, rising to a height of sixteen feet. Although Governor William Bradford of Plymouth reported a twenty foot tide in 1635, it was not in Boston but around the shores of Cape Cod.[1]

The prolific and versatile writer, Cotton Mather, was so impressed by the power of the elements during that Sunday gale that he thought the event of enough significance to write a lengthy paper on it for the Royal Society of London. It is probably the first storm so honored in the entire history of America.

The effects of the gale were seen first when the tide came in Saturday night, February 22, much higher than usual. At noon the next day it rose two feet higher than anyone then living could recall. The people had managed to arrive at church that morning without extraordinary difficulty, but when the services ended found they were marooned in the meeting houses by the ocean.[2]

Cape Cod bore the brunt of the gale. At Chatham the marshes overflowed and a fine harbor was destroyed, with the sea sweeping up over the banks to inundate hundreds of haystacks, which had been securely standing on their staddles. The water rose four feet higher than usual on the Bay side of the Cape, while it went ten to twelve feet above normal on the Back side. In Plymouth the tide was four feet higher than the previous record.

Along the New Hampshire shores the waves broke across the tops of natural banks for miles near Hampton, flooding the surrounding marshes and meadows deeper than it had ever been known before. The results of the gale of 1723 were seen for many years in this vicinity. Piscataqua was flooded, the wharves being several feet under water. Supplies stored on the piers suffered heavily.

At Gloucester, Massachusetts, the storm swept many craft ashore, but there was no outstanding loss of life. The waves pushed the sand up into the cut at Gloucester, blocking it completely for marine traffic. Farther up the coast, at Marblehead and Salem, the high water flowed inland for miles and there were many narrow escapes from the ravages of the sea. It is said that in several instances people took shelter in trees to escape the high tide.

In Falmouth, now known as Portland, Maine, damage to wharves and warehouses located along the harbor front was probably more severe than in any other storm of the town's history. The merchants did not recover financially for almost a lifetime from the great storm of 1723.

Comparatively few vessels were in trouble in the storm, which occurred well along in the winter time when sea travel was light. Many outlying islands and districts were heavily damaged, however. Boston Light, then in its seventh year, was feared to have suffered greatly, but after minor repairs, was adjudged by its keeper John Hayes[3] to be in satisfactory condition.

Perley tells us that Dorchester, Massachusetts, suffered a severe flood in this storm, one which was not equalled until the Minot's Light Storm of 1851. In Bos-

ton the residence of Mr. Hunt on Union Street was reached
by the grasp of the sea, which did terrific damage in that
town.[4]

The Reverend Cotton Mather's account was given considerable attention when it arrived in England, so we quote
most of the minister's letter describing the "Tide and Storm
of Uncommon Circumstances." The communication is addressed to Dr. John Woodward of the Royal Society in
London:

> "The reading of a storm is not so bad as the
> feeling of it; I shall therefore think it no trespass
> on civility to entertain you with a short relation
> of a storm and tide, wherein these parts of the
> world saw what no man alive remembers to have
> seen before, and suffered incomputable dam-
> ages. It was on February 24th, 1723, when our
> American philosophers observed an uncommon
> concurrence of all those causes which a high tide
> was to be expected from. The moon was then
> at the change, and both sun and moon together
> on the meridian. The moon was in her perigee,
> and the sun was near to his having past it, but a
> little before. Both the sun and moon were near
> the Equinoctial, and so fell within the annual
> and the diurnal motion of the terraqueous globe.
> There was a great fall of snow and rain, the
> temper of the air was cool and moist, and such
> as contributed unto a mighty descent of vapours.
> A cloudy atmosphere might also help something
> to swell and raise the waters. Finally the wind
> was high, and blew hard and long, first from
> the southward, and it threw the southern sea in

a vast quantity to the northern shores: Then veering eastwardly, it brought the eastern seas almost upon them. And then still veering to the northward, it brought them all with even more accumulations upon us. They raised the tide unto a height which had never been seen in the memory of man among us. The tide was very high in the night, but on the day following, it being the Lord's day, at noon, it rose two feet higher than ever had been known unto the country, and the city of Boston particularly suffered from its incredible mischiefs and losses. It rose two or three feet above the famous long wharf, and flowed over the other wharves and streets to so surprising an height, that we could sail in boats from the Southern Battery [Rowes Wharf] to the rise in ground on King Street [Merchants Row], and from thence to the rise of the ground according to the north meeting house. It filled all the cellars, and filled the floors of the lower rooms in the houses and warehouses in town. The damage was inexpressible in the country. On the inside of Cape Cod the tide rose four feet, and without, it rose ten or a dozen feet higher than ever was known."

If, as Cotton Mather says, the tide was two feet higher than ever known, then the 1723 storm caused a greater flood from the ocean than even the 1635 tempest. Conclusive evidence is naturally impossible, but it is safe to place the 1723 gale in the "Big Four" of New England storms, along with the 1635, 1815, and 1938 hurricanes.

THE GRAND DESIGN

ON July 28, 1741, the ship *Grand Design*, commanded by Captain Rowen, sailed from Ireland with about 200 passengers, bound for America. On board were many persons of wealth and distinction, who had brought along their servants and attendants. They were going to Pennsylvania, where many of them had relatives, and were to begin life again in the new world.

The *Grand Design* sailed for ten weeks before sighting land. Mighty storms she encountered, her masts going by the board, until finally the cliffs of Mount Desert loomed ahead. Captain Rowen's first landfall was the Cranberry Islands near Mount Desert. As he approached land, a southeast gale caught the ship and pushed her by the Thumper, where she slid in near Baker's Island and Dead Man's Point.

Captain Rowen now tried to maneuver the *Grand Design* into the lee of Great Goff Island, but when the vessel smashed against the Nubbles, her voyage was over.[1] Since it was not too rough to land the passengers, the 200 Irish people reached the safety of lonely Mount Desert Island, and camped on the shore. At that time the island was inhabited only by roving tribes of Indians. Months might go by before the survivors of a shipwreck could be discovered.

Taking a small sailboat with him, Captain Rowen left the group on the shores of the island, saying that he would soon return with food. It is believed that he had no intention of helping the starving people, as several weeks passed before he did come back, and his return was for another purpose. Meanwhile most of the men decided to leave the island in search of help. Except for the weaker men who were left behind, the women were alone. To this day not the slightest report has ever been heard of the eighty men who gave their lives in a futile attempt to bring aid to the women survivors of the *Grand Design*. That they were massacred by hostile Indians is the usual belief.

The captain finally returned with two small shallops, but brought no food. He began to plunder the ship, and when he had loaded his shallops with everything movable from the *Grand Design*, he invited several of the women to accompany him to one of the settlements farther down the coast where they would be placed in bonded positions as servants. A number accepted, and when they left the camp with the captain it was a pitiful group of women who remained.

Two months more went by, a period in which they lived on mussels and seaweed, gradually becoming weaker and weaker. Death was a common event among the Irish immigrants, occurring almost daily. The Indians paid a visit to the camp, taking what they wished from the women who could not defend their property.

One of the families had placed their fine clothes in the tree branches as a shelter from the snow. An Indian began stealing the attractive clothing which he saw hanging there, when a young woman rushed at him to remonstrate, but by swinging his tomahawk at her, the red man forced her to step quickly out of his way. The Indian continued to rob the family without further interference.

Mrs. Asbell or Isabell[2] Galloway had brought a nursing baby from Ireland with her, but gradually the condition of her body weakened so that the baby suckled blood instead of milk from its mother's breast. The father became so unhappy that he is said to have desired his infant's death; both the baby and the mother survived him, however, as the father soon died from exhaustion. The sorrowing and starving wife was obliged to dig her husband's grave and bury him without help. Mrs. Galloway, at the death of her husband, became acquainted with Mrs. Sherrer, who had also lost her husband.

Shortly after the shipwreck, the woman who later became Mrs. Sarah Porterfield was standing on the beach after being rescued. A little baby was placed in her arms. She asked who the person minding it was, whereupon a twelve-year-old boy spoke up. "Nobody, ma'am, but I," said the little fellow bravely. All the others in his family had perished.

Finally some friendly Indians visited the survivors at Mount Desert Island, and promised that they would let the people of Saint George's know of their shipwreck and suffering. Men from Saint George's finally arrived at the camp, and brought all the survivors back with them. One of the Saint George men, Archibald Gamble, who was also from Ireland, became interested in the Mount Desert widow, Mrs. Isabell or Asbell Galloway. His friend, John McCarter of McCarter's Point, began to feel the need of the friendship of the other Mount Desert widow, Mrs. Sherrer, at the same time, so when the ladies were established at Saint George's, the two men began their courting. Because of the unusual circumstances Mrs. Galloway quickly accepted the proposal of Archibald Gamble, while

McCarter's similar request was granted by Mrs. Sherrer.

Down in Pennsylvania, the brother of the late Mr. Galloway was offended when he heard of the marriage, and demanded that he be given Mrs. Gamble's baby boy. The Mount Desert widow wrote to him that she would keep the child until he was old enough to decide for himself.[3]

The widow experienced many other adventures in her colorful life, being captured by the Indians in 1757, two years after her husband joined Roger's Rangers. The couple had seven children, and their descendants today, including the writer, are numbered in the thousands.

Mrs. Sarah Porterfield also survived the harrowing experiences at Mount Desert. Her father came up from Pennsylvania the next summer to take her back with him, but she had consented to marry a Mr. Porterfield, who lived at Newharbor. They were married in November 1742. When she was an old lady, Mrs. Porterfield wrote out her experiences, ending the story[4] with the thought which she said gave her the courage to live through the terrors of the Mount Desert wilderness:

"I am now seventy-six years old. My anchor of hope has been for many years cast within the veil. My faith rests on the Rock of Ages, against which the gates of hell can never prevail."

THE WRECK OF THE GENERAL ARNOLD

ONE of the most melancholy disasters in the entire history of Plymouth, Massachusetts, was the shipwreck of the armed brigantine *General Arnold* in 1778. More people perished in this marine tragedy than died in that first terrible winter which the Pilgrims endured back in 1620.[1]

The *General Arnold* sailed from Nantasket Road, Boston Harbor, on Thursday, December 24, 1778, in company with the privateer *Revenge*. Bound for the West Indies, the two vessels were still inside Cape Cod when a snow storm began. The superior sailing qualities of the *Revenge* enabled her captain, Barrows by name, to beat around the Race at Cape Cod and escape the worst of the storm so that she does not figure again in our chronicle.

Captain James Magee of the *Arnold*, unable to follow the other craft, sailed for Plymouth but arrived off the Gurnet, the outer arm of Plymouth Harbor, after night had fallen. Although less than a mile from the friendly gleam of Gurnet Light, he anchored his vessel rather than risk the treacherous waters of the inner harbor without a pilot. By midnight the storm had intensified to a gale, and the *General Arnold*, off a lee shore, was now in great danger.

The master prepared his brigantine against the increasing fury of the sea. Sixteen of the vessel's twenty guns were lowered below decks, the topmasts were struck, and the sails snugly furled. Long scopes were given to

the cable holding the anchor, and every other possible pre-
caution was taken. The waves rose higher and higher.
As the great breakers crashed against her, the vessel
quivered and shook until finally the *General Arnold* began
to drag anchor. Slowly but surely she drifted toward the
shoals of Plymouth Bay, and Captain Magee realized there
was little hope of saving his craft.

Uncertain of their fate, the men stood ready for the
moment when the brigantine would scrape bottom. Suddenly, with a tremor that jarred the ship from stem to
stern, the *General Arnold* grounded on the sands of White
Flats. The captain ordered the masts cut away, and the
crew disappeared below for axes. An unfortunate incident now occurred.

After what seemed an unnecessarily long interval,
Captain Magee heard a loud clamor coming up through
the hatchway, and went down to investigate. There he discovered that several members of the crew, instead of coming up on deck with their axes, had smashed into the liquor
stores and were drinking heavily. It was truly a desperate
situation, with his vessel ashore on a lee beach, the waves
getting higher every hour, the ship slowly sinking into the
sands, and now his crew drunk below deck.

Captain Magee, however, did not falter. Pleading
with some, bullying others, and physically assisting those
who needed it, he managed to get his men back on deck,
and finally the masts were cut away. All hands were
allowed to go below into the cabin where they settled themselves for the night, but few were able to fall asleep.
Hour by hour the storm increased in fury, until it reached
an intensity seldom equalled in the annals of Plymouth
history. For years afterwards other storms of unusual

severity were compared with the Magee Gale of 1778.[2]

Rolling and thumping, grinding its way lower and lower into the White Flat sands, the *General Arnold* was enduring a terrific battering from the sea. The seams began to open. Water first trickled, then poured into the crowded cabin where within an hour it had reached a depth of three feet. Since there was nothing else to do but to return to the wave-swept deck of the brigantine, the 105 men and boys started for the companion hatchway and soon reached the comparative safety of the quarter deck.

It was apparent, however, that there was not room for all of them without extreme discomfort as they had to lie on top of each other three and four deep. Several men were knocked down in the mad scramble for places. To give some protection from the elements, a sail was stretched from the topsail boom on the port side to the starboard quarter rail, and under this tentlike covering the men huddled together. Meanwhile the ship was gradually working itself lower and lower into the sand.

With the coming of dawn, Saturday, there was no letup in the severity of the tempest. The snowfall was so heavy that some of the men, unable to move, were suffocated where they lay. Instead of getting lighter as the day wore on, the sky actually grew darker and darker, while the flakes were so thick that objects a few feet away became invisible. The sea mounted in fury, until each wave which hit the ship drenched the shivering men with icy spray, and the men could do nothing except lie still and endure their suffering.

As the afternoon wore on, the officers gradually abandoned any thoughts of disciplining the sailors and prepared themselves for death. Captain Magee portioned

out the remainder of the rum, advising the sailors to pour
it down their boots as the alcohol had a lower freezing
point than the water which was soaking them. The use
of the rum in this manner is said to have saved the lives of
several of the men.

But the strain of the unequal struggle with the sea was
starting to tell on the men. Captain John Russell, a tall,
powerful officer, was the first to die. Capable of tremendous endurance, he had been calling on his followers
for patience and fortitude when he suddenly fell heavily
on the deck and rose no more.

By now the water on the main deck was ankle deep,
and the men prayed for the tide to turn. If the sea rose
a foot or two higher, the brigantine would break up. Just
as daylight faded, however, the tide began to go out, and
the survivors were heartened considerably. Many said
later that the receding waters gave them the courage to fight
for their existence during the night.

At dead low water the wreck was half exposed on
White Flats. Although the spray did not hit the men on
the quarter deck now, another danger threatened. When
the wind veered to the northwest around midnight, the
weather grew much colder, and the clothes of the men stif-
fened on them. Many froze to death before morning,[3]
and together with those who had fallen overboard or had
been suffocated by the snow, more than thirty had now
perished.

But the blackness of the night finally ended, and the
men looked out on calmer seas. The brigantine's yawl
under the port gangboard was put over, and three volunteers offered to row for help. They started away from
the vessel with the cries and prayers of the others in their

ears, but the three never returned.   Those left on the *General Arnold* watched the men row over to the edge of the solid ice, climb out of the yawl, and walk toward a schooner a half mile away.   Disappearing aboard the schooner, they evidently abandoned their comrades to their fate, for they were not seen afterwards.

Bitterly disappointed with the turn of events, the freezing survivors decided to try to attract the attention of the residents of Plymouth and raised a great cry for help.   Captain Magee tied a handkerchief to a stick and waved it frantically in an effort to be seen.   The people in Plymouth had seen them hours before, however.   Small dories which had set out had been trapped in the heavy ice floes, and the attempts at rescue by boat had to be abandoned.   A causeway was begun out over the floe to the brigantine but was still a long way from the vessel when darkness fell.   Now began the coldest night of all.

When the last glimmer of daylight had gone and there was still no help from shore, the more discouraged of the sailors collapsed on deck and quickly perished.   In a few hours only half the 105 who had sailed from Boston were still alive.   That night below zero weather together with a biting, icy wind swept the Massachusetts coast, and the survivors aboard the wreck of the *General Arnold* had to take unusual measures to resist the cold.

Working desperately, the men piled up the bodies of their dead comrades in a protective heap around them to keep out the wind, and then sat down in a circle, their legs crossed over one another.   By constantly moving their legs back and forth they kept alive the circulation in their bodies.   When one of them fell asleep, he would receive a violent shove from his nearest companion, and thus would be brought back to life.   In this way the survivors passed the night.

The first gray streaks of dawn appeared, and Monday's sun rose in a cloudless sky.   The *General Arnold's* quarter deck that morning was covered with the dead and the dying.   Many of the bodies lay just as the men had perished, with their arms and legs bent in grotesque positions.   Some were erect, others sitting, some half crouching with their hands on their knees, and still others frozen to death with their hands straight out from their bodies.

The men from Plymouth renewed the building of the causeway at dawn and were making rapid progress out over the ice floe.   Two hours before noon they were within hailing distance of the death ship.   Soon the sleds and boards were pushed close to the brigantine, and contact was at last established.

It is said that the Plymouth men who stepped aboard the *General Arnold* that bitter morning never forgot the sight which greeted them.   The victims were all huddled together in various positions on the quarter deck, and it was impossible to distinguish between the dead and those still alive.

One of the survivors, Barnabas Downs of Barnstable, was lying helpless on the deck as the rescuers walked around him.   This Cape Cod lad was so numbed by the cold that he was unable to indicate in any way that he was still alive.   He heard himself referred to as one of the dead and feared that he would be left behind until too late. As one of the Plymouth men walked toward him, Downs made a supreme effort and succeeded in rolling his eyes at the man, who noticed the movement.   The Barnstable sailor was then taken down over the side and placed on a sled, which was pulled over the causeway to the shore.

Barnabas Downs was taken into one of the Plymouth homes, where a large tank of cold water was waiting. After three hours' immersion in the cold water, he revived enough to suffer excruciating pains as the blood began to circulate through his thawing limbs. He later said that the pain was much worse while he was regaining his circulation than when he was freezing out on the brigantine. All the other survivors were brought ashore and given the same treatment.

When Captain James Magee was brought ashore, he attributed his survival to the fact that he poured the rum down his boots instead of down his throat, as some of the others had done. Those who drank the rum to excess died within a few hours.

Seventy of the dead men were brought to Plymouth, where over a score were placed in the town brook to thaw out their bodies. It was arranged to have a mass funeral at the Plymouth Court House. The strain was so great during the services that the preacher, Reverend Mr. Dobbins, fainted. A large grave to hold the seventy men was prepared in the town cemetery, but not until 1862 was a monument erected to these Revolutionary War heroes.

Many of the men aboard the *General Arnold* came from Cape Cod, but the deep snow prevented word of the disaster leaving Plymouth for several days. The terrible tidings finally arrived at Barnstable, where twelve of the men lived. Barnabas Downs, Senior, Mr. Oris Bacon, and others, started out by horseback to Plymouth, but when they reached the scene of the wreck only the young Downs boy was still alive. All the other eleven men had perished.

Downs expressed a desire to be taken back home, but

the roads were still impassable for a carriage. John Thacher constructed an improvised ambulance which he slung between two horses. After a feather bed was placed on the sling, young Barnabas was tenderly lowered upon it. The lengthy and painful journey to Barnstable now began, but the boy was in great agony long before the lights of Barnstable were seen that evening. Although given the best of medical attention and care, Barnabas Downs never fully recovered as he lost the use of his feet altogether and had to walk on his knees for the rest of his life.[4]

Of the 105 men who sailed from Boston Harbor, only thirty-three were brought ashore alive, and nine of them died shortly afterwards. Fifteen men recovered completely from their experience, while eight others were crippled for life.

At the time it was remarked that the "moon-cursers" were not present in Plymouth, as later on every article taken ashore from the wreck was restored to its proper owner.[5] To the everlasting honor of the Plymouth men, they had not forgotten their Pilgrim traditions. Elsewhere along the New England coast the records were not always as satisfactory.

Some eighty years after the tragedy a benevolent gentleman of Plymouth noticed the unmarked graves in the Plymouth cemetery, and paid for a monument erected in 1862 to the memory of those who perished in the gale. But for those who had gone aboard the shipwreck that December day in 1778 to rescue the survivors, no monument was needed to remember the occasion, for they never forgot the terrible scenes they witnessed aboard the brigantine *General Arnold*, and their descendants still tell today the story of the "Captain Magee Storm of 1778."

THE FRIGATE ERFPRINS

THE worst disaster in New England's maritime history is also almost its least known. But few have heard of the Dutch frigate *Erfprins*, yet when that ship went down off Cape Cod in 1783, she carried with her 303 members of the crew.

The *Erfprins* was one of a convoy of three Dutch men-of-war which the Netherlands government provided to escort their newly appointed Minister Plenipotentiary to the United States. The new minister, Pieter Johan van Berckel, the brother of the Pensionaris of Amsterdam, sailed from Texel on either the ship-of-the-line *Overijssel*, carrying 68 guns, or the frigate *de Briel* of 36 guns. The *Erfprins*, with 54 guns, was the third ship-of-war. The brigantine *de Windhond* completed the convoy, which, according to plan, was to stay a unit during the voyage.

The minister reached his destination, and of his voyage the standard history of the Netherlands Navy says that nothing unusual happened except the loss of the *Erfprins*. This is a masterpiece of understatement in view of the magnitude of the disaster. What happened makes a most unusual story.

The *Erfprins* was not the most seaworthy of vessels. It had been one of eight battleships of the Dutch navy which on July 20, 1781, against heavy odds, furiously fought an English fleet off the Dogger Bank, giving shot for shot,[1] and giving and receiving damage which forced

both fleets to retire without victory. The *Erfprins,* the
special target of the British, suffered serious injury. In
the two years after the Dogger Bank engagement, other
ships in the Dutch navy were coppered but not the *Erfprins.*
Does the fact that her wooden hull was left without protection indicate that her seaworthiness was in question?

When the convoy reached the English Channel, the
Erfprins sprang a leak which necessitated the operation
of five pumps.[2] In spite of this overwhelming handicap
Commander Louis Aberson began the long sail across the
ocean. The water began to come in faster, so the captain
signalled to the squadron commander, Captain Riemersma
of the *Overijssel,* for advice. The squadron commander
told Aberson that the orders left no alternative; they must
all continue across the sea until they reached Philadelphia. The only concession Riemersma made was that each
vessel could now choose its own route.

One by one the other ships left the *Erfprins.* It must
have been a trying period to the officers and crew members as they watched the brigantine *Windhond* slide over
the horizon and out of sight. Soon the other vessels followed, until the leaking battleship was left alone on the
wide expanse of ocean.[3]

The *Erfprins,* left to her fate, sailed along in clear
weather for several weeks, but on September 19 in latitude thirty-seven a violent storm hit the ship, causing
terrific damage and much suffering aboard the vessel. The
fore topmast crashed down on the deck, the mizzenmast
went by the board, and the mainmast followed shortly
afterwards. Wallowing in the trough of the sea, the
Erfprins sustained a terrific battering from the waves,
which swept headlong against the sides of the stricken

vessel. The men on deck pumped furiously, barely holding their own against the water pouring in through the
leaking seams.

When the storm died down the discouraged and dis-
heartened commander ordered the rigging of a jury mast
and had the ship made as seaworthy as possible. The
sailors pumped on night and day in their efforts to keep
the *Erfprins* afloat, but it was a hopeless task. The ship
was still out of sight of land, drifting almost at the wind's
will, the water now began to gain slowly in the hold of the
warship, and there was no help from any other vessels.
In this manner the *Erfprins* approached America.

Nine long weeks this voyage of hopeless terror continued. Supplies grew low, water became unfit for drinking, and the sea slowly, steadily gained inch by inch.
Storm after storm hit the *Erfprins*, each battering leaving
the man-of-war in a more hopeless condition. Finally,
by November 25, 1783, the ship had drifted and sailed to
a point only twenty-four miles from Cape Cod.[4] That
afternoon the vessel reached a position so low in the
water that she was making no headway at all. Captain
Aberson, knowing that the *Erfprins* would not stay afloat
many hours more, decided to try to reach land. Choosing
thirty-nine picked men to form his longboat crew, he
pushed away from the ship. Three minutes after they
left the vessel, the *Erfprins* sank beneath the waves, carrying to their death 303 members of the ship's company.

Rowing strenuously for several hours, the captain
and the longboat crew finally sighted a brig outward
bound, hailed it, and were soon rescued. Shortly afterwards they were transferred to a Gloucester-bound sloop,
which landed them at Cape Ann a short time later.

Just what happened after the Cape Ann landing is not clearly known. The Gloucester records speak of the forty men who brought the news of New England's worst shipwreck, the *Boston Gazette and Country Journal* also reports the incident, but from then on their whereabouts are in doubt. Captain Aberson wrote a long letter to Van Kinsbergen, which is printed in the *Nedelandsche Jaarb. 1784,* but other than brief mention of honors bestowed upon him for saving the forty men, nothing is certain.[5] Whether he ever tried to find others aboard the *Erfprins* who might have escaped, how he returned to Holland, what parts of the coast he traversed on his journey, we can only surmise. No other members of his crew aboard the ill-fated man-of-war ever reached shore.

THE FRIGATE ERFPRINS SANK IN 1783
THE GREATEST MARINE DISASTER OF NEW ENGLAND.

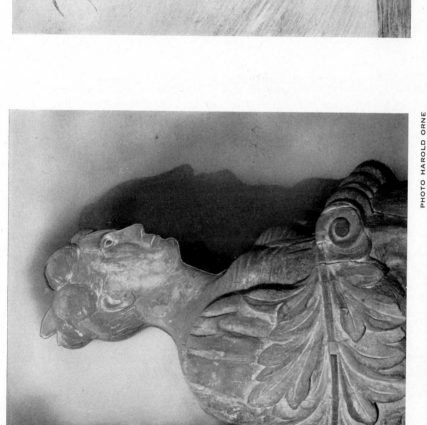

PHOTO HAROLD ORNE

THE FIGUREHEAD OF THE MARITANA
NOW AT THE OLD STATE HOUSE IN BOSTON.

CAPTAIN JOSHUA JAMES
WHO MADE MANY HEROIC RESCUES DUR-
ING THE PORTLAND GALE.

CAPTAIN MICHAEL F. HOGAN
PERHAPS THE LAST MAN TO
SEE THE PORTLAND.

THE PILOT BOAT COLUMBIA
WRECKED DURING THE PORTLAND GALE AT SCITUATE. ALL ON BOARD WERE
DROWNED. WHEN W. SIDNEY DAVEY MADE THIS PICTURE
THE BOAT HAD BEEN A MUSEUM FOR MANY YEARS.

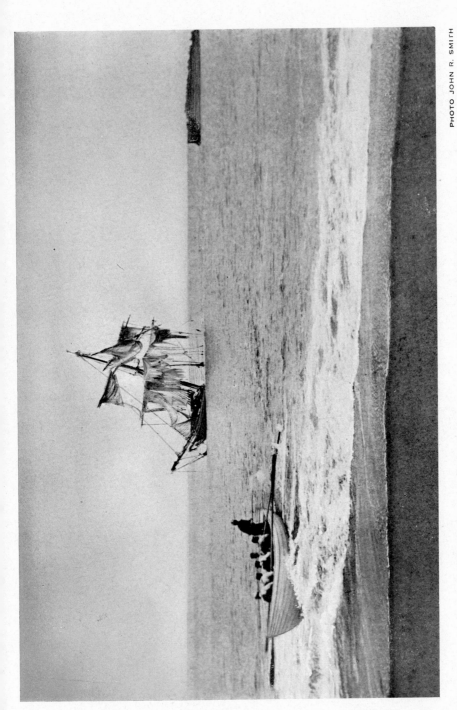

PHOTO JOHN R. SMITH

A LIFEBOAT RETURNS FROM THE WRECK OF THE SHIP JASON. DECEMBER 1893

AN AP PHOTO

PROVIDENCE DURING THE 1938 HURRICANE

A BOSTON POST PHOTO

THE ICE-INCASED NORTH STAR
WHICH RESCUED THE SURVIVORS OF THE MARY E. O'HARA.

THE DECEMBER STORM OF 1786

THERE is an almost unbelievable sequence of freak events and terrible occurrences all along the New England coast because of the December gale of 1786. In Plum Island Sound two men floated for hours on a haystack before they were rescued. Thirteen persons in Boston Harbor were frozen to death, while near Plymouth a shipwrecked party on the Gurnet Beach walked five miles before reaching safety.

The strange story of Samuel Pulsifer and Samuel Elwell is about two men who had journeyed down to Hog Island on the marshes of Rowley to stay for the night. Arriving Monday morning, they spent the forenoon digging clams on the low tide flats. When the snowstorm began, they stopped their work and returned to the island, only to find the storm increasing in violence. Because of the weather they started out at once to return home while the tide was still low, but the snow fell so thick and fast they became completely lost in the blinding storm.[1]

After wandering helplessly through the swirling flakes for several hours trying to find a landmark, Pulsifer and Elwell climbed a nearby haystack to rest their weary limbs. The stack was so warm and comfortable that they agreed to spend the night there and make a fresh start in the morning. When morning came, however, the storm had risen to new intensity, and the tide was coming in around the staddle on which the haystack rested. As it was several hours before high tide, the men began to worry. Higher and higher the sea came, until the staddle began to rock. Pulsifer and Elwell dug themselves places at the top of the stack and there awaited the oncoming tide.

Soon the waters lifted the stack entirely off the staddle, making the men unwilling sailors on as strange a voyage as was ever experienced in Plum Island Sound. The two men could not ascertain in which direction the wind and tide were taking them, but they whirled and twisted back and forth around other stacks and ice cakes with extreme rapidity. Hour after hour passed. Gradually the haystack was going to pieces because of the buffeting of the waves. The men, believing that they would soon be thrown into the icy waters of Plum Island Sound, prepared for death.

Suddenly there was a terrific shock as another larger stack crashed into them. Pulsifer and Elwell leaped into the new haystack in time to watch their former conveyance go to pieces before their eyes. They had been just in time. Now began another strange journey. Hour after hour they floated, never knowing where they were, death always in their thoughts.

Some time later the churning of the sea seemed to abate, and they found themselves grounded at a location later identified as Smith's Cove, Little Neck, Ipswich.[2] They had journeyed on the two stacks at least three miles from the start of their voyage. At first neither Elwell nor Pulsifer made any effort to leave the stack until each realized it was moving out toward the open sea. Pulsifer then jumped to an ice cake and tried to walk ashore in the knee-deep water. Elwell, almost completely benumbed by the cold, finally climbed on an ice cake and pushed himself ashore. Pulsifer was able to touch the bottom with his feet, but could not move his legs and seemed about to perish a few feet from shore. Finally, grasping his trousers firmly at the knees, he lifted his feet one at a time. In this strange manner he negotiated the short distance to shore, where he fell exhausted.

The men soon realized the importance of keeping up their circulation, and after walking rapidly up and down the shore for a time, they were finally able to run a short distance. Making their way to the top of a hill, Pulsifer and Elwell discovered they were on a small island. A large haystack stood close at hand, into which they crawled for warmth. Later the men climbed to the top of the island again. Pulsifer saw a man walking on the mainland about a mile away but failed to attract his attention. They became utterly discouraged. It had been two days since they had eaten, and there seemed no hope of rescue.

When an hour later three persons were seen walking along near the shore of the mainland, their hopes revived. Elwell, waving his hat and shouting for help, was seen. The persons walking on the mainland were Major Charles Smith of Ipswich and his two sons.[3] Major Smith waded across to the island on a causeway covered with water three feet deep and helped the men back to the mainland. After a short rest of several days at the home of Major Smith, Samuel Elwell and Samuel Pulsifer returned to their homes, thankful that they were still alive after their most unusual adventure.

During the same storm a sloop from Damariscotta, Maine, crashed on the beach at Lovell's Island, Boston Harbor. All the passengers and crew, thirteen in number, reached the safety of the island but looked in vain for shelter. At the top of the hill there was a large rock which gave them some protection against the fierce blizzard then raging, and there the people huddled in their wet clothing. The temperature in surrounding towns and villages dropped far below zero that bitter night. One by one the freezing cold claimed its victims.

With the coming of dawn, a fisherman on a neighboring island, Thomas Spear by name, crossed over to Lovell's Island. Up by the rock he saw shapeless forms outlined under the snow and found the entire party apparently frozen to death. Among the group were two young lovers, Miss Sylvia Knapp and a young man whose name is not known, who were on their way to Boston to purchase furniture for their new home. The lovers were found locked in death in each other's arms.

Although the usual belief was that all were frozen to death, the *New England Courant* told of one man, Theodore Kingsley of Wrentham, who lived for almost two weeks after the shipwreck before succumbing. Captain Oliver Rouse, a former officer in the American Revolution, was also among the victims. John and Joseph Cowell, brothers, had just returned on the packet from a hunting trip in Maine. Their remains, together with those of a friend, Joseph Robichaux, were taken to Wrentham, where their graves can still be seen.[5] Fifty years to the day after the tragedy one of their friends wrote a letter of condolence to the family, the manuscript of which is still preserved by Mr. David H. Cowell of Hingham.

The story of the tragedy was told by Frederick William Augustus Steuben Brown, the Boston Harbor poet.[6] A few verses must suffice:

The tempest hid the cheering Light
So thickly flew the snow;
Alas, what horror fill'd the night
With bitter, piercing woe.

At length they gained the sea-beat strand
And rescued from the waves;
On Lovell's Island only land,
To find more decent graves.

Among the rest, a youthful pair,
Who from their early youth;
Had felt of love an equal share,
Adorned with equal truth,

Lay prostrate mid the dire alarms,
Had calm resign'd their breath;
Fast lock'd within each other's arms,
Together sunk to death.

The rock where the two lovers perished, still pointed out to visitors at the island, is now known up and down Boston Bay as Lover's Rock.

Three miles away from Lovell's Island, the brig *Lucretia*, under Captain Powell, was being pushed ashore at Point Shirley by the waves. The brig crashed on the beach about nine in the morning, and five of the men jumped into the raging surf. They succeeded in reaching the deep snow on Shirley Gut Plain and disappeared from the view of others aboard the brig. Floundering around in the waist-deep snow, the men were quickly exhausted, sinking into the drifts. All five perished, including Mr. Sharp, a part owner of the vessel.

Captain Powell and the rest of the crew survived the night aboard the wreck without incident, going ashore after the storm ended the next day. The bodies of the five victims were dug out of the snow the following week. Mr. Sharp, a prominent merchant, was given a funeral at the American Coffee House on State Street, Boston, December 12, 1786.[7]

A coasting sloop under the command of Samuel Robbins was thrown up on the sands of the Gurnet Beach, off Plymouth, Massachusetts. Sixteen persons were successful in reaching shore, where they found themselves on the beach at the northern end of the Gurnet peninsula. Wet and cold, the party separated, some going north and the others south. Those heading south eventually reached the Gurnet Lighthouse, where a rescue party set out to find the others. The survivors who had started to walk northward were finally found in a small hut about two miles from the wrecked vessel. Five refused to leave the hut, preferring to sleep there in their exhausted condition rather than walk the five miles to Mr. Burgess's home at Gurnet Light. They were found safe the next day, when the entire group was given transportation to the town of Plymouth.

This storm covered New England with a white blanket from five to six feet deep.[8] With its record of freezing cold, shipwreck, and death, the December gale of 1786 was one of the outstanding New England storms of all times.

THE TRIPLE SHIPWRECKS

UNTIL seventy-five years ago a spell of unseasonably warm weather in February would remind the older Salem and Marblehead residents of the wreck of the three East Indiamen back in 1802. It was a tragic disaster with a strange sequel. When such a spell came, the people of that period would gather their children around the fireside to tell of the start of that voyage from Salem Harbor which ended with the triple shipwrecks in the sands of Cape Cod. By now even those children have grown old and passed away, and the present generation knows very little of the wrecks of the *Ulysses,* the *Brutus,* and the *Volusia.*[1]

The winter was very mild until the 21st of February. Ice began to go out to sea from the rivers on January 24, with the temperature at sixty above zero four days later. There had been but little snow, and the people were congratulating themselves on having escaped the extremities of a New England winter. If they had been able to look ahead, they would have been more apprehensive.

Sunday, February 21, started in as a pleasantly warm day, but suddenly the storm clouds gathered and the wind shifted to the northeast. Snow began to fall, and in a few hours a frightful blizzard was sweeping the coast. This storm lasted nearly a week. Out at sea many vessels were caught.

All along the coast wrecks came ashore. A ship and a schooner slid up on the sand at what is now Revere Beach,

Massachusetts, while two vessels crashed on the rocks at Cape Ann. Two schooners and a brig smashed ashore around Boston Harbor. The boats of the Boston pilots suffered during the gale. Pilot Cole's vessel was driven up on the rocks, and the craft of Thomas Knox,² Boston Light keeper, was likewise sent ashore with heavy damage. Another luckless schooner hit Minot's Ledge while the ship *Florenzo* was lost at Marshfield.

The storm, however, is remembered principally for the loss of the three Salem ships. As has been mentioned, it was a fine Sunday morning when the vessels sailed. The three ships passed Baker's Island lighthouse, heading for the open sea. The wives and families, together with many friends had gone down to the wharves to say their fare-wells, confident that a pleasant voyage was ahead.

At dusk that evening the three square-riggers were still close to each other. Captain James Cook of the *Ulysses*, William Brown of the *Brutus*, and Samuel Cook of the *Volusia* spoke to one another at a point ten miles south southeast of Thacher's Island, with all three ships sailing east northeast. The storm which began later that evening necessitated another conference of flags, as the captains dreaded the dangers of snow at sea. They finally agreed to continue the voyage, changing their course to due east. Extra canvas was added in their efforts to get away from land, but the breeze continued light, at times dying away completely. By midnight the storm hit in earnest from the northeast, and the sailors realized their danger.

At two thirty in the morning Captain Samuel Cook of the *Volusia* became worried and put about for a return to Salem. When he thought he was off Gloucester, the storm was so bad that he could not see a harbor entrance, so ran before the wind. With reefed topsails the *Volusia* kept off the coast until late that morning, when the dreaded spectacle of Cape Cod loomed before them on a lee shore. The captain, realizing then that he could not weather the Cape, tried to reach Provincetown Harbor. At this moment a terrific gust of wind swept through the sails of the ship, parted the foretopsail, and tore it to shreds.

The slings of the foreyard were carried away, and the yard crashed down on the deck rendering the headsails useless. The vessel drove toward shore. Knowing that their chances were slight, the sailors thought of their loved ones at home who had waved farewell just a few hours before; they made their prayers for a safe landing on the dangerous beach ahead.

The *Volusia* hit the Peaked Hill Bars and bumped across the outer reefs, soon becoming a hopeless wreck. The masts were cut away, and the ship slid over the last of the bars to head for the shore itself, grounding a short distance from safety. The tide was going out, however, so a more hopeful condition presented itself. Watchers on the beach had noticed the wreck. If the ship held together until low tide, the men could reach shore. Hour after hour passed, with the seas gradually going down. Finally at extreme low water the men scrambled ashore. The people of Cape Cod who were waiting for them took the sailors to their homes where the men of the *Volusia* were soon warm and comfortable. Later the *Volusia* was successfully got off the beach and sailed away.

When the *Volusia* parted from the other two ships the captains had continued their conversations as they sailed along. Finally, they agreed to keep on a north northwest course until daylight. At six o'clock the *Ulysses* headed for Cape Ann, while the *Brutus* turned to the southeast. The storm soon increased to put both ships in its power, with the *Ulysses* the first to sight the Cape Cod shore. In spite of all efforts of the crew the ship crashed on the northern pitch of Cape Cod shortly after five o'clock in the afternoon. The men from the *Ulysses* leaped down into the sand just as the waves battered to pieces their proud ship. The *Ulysses* had struck only a mile from the *Volusia!* While the vessel was a total loss, the men were all saved.

The men of the *Brutus* were not so lucky. The ship had weathered the gale all that day, and when nightfall came the sailors had hopes of final victory over the storm. But it was not to be. Sailor Andrew Herron of Salem fell from aloft and was killed. The *Brutus,* now in the trough of the sea, soon hit the Cape Cod bar two miles from the lighthouse. To lighten the vessel, a large part of the cargo was thrown overboard allowing the *Brutus* to come on the beach near the Highland Light. The waves soon had complete possession of the ship. She started to break in two, the mainmast falling toward the beach just as the stern separated from the bow.[3] The sailors climbed over the mainmast to drop nearer to the shore. One by one they reached land, but George Pierce of Marblehead slipped off the mast into the surf, where the undertow soon sucked him down. He was the only one lost at this time.

The trials of the survivors were just beginning. Having reached shore in the blackness of a February night, they had no watchers on the beach to aid them. By this time the swirling snow had created great drifts, obliterating roads and paths alike. Wet and exhausted, the men started their search for shelter. It was the coldest night of the winter, with the temperature far below zero. Captain

William Brown was thinly clad, and soon succumbed to the elements. First Mate Ruee had tried to save him, but Brown was beyond help. One by one others in the crew succumbed to the cold, sinking to the ground where they froze to death. At this time the men had reached a point on the western side of the bay between Provincetown and Truro. It was later found that the men had passed a few yards from a man's home, but in the thick snowstorm had failed to see it.

At four o'clock in the morning of Tuesday, February 23, the survivors reached some outhouses and fences, and soon were knocking at the door of the keeper of Highland Light. Only five of them were left. They had walked over twenty miles in the terrible blizzard before reaching the light, crossing and recrossing their steps in their efforts to reach safety. The keeper gave them every possible assistance, and sent his men out into the gale to search for survivors who might still be alive in the snowdrifts.

Benjamin Ober, a sailor from Manchester, was found buried alive in the sand and snow, where he had been watching attempts to locate his body. In the snowdrift for thirty-six hours, so frozen that he was unable to communicate with the men who walked by him, he was in great agony. Finally a little boy saw Ober's hand protruding from the snowdrift, and Ober was immediately taken into a nearby home. But it was too late, for although every care and attention was given him Benjamin Ober soon passed away.

There is a sequel to this story. During a great easterly storm which swept along the Cape Cod coast seventy-eight years later, the waves washed away part of the sand bank where the wreck of the East Indiaman *Brutus* had lain, and the skeleton of a sailor was exposed under the beam ends

of the vessel. It is probable that the remains were those
of George Pierce. Some silver coins were found near his
skeleton. When these were moved, there was revealed a
watch, the hands of which still pointed at two o'clock, the
time Pierce had fallen from the mainmast into the sea.
Shebnah Rich, who wrote the history of Truro[4] sixty years
ago comments on the story, saying that the wheels of
the watch and the wheels of life stood still, having been
wrapped in their sandy winding sheet for seventy-eight
years.

THE STORM OF OCTOBER 1804

ONE of the outstanding October gales of all times swept across New England on the morning of October 9, 1804. The tempest brought heavy rain in the southern part of New England, while the people in Massachusetts and to the north experienced a snowstorm. The wind blew from the southeast, and then early in the afternoon veered to the north northeast, increasing in intensity until sunset, when its terrific force blew down houses, barns, trees, and hundreds of chimneys. Before midnight the worst of the gale had passed, although the snow and wind continued for two days.

It was one of the worst October storms ever witnessed in Massachusetts, the fall of snow averaging from five to fourteen inches. At Concord, New Hampshire, the snow was two feet deep, but in Vermont only five inches fell. Farmers were among the worst sufferers. Fruit orchards were blown down everywhere. Cattle and sheep died by the hundreds, with thousands of fowl perishing. At Thomaston, Maine, a sixty-acre timber lot was almost completely blown down. Such great sections of timber were destroyed that entirely new views were possible; houses and other buildings never before visible from a distance could be seen across valleys and townships. The change was so pronounced in certain sections, according to Perley, that the surroundings seemed to have become entirely different, people feeling that they were in a strange place.[1]

The South Church in Danvers lost its roof, while in Peabody over 30,000 unburned bricks were ruined by the gale. The spire of the Beverly meeting house broke off.

In Boston, the wind blew the battlements from a new building upon the roof of a residence occupied by Ebenezer Eaton, who had left the house with his wife just in time. Four others were crushed in the ruins, one dying later. The roof was ripped off King's Chapel, dropping it to the ground two hundred feet away. The handsome steeple of the Old North Church was toppled over into the street, landing partly on a building nearby and demolishing it. No one was inside. Paul Revere's buildings over his copper furnaces were destroyed.

Shipping in the harbor suffered considerably, with several persons losing their lives. The schooner *Dove* was wrecked on Ipswich Bar, all seven on board perishing. The sloops *Hannah* and *Mary* were driven on Cohasset at about the same time. Captain Gardner of the *Hannah* was swept off the deck and drowned, but the others aboard were saved. The crew from the *Mary* were successful in reaching shore alive. The ship *Protector* hit on Cape Cod five miles south of Cape Cod Light, with a cargo valued at $100,000. Only one man was lost.

The Reverend William Bentley of Salem said that this gale was the heaviest blow ever known in that town. He could find no record of previous storms in which wharves, ships, trees, houses, fences, and outhouses were so totally destroyed. "I cannot refuse to adopt the belief that the late storm was the most severe ever felt in this part of America. All the accounts which I have seen represent nothing like it," were the words[2] Bentley wrote in his diary.

THE SEPTEMBER GALE OF 1815

THE most severe storm of the nineteenth century, the September Gale of 1815, centered its destruction in Providence, Rhode Island, although the effects were felt all over New England. Beginning around eight o'clock on the Sunday morning of September 23, the wind swept Narragansett Bay with a force seldom approached, causing death and disaster for miles around. By ten o'clock utter confusion reigned around the wharves of Providence as large vessels, torn from their moorings by the wind and tide, swept across streets and wharves which in normal times would be ten and twelve feet above the usual high tide.

The great bridge connecting the two parts of Providence was swept away as the vessels crashed into it and continued up the cove. After the storm four ships, nine brigs, seven schooners, and fifteen sloops were found from five to six feet above the usual high tide mark. One sloop stood upright before the door of a Mr. Webb, while a ship was found in the garden of General Lippet.[1]

On the west side of the river the water rose nearly to the tops of the first floors of the residences. On the east side, the water swept up Weybosset Street three feet deep. Masts, cotton bales, coffee, grain, and wreckage of boats were all carried along Providence's main street as the water rose higher. The Second Baptist Church collapsed when the tide came up around the foundations, while the meeting house of the Reverend Mr. Williams barely escaped the same fate as the tide began to recede. Along the higher ground lumber, candles, grain, flour, household furniture, and endless other articles were heaped in hopeless confusion. Those who witnessed the storm in Providence later said it was a sight of such widespread desolation and havoc that it defied description.

The Exchange and Union Banks, leading investment houses, were literally inundated. The ship *Ganges*, forced up the river by the tide, crashed into the Washington Insurance Building, smashing her bowsprit into the third story of the edifice. India Bridge at India Street was swept away, as was Mill Bridge at the foot of Constitution Hill. More than 500 buildings, valued at $1,500,000, were completely destroyed. It is impossible to estimate the loss of life in Providence during the 1815 gale, but it was extremely heavy. After the storm a force of 300 armed men were stationed in the town to prevent looting.

At Bristol, Rhode Island, every vessel in the harbor was driven ashore. The post office and several other buildings were carried away. A grist mill at Glenrock Village was destroyed, while a similar fate befell the Point Judith Lighthouse.

Buzzard's Bay also felt the full force of the hurricane. No rain fell there, but the tide was eight feet higher than usual, with tremendous damage as a result. At New Bedford all the vessels except two went ashore. A merchant named Russell, who was in his store when it was swept away, had an unusual experience. The store crashed into a vessel and Russell leaped aboard. The vessel soon smashed to pieces, but Russell escaped unhurt. The storm carried away the salt works, one small building sailing for several miles before grounding at a location usually nine feet above the high tide mark.[2]

At Stonington, Connecticut, the tide rose seventeen feet higher than usual, and swept across the town. Twenty ships in the harbor were either sunk or driven ashore. At New London the tide was higher than ever before in its history. Wharves were everywhere demolished; that of M. Ledyard was entirely destroyed with the merchandise upon it. Groton and Norwich also suffered heavily, the market house in the latter place being carried away.

The storm seems to have spent itself before reaching northern New England, as no portion of the coast north of Cape Cod suffered from the gale except the area between Boston and Cape Ann. In Boston the only building entirely destroyed was the Glass House, a huge rickety affair which blew down around eleven o'clock Saturday morning. It immediately took fire and was completely consumed. About sixty chimneys were blown down, three or four of the smaller chimneys of the State House among them. Twenty stately trees on Boston Common were levelled, and five of Paddock's famous elms shared the same fate. In Chelsea the well-known elm near the ferry, seventeen feet in girth, which had a portico built about it, was blown down. The Danvers pear tree, which Governor Endicott planted in the seventeenth century, lost half its branches.

Shipping damage in Boston Bay was severe. About sixty vessels were included in the list of those affected by the gale in Boston Harbor alone, while at least an equal number met trouble elsewhere along the Massachusetts coast. Salem, Marblehead, and Gloucester suffered severely. Compared to Providence, and other locations in southern New England, however, the Massachusetts towns were very fortunate.

Oliver Wendell Holmes remembered well the September Gale of 1815.   His story[3] follows:

"The wind caught up from the waters of the bay and of the river Charles as mad shrews tear the hair from each other's heads.   The salt spray was carried far inland, and left its crystals on the windows of farm-houses and villas.   I have, besides more specific recollections, a general remaining impression of a mighty howling, roaring, banging, and crashing, with much running about, and loud screaming of orders for sudden taking in of all sail about the premises, and battening down of everything that could flap or fly away. . . . It was hard travelling that day.   Professor Farrar tried with others to reach the river, but they were frequently driven back, and had to screen themselves behind fences and trees, or 'tack' against the mighty blast, which drove them like a powerful current of water."

In that September gale which occurred when he was a small boy, Oliver Wendell Holmes suffered an unusual loss.

It chanced to be our washing-day,
And all our things were drying
The storm came roaring through the lines,
    And set them all aflying;
I saw the shirts and petticoats
    Go riding off like witches;
I lost, ah! bitterly I wept, —
    I lost my Sunday breeches!

THE LOSS OF THE ROYAL TAR

DURING the summer of 1836 a circus and menagerie toured the Canadian province of New Brunswick and the surrounding areas. At the close of a successful season the entire circus embarked on the *Royal Tar*, a steamer bound from New Brunswick to Maine. It was a new vessel, named for King William IV of England,[1] and built at Saint John that spring.

Captain Thomas Reed was in command of the Portland-bound *Royal Tar* as she sailed out of Saint John Harbor on Friday, October 21, 1836, with a strange cargo of assorted animals. The shows were billed as Dexter's Locomotive Museum, and Burgess' Collection of Serpents and Birds. The circus carried a brass band and included horses, two camels, Mogul the elephant, two lions, one Royal Bengal tiger, a gnu, and two pelicans. The 164-foot vessel soon reached the open sea and headed south.

When the steamer began her voyage that Friday morning, the weather had been fine in every respect, but before the sun set a high westerly wind started to blow. Continuing several days, the wind forced the *Royal Tar* to seek shelter in Eastport Harbor, where the steamer remained until the following Tuesday. She left port that afternoon, but the rising winds again forced her to seek shelter, this time behind Fox Island. The *Royal Tar* anchored about two miles off Fox Island Thoroughfare to fill her boilers.

Evidently the water in the boilers was much lower than had been believed, for when the pilot's son tested the lower cock he found it dry. The boy told his father, who mentioned the fact to Mr. Marshall, the second engineer in charge. Both father and son were made to understand that they were mistaken in believing that the boilers were dry, as everything was in order. It was later learned that the regular engineer had been up all night working on the boilers. Tired, he had entrusted his position to the second engineer, who in turn had given the task of watering the boilers to the fireman.

A few minutes after the discussion, the empty boiler became red hot, setting fire to two wedges supporting the elephant stall. The fire gained headway rapidly, for by the time Captain Reed looked down the grating the flames were beyond control. Realizing that the *Royal Tar* was doomed, he ordered the men to slip anchor, hoist a distress signal, and lower the boats.

Taking charge of the jolly boat, Captain Reed came alongside the *Royal Tar*, where two able men, Mr. Sherwood and Mr. Fowler, joined him. Sixteen other men jumped into the long boat, cut the ropes to drop their craft into the water, and started for shore. The strong wind rapidly swept them leeward in the direction of land, which they reached safely four hours later.

A man in the circus escaped from the pandemonium which had broken loose on deck by jumping into the water and swimming to the jolly boat. It was a strange tale he told the others of wild animals and frightened people milling together on the burning ship, man and beast alike frantic in their desire to escape the spreading flames.

The revenue cutter *Veto* was seen in the distance, approaching rapidly. Captain Dyer of the cutter soon drew near, and Captain Reed in the jolly boat ordered his men to row over to the *Veto*, then lying to windward. The men refused, infuriating Captain Reed.

"I was captain of the big boat," said Reed, "and damn me if I will not be captain of the small one, and if any man refuses to run for the cutter I'll throw him overboard." Without further interruption, the jolly boat now made for the cutter where the passengers received treatment.

The revenue cutter's pilot arrived near the *Royal Tar* with the *Veto's* gig, but the flames of the burning vessel so frightened him that he dared not approach closely enough to effect the rescue of anyone. Passing around in back of the stern, the pilot saw the passengers and crew hanging over the sides, clinging to the ropes. Terrified by their cries for help, he lost his nerve and steered back to the cutter without saving a single person. The cutter itself, with a heavy deckload of gunpowder, was unable to approach any closer to the burning steamer.

Working desperately to construct a substantial raft from the deck boards of the *Royal Tar*, a group of men aboard the burning ship managed to launch a makeshift float which supported them fairly well. Just as they were about to push off from the vessel, the huge form of the elephant loomed directly over them, balanced for a terrifying moment at the taffrail, and smashed down through the air to land on the raft, sinking the float and drowning the men. The body of the elephant was found floating a few days later near Brimstone Island. It was said that every animal belonging to the menagerie was lost.[2] Other accounts mention that when the horses jumped overboard they swam round and round the burning vessel until they sank, instead of making for shore where they might have been saved.

Captain Reed now took charge of the revenue cutter, as the regular captain was not aboard. Steering the cutter in closer to the *Royal Tar*, he went across in the jolly boat for those still left on board. By this time some of the passengers had been on the wreck for almost two hours, hanging to ropes in the water. One by one the ropes would burn through, dropping the victims into the sea to their death. Another element of delay had been the elephant which had appeared at the rail several times as the jolly boat drew near, seeming ready to leap.

One of the passengers, Mr. H. H. Fuller, clung to the rope over the stern until his strength failed him; then he twisted the line around his neck to prevent slipping into the sea. Four others grabbed hold of his body, causing terrific pressure on his throat. Lifting his leg high out of water, in some way he transferred the rope from his neck to his leg. A woman grabbed hold of his other leg and clung desperately to him. They were still in this awkward position when rescued a short time later.

Of the ninety-three persons on board, thirty-two passengers and members of the crew perished. One of the most unusual deaths was that of a man who lashed his small trunk to a plank, which he slid off into the sea successfully. Fastening $500 in silver to a money belt around his waist, he mounted the taffrail and leaped into the sea. What he did not realize was the tremendous weight of the $500 in silver! When he plummeted down through the waves he was so heavy that he never rose to the surface again.

The passengers were high in their praise of the acts of Captain Reed, who did much to reduce the loss of life aboard the *Royal Tar*. One of the prominent passengers[3] on board was quoted as follows:

"Captain Reed took charge of the stern boat, with two men, and kept her off the steamboat, which was a very fortunate circumstance, as it was the means of saving from 40 to 50 persons, and to him all credit is due for his deliberate and manly perseverance throughout the whole calamity.

"It is impossible to describe the appalling spectacle which the whole scene presented—the boat wrapped in flames, with nearly 100 souls on board, without any hope of relief, rending the air with their shrieks for help; the caravan of wild beasts on deck, ready to tear to pieces all that might escape the flames."

Shortly before sunset the last rescue boat with a single survivor on board left the *Royal Tar*. The passenger was a woman who had seen her sister and daughter perish before her eyes. After taking aboard the unfortunate woman, the revenue cutter started for the Isle of Haut[4] to land the survivors. The passengers then obtained a schooner to take them to Portland while the master and crew went to Eastport on another vessel.

On November 3, 1836, Captain Reed was presented with a purse of $700 for his heroic work during the fire. A few years later he was appointed harbormaster at Saint John. He became a picturesque figure around the Saint John waterfront, where he was often seen with his faithful dog walking at his side.

THE TRIPLE HURRICANES OF 1839

PERHAPS the only account of three gales in one month is that of the triple hurricanes of December 1839. The first two weeks had been unusually mild, suggesting September or October weather. At midnight on Saturday, the fourteenth, snow began to fall and the wind veered to the southeast. By noon of the fifteenth a bad storm had set in. All along the coast vessels were blown ashore or capsized at their anchors. Many crews cut away their masts in time, while others steered their craft ashore on sandy beaches, thus saving their own lives. At two o'clock the next morning the storm went down a little after the wind had swung to the northeast.

When the gale ended, the whole of the Massachusetts shore was covered with wreckage from scores of vessels, and no accurate survey of the loss of life was ever made. The harbors of Boston, Salem, Newburyport, Gloucester, Cohasset, Lynn, Marblehead, and Provincetown were filled with disabled vessels. On land many buildings were blown down and hundreds of chimneys were toppled over.

The tide in Boston swept across Boston Neck, isolating the city and making it a temporary island. The force of the tide was so strong that there was no apparent fall of the sea for three hours after high water. In East Boston a corner of the Maverick House roof was ripped away, as was the roof of the car barn there. The schooner

Davenport was pushed high and dry on Rainsford's Island, Boston Harbor.[1]

Perley avers the scene in Gloucester Harbor has never been equalled in any other New England port. Of course Perley wrote before the 1938 hurricane, but the 1839 storm was nevertheless an awesome sight. Sixty vessels were there during the gale, and one by one they broke loose and drifted across the bay. By Monday morning only a single mast was left standing in the harbor. Twenty-one vessels were driven ashore, three schooners went down, and seventeen others were broken up into kindling wood. Twenty vessels still were straining at their moorings out in the harbor, all but one having had their masts broken or cut away.

About forty lives were lost around Gloucester Harbor. The worst disaster was at Pigeon Cove, where twenty people were drowned from a schooner. It is believed that Henry Wadsworth Longfellow obtained the idea for his poem, *The Wreck of the Hesperus,* by watching the wreckage and bodies that came up on the beach after the storm. Not satisfied with the poetic possibilities of any name on the ships wrecked at Gloucester, he noticed the results of a peculiar disaster when he returned to Boston. A schooner from Gardiner, Maine, had driven into a four-story building on the waterfront, with the schooner smashing her jib boom through the fourth story. While he was down near the wharves, Longfellow looked up at the unusual accident and noticed the name of the vessel. It was the schooner *Hesperus.*[2]

The schooner *Deposit* came ashore at Ipswich, but the surf was so heavy that no boat could live in the angry sea. The waves broke over the wreck all night long. By morning two sailors had died. Keeper Greenwood of Ipswich Light and a friend, Marshall, tried to approach the vessel. Tying one end of a rope to a dory and the other around his waist, Greenwood swam out to the wreck and then signalled for Marshall to climb into the dory on the beach. Marshall launched the dory just as a wave started to recede, and Greenwood pulled his friend out to the schooner. The exhausted captain was first lowered into the dory, and after several narrow escapes from swamping, was landed safely on the shore. Two others of the crew were then rescued.

The second of the December hurricanes hit the coast on Sunday, the twenty-second. Terrific damage resulted in many sections of New England. In Boston Harbor the schooner *Davenport*, which had just been floated from Rainsford's Island, was again thrown up on the beach there. The brig *Pocohantas* was another victim of the storm.

The *Pocohantas* was bound from Cadiz to Newburyport but crashed against the sandbar off Plum Island. Her masts were carried away by the gale, and the anchors dragged. Stern first she drove up on the reef, 150 yards from the beach itself. Soon after daylight the next morning Captain Brown of the hotel on Plum Island discovered the disaster and notified the people of Newburyport. When the vessel was first seen, there were three men still on it, one of them at the taffrail and two others clinging to the bowsprit. Several of the bolder men ashore hauled a dory three-quarters of a mile to the beach near the wreck, but finally gave up their efforts to launch it after several vain attempts. A short time later another view of the ship disclosed one man still clinging to the bowsprit, the other two having vanished.

Just before noon the man at the bowsprit lost his hold and was seen no more. A few minutes later the wreck washed ashore on the beach. A man found lashed to the vessel was still breathing, but soon expired. Thus young Captain Cook, who perished within sight of his own home, lost his life along with ten others. Seven bodies washed ashore in all, and were buried in the Old Hill Burial Ground at Newburyport.[3]

During the middle of the week the weather moderated, but on Friday another storm, believed by some to be worse than either of the other two, smashed along the coast. The ship *Columbiana*, loaded with ice, smashed against Boston's Charlestown bridge.[4] She ripped through the structure and crashed against Warren Bridge, tearing down the drawtender's house. If the mate, then at the wheel, had not luffed the *Columbiana*, she probably would have carried away Warren Bridge as well.

With the third hurricane, December had finished its gales. As a result of these three storms over three hundred vessels were wrecked, at least a million dollars' worth of property was destroyed, and more than 150 lives were lost. Perley remarked[5] of the three storms:

"How many widows and orphans afterwards sat at the windows of their cottages at Mount Desert and many other places looking for the sails that they knew so well, yet not daring to hope that they would see them again!"

THE FIRE ON THE
STEAMER LEXINGTON

COMMODORE CORNELIUS VANDERBILT'S 205-foot steamboat *Lexington* was one of the most popular vessels on Long Island Sound during the early part of the last century. Built in 1835 to accommodate New York bound passengers from Boston to Providence, the *Lexington* made a new record on her first run, reaching New York from Providence in eleven and one-half hours, June 2, 1835. Some famous steamboat races took place during this period, inhabitants of towns and cities flocking to the waterfront to watch the steamers go by. Perhaps the most outstanding race of the period was the occasion when the *Lexington* lost to the *Richmond*.

The *Lexington* soon established herself as one of the leading steamers on the Sound. In 1840 she was running regularly between Stonington, Connecticut, and New York City. On the afternoon of Monday, January 13, Captain George Childs sailed the *Lexington* away from her New York pier on what was destined to be her last voyage. Backing out of the dock, the *Lexington* threaded her way up the East River through Hell Gate, and into Long Island Sound. The last streaks of sunset were lost in the western sky by this time, and the boisterous January winds began to lash the afterdeck.

Gathered in various parts of the steamer were coastwise travelers, merchants, and round-the-world sea captains, discussing national affairs and local matters. A few tables for the card players had been set up, and those who enjoyed the games were busy at their chosen pastime, while the returning sea captains gathered around one of the stoves to talk over their home coming. Some of these master mariners who had been away from their loved ones for several years were happy with the thoughts of the coming family reunions.

Suddenly a single cry full of alarm and terror was heard echoing through the *Lexington*. "Fire, fire," came the shout, which was picked up and repeated everywhere. Soon the passengers all knew the dreadful news. The worst marine calamity possible, a fire at sea, had broken out. A vessel may weather a thousand storms, but disaster is inevitable aboard a burning ship unless the fire is brought under immediate control.

Second Mate David Crowley rushed to the scene of the blaze near the smokestack, and quickly organized a fire bucket brigade. Pail after pail of water was thrown in vain at the growing blaze, which by now had assumed terrifying proportions. The men fought on until their burned and blackened bodies could stand no more. As the flames forced their relentless way ahead, Captain Childs finally told the bucket brigade to drop back, as the *Lexington* was doomed. The steamer was now running for the nearest shore.

Across Long Island Sound at Southport, Connecticut, Captain Meeker of the sloop *Merchant* watched the burning boat sail up the coast. Attempting to sail his sloop to the rescue, he ran her aground on the outer bar. It was not until several hours later when the tide turned, that Meeker arrived at the scene to render assistance, but by that time few were alive to be helped.

Another small boat put out from the Long Island

shore, but the speed of the *Lexington* was so great that the other vessel gave up and returned to port. The water had been rough, and the smaller craft was in danger of capsizing.

Finally the captain realized that he would have to abandon ship. In a calm voice he cried out, "Gentlemen, take to the boats." According to some, this started a rush for the lifeboats while the steamer was still making too much headway for the launching of a lifeboat into the rough seas. Regardless of this danger, the panic-stricken passengers put over a lifeboat from the forward part of the steamer. The small boat, caught in the waves, was swamped instantly. If the passengers had waited until the engines stopped they could have launched the boat into comparatively calm seas.

The testimony of a passenger, Captain Hillard, under oath, follows:

"It was about an hour after supper that I first heard the alarm of fire. I was then on the point of turning in, and had my coat and boots off. I slipped them on. I then discovered the casing of the smoke pipe, and I think, a part of the promenade deck, on fire. There was a great rush of the passengers, and much confusion, so that I could not notice particularly. The after part of the casing was burning, and the fire was making aft. I thought at the time that the fire might be subdued; but being aft at the time, could not, therefore, see distinctly. . . .

"I shortly after went on the promenade deck; my attention had previously been directed to the passengers, who were rushing into the quarter boats; and when I went on the quarter deck, the boats were both filled. They seemed to be stupidly determined to destroy themselves, as well as the boats, which were their only means of safety. I went to the starboard boat, which they were lowering away; they lowered it until she took the water, and then I saw some one cut away the forward tackle fall; it was at all events disengaged, and no one at the time could have unhooked the fall; the boat instantly filled with water, there being at the time about twenty persons in her; and the boat passed immediately astern, entirely clear. I then went to the other side; the other boat was cleared away and lowered in the same manner as the first, full of passengers. This boat fell astern entirely disengaged, as the other had done, but fell away before she had entirely filled with water.

"By this time the fire had got under such headway, that I pretty much made my mind up 'it was a gone case.' . . . The fire by this time began to come up around the promenade deck, and the wheel-house was completely filled with smoke. There were two or three on the promenade deck near the wheel-house, and their attention was turned to the life boat; it was cleared away. I assisted in stripping off the canvas, but I had no notion of going in her, as I had made my mind up that they would serve her as they had done the other boats. . . . The smoke was so dense that I could not see distinctly what they were about. I think that the communication with the fore part of the boat was by this time cut off; from the first hearing of the alarm, perhaps twenty minutes had elapsed. The engine had now been stopped about five minutes. I recommended to the few deck hands and passengers who remained, to throw the cotton overboard; and told them they must do something for themselves, and the best thing they could do was to take the cotton. There were perhaps ten or a dozen bales thrown overboard which was pretty much all there was on the larboard side which had not taken fire. I then cut off a piece of line, perhaps four or five fathoms, and with it spanned a bale of cotton, which, I believe, was the last one not on fire. It was a very snug, square bale, about four feet long and three feet wide, and a foot and a half thick. Aided by one of the firemen, I put the bale up on the rail, round which we took a turn, slipped the bale down below the guard, when we both got on to it. The boat then lay broadside to the wind, and we were under the lee of the boat, on the larboard side. We placed ourselves one on each end of the bale, facing each other; with our weight it was about one-third out of the water. The wind was pretty fresh, and we drifted at the rate of about a knot and a half."

The two voyagers decided not to lash themselves to the bale, but coiled the rope up in the middle. They then pushed away from the burning craft, as it was getting unbearably hot. Shoving the bale around to the stern, they finally left the burning *Lexington* around eight o'clock

THE TRAGEDY OF THE MARY E. O'HARA, JANUARY 21, 1941
THE POINT ALLERTON COAST GUARD CREW SECURING
A LINE TO THE FOREMAST.

A PERILOUS JOURNEY
SURVIVORS OF THE LEXINGTON DISASTER, HILLARD AND COX ARE SHOWN
AS THEY FLOATED ON THE BALE OF COTTON.
COX LATER DROPPED TO HIS DEATH.

SHAG ROCKS, BOSTON HARBOR
THE LEDGES WHICH HAVE COST THE LIVES OF OVER 100 SAILORS.   THE
MARITANA CRASHED HERE IN NOVEMBER 1861.

GLOUCESTER HARBOR DURING ITS WORST STORM
DECEMBER 15, 1839.

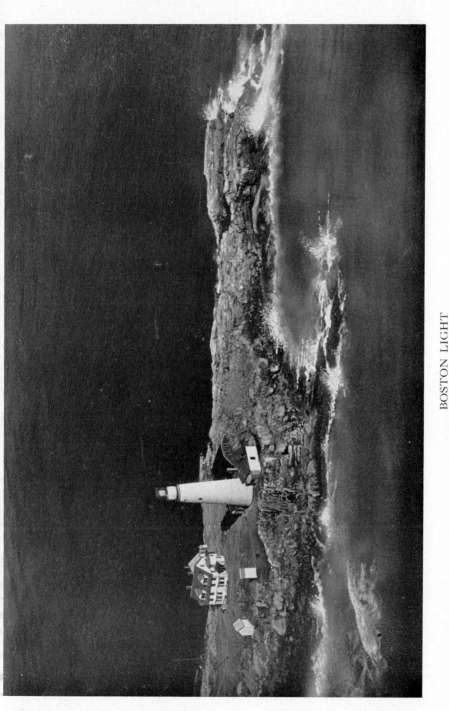

BOSTON LIGHT

AMERICA'S FIRST LIGHTHOUSE, ERECTED IN 1716 TO GUIDE THE STORM-TOSSED SAILOR INTO BOSTON HARBOR. THE
PRESENT FOG STATION IS AT THE RIGHT AND IN FRONT OF THE TOWER. THE CALVIN F. BAKER CRASHED
DURING THE PORTLAND GALE JUST BEHIND THE KEEPERS' RESIDENCE.

THE TOWER AT MINOT'S LIGHT TOPPLES OVER INTO THE SEA
DURING THE STORM OF APRIL 16-17, 1851.

THE BOSTON CUSTOM HOUSE DURING THE MINOT'S LIGHT GALE
THE WATER IN THE STREET WAS THREE FEET DEEP.   INDIA AND CENTRAL
STREETS ON THE LEFT, WITH STATE AND COMMERCIAL
STREETS ON THE RIGHT.

that night. Captain Hillard found a stick in the water, which he adapted for a paddle. In this manner he kept the bale facing into the sea.

When the men pushed away from the ship, there were few living persons still aboard the *Lexington*. Most of them had either perished in the swamping of the boats, or had jumped into the ocean. The two men sat astride their bale of cotton, the waves sloshing against their bodies until they were wet up to the waist. Every half hour Hillard glanced at his watch. The wreck did not sink until three o'clock the next morning. It was then so cold that the men kept up their circulation by violently beating their arms against their wet bodies. An hour later, whether because of their vigorous efforts or not, the great bale rolled over. The men clambered up on top of the other side, the paddle was lost, and conditions rapidly became worse. Now riding an unmanageable bale of cotton, the men were desperate. Cox soon lost courage at the turn events had taken, and lapsed into a coma. Hillard tried to revive him, but in vain. Suddenly the bale gave a quick lurch. Cox rolled off into the water and failed to come up. That was the last Captain Hillard ever saw of Benjamin Cox, the *Lexington's* fireman.

Back in Southport Captain Meeker had finally got his sloop off the bar. Sailing in the direction which the *Lexington* had taken, he came upon Captain Hillard lying across the bale of cotton. Hillard was taken aboard the sloop, where he was given every possible attention. A short time later Captain Meeker fell in with two other survivors, one on another bale of cotton, and the second floating with the help of a section of the guard rail. They were quickly revived and told their stories.

The man who had been taken from the second bale was Captain Manchester, pilot of the *Lexington,* while the other was Charles Smith, a deckhand. Captain Manchester said that when the fire broke out he had put the wheel hard-a-port to steer the *Lexington* to land. When orders came later to abandon ship, he saw a small raft floating by the side of the vessel, and jumped down on it. Several others were already there, however, and his added weight made the raft sink, so Manchester climbed back aboard the burning ship. He next noticed a bale of cotton tied to the rail, with a man whom he recognized as a Mr. McKenna sitting on it. Another person threw McKenna into the water, but Manchester pulled the man back and the third party left them. The bale now drifted away from the blazing ship. McKenna gradually weakened as the long night advanced, dying early the next morning. The seas washed him overboard. Captain Manchester's body was freezing when the sloop hove in sight, and he was barely able to wave at his rescuers.

The story Deckhand Smith told Captain Meeker gives us a vivid picture of the last moments of the *Lexington.* Asleep in his bunk at the time of the fire, Smith heard Captain George Childs call out to the engineer, asking if he could stop the engines. The engineer shouted back that the fire prevented this being done.

Smith had then gone aft, where he found Captain Childs in serious trouble. The lifeboat had been launched full of passengers, and the bow tackle cut away. The boat had swung, filled with water, and was then hanging by the stern tackle. Childs stepped down into the stern sheets, shouting to Smith to hold on to the stern tackle. Just then some one else cut the tackle, and the lifeboat fell free, swamped, and went over. That was the last seen of anyone in the small boat, and Smith believed that the captain of the *Lexington* perished in a futile attempt to save the lives of his passengers in the lifeboat.

The deckhand then went over the stern to climb on the rudder. Hanging by the nettings, he was able to kick in three cabin windows, and lowered himself down by them to stand on the rudder itself. Several others followed him. The bales of cotton now started to fall into the sea as the ship eased lower in the water. There were only ten or twelve people then alive on the craft, all men. The *Lexington* began her final plunge, thought Smith, around three in the morning. All those still alive grabbed for drifting timbers. Deckhand Smith located a large section of the guard rail, and with it kept afloat until he sighted the *Merchant* and was picked up.

The three survivors were soon landed ashore, and it was believed no other persons were still alive from the disaster. But this was not the case. The remarkable story of David Crowley, the second mate, was not learned until later. When the three men were safely put ashore at the Southport wharf, Crowley was floating on a cotton bale some miles away. He had actually seen the *Merchant* rescue two of the survivors, whereupon he had tried to wave to the captain, but could not get his attention. The *Merchant* sailed away, and the course of the bale brought Crowley to a point off Faulkland Island. As the cold was beginning to affect him, he tied his waistcoat around his head for warmth.

Crowley had hoped the bale would touch the island, but the tide carried him out to sea again. As soon as the wind and surf went down, he stretched out on the bale and soon fell asleep from exhaustion. Why he did not freeze to death he never could understand, but he awoke with the morning sun shining in his face, completely refreshed by his slumbers. All that day he drifted on, hoping and praying for rescue. As darkness fell, the bale suddenly bumped ashore, and Crowley sat up to find himself, on a beach at the foot of a high bank. Sliding off the bale, he managed to crawl to the top of the hill, where he saw a light shining from a house in the distance. Step by step he forced his weary body toward the beacon in the darkness, finally arriving at the door of the home. He was admitted just as the son of Mr. Huntington, the occupant, finished telling the story of the *Lexington's* disaster. It was said afterwards that he presented a weird appearance, with his waistcoat tied around his head while he stood explaining his adventure. He was given immediate care and later recovered completely.[1]

It was later brought out at the inquest that the *Lexington* had been on fire before, on the January 2nd run. At that time the deck did not catch fire, since only a small box had ignited. Another point discussed at the inquest was the proximity of the sloop *Improvement* at the time of the fire. Less than five miles away, Captain William Tirrell of the *Improvement* decided for himself that the boats of the *Lexington* would take off all the passengers. It was estimated that over half of the 150 lost would have been saved if Captain Tirrell had sailed over and investigated the disaster.

Among those who perished was Dr. Charles Follen[2] of Lexington, formerly a professor at Harvard College. A liberal in Austria, Follen fled to America because of his convictions. Another person lost was Robert Blake of Wrentham, an outstanding citizen in his community.

The steamer's loss made a tremendous impression up and down the Atlantic Coast. Pictures of the burning vessel were sold by the thousands. As a commentary on the age, we include[3] part of a sermon by Reverend S. K. Lothrop, preached shortly after the disaster:

"The steamboats of Long Island Sound have, till recently, been in general managed with distinguished skill and care, and all necessary, nay, even a scrupulous attention paid to the safety and comfort of the passengers. Of late years, however, the growing competition and the increased facilities for carrying freight, afforded by the rail-roads to Providence and Stonington, have produced an unfavorable change, and taken from the boats the high character of safety and comfort that once attached to them. . . . Until the fate of the Lexington is forgotten, most persons will be willing to pay something extra if they can be insured a safe, comfortable passage. It is to be hoped that this melancholy catastrophe will direct public attention to the subject, so that the reckless exposure of human life, which has marked some portions of the travelling in New England will end."

But it was many years before marine regulations were of such uniformity that they insured stringent enforcement of the safety laws. Man learns slowly and forgets quickly, especially when it is something which involves much thought and planning.

THE IMMIGRANT SHIP SAINT JOHN

THE most serious shipwreck to occur in the outer reaches of Boston Harbor was that of the British brig *Saint John* in the year 1849. One hundred and forty-three persons perished in this disaster, which took place inside of Minot's Ledge October 7 of that year. The *Saint John* had left Galway, Ireland, for Boston, September 5, running into heavy weather off Cape Cod a month later.

The storm itself was well remembered around New England for many years. Rain began to fall October 6 late in the afternoon, and by midnight a violent storm from the northeast set in. Many other vessels were wrecked at various locations along the coast, while in Chelsea, Massachusetts, the walls of the partly constructed Universalist Church on Chestnut Street blew down with a terrific crash. Many other cities and towns in Massachusetts were swept by the gale, and damage was exceedingly heavy.[1]

When the weather turned thick, Captain Oliver of the *Saint John* ordered the crew to heave to, heading northeast. At four the next morning they wore ship and stood south. Several hours later Captain Oliver reached a point off Minot's Ledge Light, and noticed the British brig *Kathleen* anchored just off Cohasset.

Hoping to gain the protection of a land-locked harbor, Oliver ran before the wind, dropping anchor near the newly completed but unlighted Minot's Ledge Lighthouse.

The wind increased, the waves grew higher, and soon the *Saint John* began to drag her anchors. Although the frightened crew cut away the masts, it was soon apparent that the brig was doomed. Slowly but inevitably the Irish immigrant ship neared the rocks. Suddenly a wave higher than the rest loomed before the terrified passengers and crew. Of gigantic proportions, the breaker rolled in toward the vessel, carrying the brig with its screaming cargo toward the rocky ledge.

Hundreds were watching the disaster from the Cohasset shore, while many others stood at the Glades House in Scituate. As they saw the vessel ready to pile up on the Grampus, they knew that the brig was doomed. They also realized that since the waves were too high to launch a lifeboat, few would be saved from the *Saint John*. The men of Cohasset and Scituate could do nothing except wait for the elements to subside.

Ripping and grinding its way over the outer rocks, the *Saint John* wallowed in the trough of the sea, buffeted by each wave as it swept by. Directly in its path was the Grampus, the grave of many a sturdy ship. With a tearing crash, the *Saint John* struck the ledge and began to break up.

The towering breakers swept over the vessel, twenty and thirty feet high, each wave carrying several victims to their death until only a few remained alive aboard the wreck. The ringbolt holding the jolly boat in place snapped, dropping the small boat into the ocean. Twenty-five persons jumped into the frail craft, which capsized, throwing the occupants into the sea. Only the captain and one boy managed to swim back to the ship, while all the others perished.[2] A great wave now swept the long boat some distance from the ship, and a number of passengers drowned trying to swim to it. The captain and eleven others reached it, landing at the Glades an hour later after a dangerous trip through the high waves.

Meanwhile the seas were going down rapidly, and a rescue boat from shore started for the wreck. Rowing through the waves, they passed the captain and the others in the long boat, and decided from the fact that only twelve were in it that all others aboard the *Saint John* had been rescued. So the lifesavers rowed on by the wreck and headed for the British brig *Kathleen*. They had not seen the survivors aboard the *Saint John* because of the high waves.

Two incidents should be mentioned here. An Irishman, Patrick Swaney by name, was aboard the *Saint John* with his eleven children, and they were all swept overboard by the same wave. Swaney, with his youngest child at his breast, swam toward the long boat. When he had almost reached his destination, a gigantic wave engulfed him, and neither he nor the child was ever seen again. Since all his other children had perished, that was the end of the Swaney family. A fourteen-year-old Irish lad had secreted himself aboard the emigrant ship at the start of the journey because his two sisters were going to America. When the crash came, he jumped into the jolly-boat, swam back when it was swamped, and was later helped into the long boat. On reaching shore he discovered that both his sisters had been lost.

The great shipwreck off Cohasset attracted the attention of Henry David Thoreau, who was planning to visit Cape Cod. When the regular boat failed to run because of the storm, Thoreau went by land, stopping at Cohasset.

On the train he noticed many Irish people on their way to the scene. Arriving at Cohasset, he made his way through Cohasset common. As Thoreau walked by the graveyard he saw an immense hole freshly dug there, where the bodies of the victims were to be placed.[3]

Reaching the ocean, Thoreau found the sea still breaking violently over the rocks. More than twenty-six bodies had been recovered from the vessel. A woman who came to Boston without her baby months before had been expecting her sister to bring the child with her on the *Saint John*. On hearing of the tragedy she went down to the scene for particulars. The men in charge advised her to examine the remains of those who had come ashore. As the mother opened the lid of one of the coffins she found her own child in her sister's arms, both cold in death. The poor lady died three days later as a result of this terrible shock.

The men who worked straight through all the excitement made a deep impression on Henry David Thoreau as they continued collecting the seaweed as if nothing else mattered. Separating bits of cloth and sticks from it, the men piled up the kelp and rockweed undisturbed by the possibility of turning up a dead body at any time. Much debris filled the cove. A man's garments were arranged on a rock, then came a woman's scarf, a gown, and a straw bonnet. A large section of the brig forty feet long lying behind one of the rocks attracted Thoreau, and he climbed down to where he could examine the wreckage. Quoting from his story[4] we read:

"I was even more surprised at the power of the waves, exhibited on this shattered fragment, than I had been at the sight of the smaller fragments before. The largest timbers and iron braces were broken superfluously, and I saw that no material could withstand the power of the waves; that iron must go to pieces in such a case, and an iron vessel would be cracked up like an egg-shell on the rocks. Some of these timbers, however, were so rotten that I could almost thrust my umbrella through them. They told us some were saved on this piece, and also showed where the sea had heaved it into this cove which was now dry. When I saw where it had come in, and in what condition, I wondered that any had been saved on it. A little further on, a crowd of men was collected around the mate of the St. John, who was telling his story. He was a slim-looking youth, who spoke of the captain as the master, and seemed a little excited. He was saying that when they jumped into the boat she filled, and the vessel lurching, the weight of the water in the boat caused the painter to break, and so they were separated. Whereat one man came away saying, — 'Well, I don't see but he tells a straight story enough. You see, the weight of the water in the boat broke the painter. A boat full of water is very heavy,' — and so on, in a loud and impertinently earnest tone, as if he had a bet depending on it, but had no humane interest in the matter.

"Another, a large man, stood near by upon a rock, gazing into the sea, and chewing large quids of tobacco, as if that habit were forever confirmed with him.

"Further, we saw one standing upon a rock who, we were told, was one that was saved. He was a sober-looking man, dressed in a jacket and gray pantaloons, with his hands in the pockets. I asked him a few questions, which he answered; but he seemed unwilling to talk about it, and soon walked away. By his side stood one of the life-boat men, in an oil-cloth jacket who told us how they went to the relief of the British brig, thinking that the boat of the St. John, which they passed on the way, held all her crew. . . . There were one or two houses visible from these rocks, in which were some of the survivors recovering from the shock which their bodies and minds had sustained. One was not expected to live.

"We kept on down the shore as far as a promontory called Whitehead, that we might see more of the Cohasset Rocks. . . . We afterwards came to the lifeboat in its harbor, waiting for another emergency; and in the afternoon we saw the funeral procession at a distance, at the head of which walked the captain with the other survivors."

Many years after the last bruised and battered body of the immigrants had been placed in the Cohasset cemetery, the Irish people of Boston visited the graveyard to dedicate a graceful granite shaft in memory of the shipwrecked victims. Because of this act of the Ancient Order of the Hibernians,[5] Patrick Swaney and his eleven children, as well as the others who perished, will probably not be forgotten.

THE MINOT'S LIGHT STORM

THE storm which began on Monday, April 14, 1851, developed into a gale which proved to be one of the severest of the century along the shores of Massachusetts. Damage to shipping was estimated in hundreds of thousands of dollars, while property all along the coast was destroyed. Many of the residents of New England remembered the gale for one reason, the total destruction of Minot's Ledge Lighthouse off the shores of Cohasset, Massachusetts.

The light had been built because of the many shipwrecks in the area south of Boston. In 1847 Captain Daniel Lothrop made a survey of the shipping losses in the vicinity from 1817 to 1847. He found that thirty-nine ships had been wrecked off Cohasset during that period with the loss of many lives, so the lighthouse was built.

Completed January 1, 1850, the tower was constructed on iron stilts which rose to a height of sixty feet above the water.[1] In the spring of 1850 several great storms weakened the lighthouse, causing the keeper to resign his position, but a new man was found willing to accept the responsibility and danger.

With the coming of 1851 John W. Bennett, the new keeper, realized that the tower was in danger. He wrote several letters asking to have the lighthouse strengthened. But since the man who built the tower, Captain William H. Swift, scorned any suggestion that the light would fall, nothing was done.

A terrific tempest swept the Atlantic in March, and the tower swayed four feet in the gale. Damage was great, but the storm finally went down. The assistant keeper, Joseph Wilson, visited Boston on leave a few days later. During his stay in the city a friend asked him whether it would be difficult to hire another capable man for the position in the event that Keeper John W. Bennett gave up his post at the lighthouse.

"Yes, sir," he replied. "I shall stay as long as Mr. Bennett does, and when we leave the light, it will be dangerous for any others to take it." The young man, only twenty, was feeling rather happy that the winter was over. He was looking forward to being at the light the coming summer, with the warmth and sunshine making up for the winter of terror he had recently experienced. But the summer never came for Assistant Keeper Wilson.

While he was in Boston, he was also asked what he would do if the light should fall. He answered that he was quite confident of reaching the shore. In view of what actually happened three weeks later his remarks take on special significance. His final statement was that he would stay at the light as long as the tower stood. When the time came, that is exactly what happened.

The head keeper, John W. Bennett, spent the next few days at the light tightening and strengthening the braces. He found the dory smashed beyond all hope of repair, however, and made arrangements to go to Boston to purchase a new one as soon as Assistant Keeper Wilson returned from his leave. A relatively calm spell was enjoyed the first week in April, but around the 8th of that month easterly winds began to blow. Bennett decided to leave the light when the east wind diminished somewhat, and on the morning of Friday, April 11, he flew the signal for the boat to come out. Leaving the weakened structure in charge of the two assistant keepers, Joseph Antoine and Joseph Wilson, Head Keeper Bennett sailed away from the lighthouse never to return. It was the last time he saw either man alive.

Arriving on the mainland, Keeper Bennett proceeded to the Custom House in Boston where he interviewed Collector Philip Greely concerning the purchase of his new boat. The next day he returned to Cohasset and made an effort to reach the light, but the easterly wind had increased so that a heavy sea was running at Minot's Ledge. Sunday the wind grew stronger, and by night the surf was seen hitting fairly high against the structure on the lonely ledge. Late Monday the wind had developed into a gale which intensified to hurricane force by Wednesday morning. The exact course of the storm on April 16, 1851, was east northeast.

On the mainland the storm was causing considerable destruction up and down the coast. Scituate Harbor was damaged to an extent of $5,000. Several houses on Pleasant Beach in Cohasset were entirely swept away. A large three-story hotel was floated right out from its underpinning, with almost a score of guests escaping in time. A few moments after the occupants had left the building, the sea broke over it, smashing the hotel into four great sections in a comparatively short time. The storm raged all along the coast from New York to Portland, Maine. The feeling was general that the storm brought a higher tide and greater gale than any since December 1786, when thirteen people froze to death on Lovell's Island in Boston Harbor after their ship had been wrecked.[2]

The tide at Dorchester, Massachusetts rose seven feet higher than usual, while a Brighton man crossing the Cambridge Bridge was blown into the Charles River but saved himself from drowning. The old railroad depot at Wilmington Junction and two barns at Tewksbury were demolished, with a house and many chimneys blown down at Danvers.

Church steeples suffered in many localities. That of the new Baptist church in Charlestown was blown down, the steeple crashing on a Mr. Locke of Lexington, who died shortly afterwards. The steeple of the Catholic Church in Pawtucket, one of New England's tallest, was blown down. East Boston's new Episcopal church at the corner of Decatur and Paris Streets was moved from its foundations on Tuesday night, and blown down altogether the following day.[3]

Deer Island in Boston Harbor was in the direct path of the tempest. The new seawall was destroyed, and the water swept right across the island to carry three buildings out to sea. The boys at the Deer Island school had a narrow escape, as they were caught in their dormitory with the water steadily rising around them. The instructor waded through water three feet deep to warn them of the danger. By midnight the water had risen to a height of five feet, and the roof of the building fell in. The instructor and the boys feared they would be drowned as the waves battered the house, but by dawn a team of oxen arrived and took them to higher ground. A few hours later the boys watched their dormitory swept out to sea. The passage through Shirley Gut was widened to twice its former size.

Winthrop, Massachusetts, across Shirley Gut from Deer Island, was heavily hit by the gale. In the Point

Shirley district Taft's Hotel was inundated, the waves breaking completely over the structure to destroy the front of the hotel. The occupants fled to the higher ground, stopping with a Mr. Wyman for the night. At the height of the storm the roof of the Taft barn was carried away, crashing on a pleasure yacht on the back beach, completely demolishing the craft. At Pleasant Beach, Isiah Baker had a public house. Mr. Baker was able to escape with his boarders before the building broke up completely. Several vessels were pushed ashore onto the beach, with a number of sailors drowned. The Fay family, then living at Winthrop Beach, were rescued just in time as their house was hit by the surf.

Derby Wharf in Salem was ruined. The railroad track at Collin's Cove and the bridge between Forrester Street and Northey's Point were carried away, and the sea rushed into the tunnel. In Beverly the sea washed over Tuck's Point and over Water Street, while the tide in Gloucester was said to have been the highest in fifty years. Michael Duley's store there was carried away.[4]

The Merrimac River rose twenty-two inches higher than the record of December 1839, flooding warehouses and cellars on the lower side of Water Street, Newburyport. $20,000 damage was sustained in that town. Below South Street the river swept over the whole length of the turnpike road to Plum Island.

The brig Primrose went ashore off Plum Island. Captain Bokman, not able to take an observation for several days, supposed the craft in Boston Bay. The Primrose hit a reef near the Emerson Rocks, and began to break up. For three hours rescuers tried to make fast lines thrown from the brig. At two o'clock in the afternoon the rope was made fast, and the nine shipwrecked men made their way to safety.

At Newcastle, New Hampshire, the ocean washed across the roads, making an island of Jaffrey Point. Several families, believing that another deluge had come to destroy the world, did nothing to escape, as they felt they were doomed. The next day, however, the tide went down, and they returned to their regular pursuits.

Many schooners were driven ashore at Rockport, Nahant, and Salem Harbor. Seven vessels were wrecked at Marblehead, while it is known that a number of mariners were drowned off Marshfield.

The City of Boston actually became an island during the Wednesday high tide as the water swept across the neck, cutting the city off from the mainland completely. On Harrison Avenue the water was four feet deep, and the tide flowed entirely across Washington Street near the corner of Waltham Street. In downtown Boston the waves swept right up State Street, with the area around the Custom House three feet under water. Broad Street was partially submerged, the waves continuing up Central and Milk Streets. It is said that Merchants Row was reached by the great tide. The record high tide submerged both the Charlestown and Chelsea bridges. The evening *Transcript* for April 16, 1851, reported that no cars were operated over the Old Colony Railroad line that morning.

"The rails have been washed up, so that they lie crosswise hundreds of feet in many places. . . . This is believed to be the highest tide ever known in Boston. It began to recede slowly about twelve o'clock. Thousands of spectators flocked down to the wharves to witness the grand spectacle which the waters . . . presented.

"Great apprehensions are felt in regard to the lighthouse at Minot's Ledge. The weather is still too misty to distinguish if it is still standing."

At the time this article was written, however, Minot's Light was still fairly upright. The two heroic keepers had continued to carry out their tasks in spite of the terrific odds against them. They kept the bell ringing and the lamps burning for the ships in distress outside the ledge. Their worst night was about to begin. The storm seemed to have spent its fury, but as is so often the case, the great seas grew even higher as evening came.

No one will ever know the exact circumstances of the tragedy which befell the two brave keepers out on the rock. The following explanation is offered as a possibility. It is, however, an account in which all the known facts are put together in a sequence that may be considered reasonable.

We know that several families living at the Glades in Scituate saw the gleam of Minot's Light about ten o'clock that fateful Wednesday night. Thus we may naturally assume the light was still standing at that time. The two men, realizing their danger would be greatest around high tide at midnight, prepared a message for the outside world in case they failed to survive the storm. Casting the bottle containing the message out from the lighthouse, Wilson and Antoine now made their plans for what proved to be their last night in this world.

The wind had abated appreciably, but the great tide was slowly rising, sending wave after wave through the upper framework of the tottering structure. There was still that terrifying surge of hundreds of tons of foaming surf just below them. The doomed tower, rocking perceptibly back and forth, seemed about to crash at any time. Higher and higher the billows swept, until almost every wave smashed against the keepers' quarters sixty feet above the ledge. Probably around eleven o'clock that night the central support snapped completely off, leaving the top-heavy, thirty-ton lantern tower to be upheld by the already weakened outside piling.

The large five and one-half inch rope hawser, which had been fastened into position by Keeper Bennett, ran from the top of the tower to a seven-ton granite rock located about two hundred feet in the lee of the lighthouse. Keeper Bennett used this cable to get on and off the tower whenever a turbulent sea was running.

Many believe that this cable, pulled by the huge rock as the boulder in turn was pushed toward shore by the sea, was a contributing factor in the destruction of the edifice. Keeper Bennett usually slackened the hawser when a storm came up, but it is a question whether this was beneficial to the lighthouse. If the rock started moving, the slack would soon be taken up.

With the central support cracked off, the tower became more and more dangerous. The cable attached to the rock probably had the same effect that a rope would have tied to the top of a high tree after it is almost chopped through, with the granite block creating a pull like men trying to bring the tree down. Inch by inch the granite block moved toward the shore, gradually increasing the strain on the eight remaining iron supports. Without question the lighthouse slanted at an angle of twenty degrees from the perpendicular by midnight. The previous afternoon a man with a telescope, standing on the beach at Cohasset, was peering anxiously in the direction of the ledge. He detected a decided list toward shore when he occasionally saw the structure through the mist, and felt that the lighthouse was doomed.

Just before one o'clock on the morning of April 17, 1851, because of the combined forces of wind, sea, and straining hawser, the Minot's Ledge Lighthouse toppled over into the sea. One by one the pilings broke, snapping like pipe stems, until only two or three remained. There the tower rested for a time.

The keepers realized that the end was near. Wishing in some way to communicate with their loved ones ashore, they seized the heavy hammer and began to pound furiously on the lighthouse bell. We know that this signal was heard, for many residents at the Glades later recalled the sound of the bell which came over the water to them even above the roar of the surf at one o'clock that wild morning.

With the tower so bent over that the storeroom and capping received the full force of each breaking wave, the remaining supports soon gave way, and the great tower plunged beneath the ocean waves. The Government had made a costly mistake. The sea reclaimed the ledge for its own.

But what of the two keepers?

Letting themselves down by the hawser into the water, the two men, each with a life-preserver strapped to his back, dropped into the boiling surf. We believe that Antoine and Wilson did come down the hawser, for the stay was later found, and from its appearance it seemed probable that the lanyard connecting it to the lighthouse had been let loose. It had been tied in such a way that only human hands could have loosened it.

The body of Joseph Antoine was washed ashore soon

afterward at Nantasket. The writer believes it possible that young twenty-year-old Wilson tried to live up to his expressed determination to reach land.

A short distance from the Glades lies Gull Rock. Here it was that Joseph Wilson was washed ashore, more dead than alive, terribly chilled and bruised by the battering of the icy waves. He crawled up to the top of the rock, and discovered he was not on the mainland. This disappointment, after his long swim from the lighthouse, was too much for Wilson, and he sank, exhausted, in a cleft of the Gull Rock far above the reach of the outgoing tide. He probably died before morning of exhaustion and exposure. It is not all conjecture, however, for when the body of Joseph Wilson was discovered, the position and condition indicated that the young man reached the rock alive.[5]

When Keeper Bennett had been prevented from going out to the tower, he went to his home on White Head, near the Glades. As the storm increased, the water swept across the shore and surrounded his residence, forcing the keeper to leave his home. Restless and uneasy about the fate of his fellow workers out on the lighthouse, he wandered along the beach. Around four o'clock the next morning, perhaps at the very time when his assistant, Wilson, was near death on Gull Rock, John Bennett began to notice debris coming ashore. He went down to the edge of the sea. To his amazement Bennett recognized some of his own clothing which he had left at the lighthouse. Wreckage was also coming in, and he gathered two or three fragments from the rolling breakers. His worst fears were realized when he saw that pieces of timber were actually from the light itself, proving that without question it had fallen.

Captain William H. Swift visited the ruins of Minot's Light on April 22, 1851, and made a sketch of the ledge with the broken piling. He also drew the lighthouse tower itself, as it lay in the water with only a part of the side showing. He probably experienced the bitterest moments of his life when he stood on the rolling deck of the boat and sketched the symbol of his costly failure.

The gale which caused the destruction of the lighthouse off Cohasset has since been referred to as the *Minot's Light Storm of 1851.*

Minot's Ledge Lighthouse was rebuilt. A fine stone beacon, rising to a height of 114 feet, was erected on the site of the old tower, and after a wait of nine and a half years, the welcome gleam of its rays flashed out on November 15, 1860.[6] Although many fear that this tower may some day fall into the sea, the keepers feel that nothing less than an earthquake can ever shake it from its foundations.

During the many yearly storms at the new lighthouse, the surf often goes over the very top of the tower, and one may well imagine the lonely lives the keepers pass on the ledge. As the gales roar in from the depths of the Atlantic with gigantic waves sweeping up the sides of the tower, the men in the lighthouse often think of that night, now so long ago, when two brave men stood side by side to keep their last faithful watch that ended in eternity.

THE CITY OF COLUMBUS

ONE of the most terrible marine disasters in the annals of Massachusetts steamship navigation was the loss of the Boston and Savannah liner *City of Columbus* at Martha's Vineyard in 1884, with the death of one hundred passengers and members of the crew.

When she sailed from Nickerson's Wharf[1] in Boston, the steamer had eighty-seven passengers and a crew of forty-five. The *City of Columbus* possessed the highest rating possible, with an A 1 classification and was amply provided with fixtures, life preservers, and boats as required by law. It was a happy group of travelers who sailed away from Boston that January afternoon, for they were leaving the wintry weather for the South's warm, sunny climate.

As the steamer rounded Cape Cod, the night was clear and cold. The *City of Columbus*, all her lights visible, continued down the coast. The weather was getting colder, with a strong wind blowing from the northwest. By one-thirty in the morning the captain, constantly on his feet since the ship had sailed, believed it safe to turn in. The dangerous part of the journey, around Cape Cod, lay behind, and the vessel was now halfway through Vineyard Sound. Captain S. C. Wright told his first mate, Edwin Fuller, the course to follow:

"When Tarpaulan Cove bears north, change the course to west southwest."

It later developed that the man at the wheel, Quartermaster MacDonald, had not heard the low-voiced instructions the captain gave the first mate. Captain Wright then retired to his cabin in the rear of the pilot house, but for some reason did not go to bed. He sat down on the floor with his back against a stanchion. The wind was now north northwest. Robert Bennet Forbes, master mariner of the nineteenth century, said later in referring to the ship that "any ordinary landsman without chart or compass could have taken her clear of all danger." The passage in the Vineyard Sound at this point is almost five miles wide, but the tired and overconfident mate did not realize that the combined force of wind and tide near Menemsha Bight was slowly dragging the great steamer to disaster.

At a few seconds before quarter of four that morning the lookout was pacing the deserted deck forward of the wheelhouse when he suddenly noticed a buoy on the starboard side of the ship. Shouting a warning at the top of his voice, he received no answer from the pilot house, so rushed toward the man at the wheel. First Mate Fuller, however, hearing the cry, excitedly ordered Quartermaster MacDonald to port his helm.

The shouting aroused Captain Wright, who was still sitting on the floor of his cabin. Rushing into the wheel house, Wright cried out, "Hard a port!" and ordered the engines stopped. It was too late, for in less than thirty seconds the *City of Columbus* crashed on the hidden rocks of the Devil's Bridge at Martha's Vineyard, and disaster followed.

At this location there was a murderous double ledge which projected out under water. The outer reef where the ship hit was locally known as the Devil's Back. And such it proved on that luckless night of 1884. The ship remained afloat barely four minutes after she hit, for the captain now made his greatest mistake.

"I . . . saw the buoy on the port side[2] about two points forward of beam and about three hundred yards distant," said the captain later. "She immediately struck. I ordered the engines reversed, and she backed out about twice her own length. The steamer stopped immediately, and I ordered the jib hoisted and endeavored to head her for the north, but she filled forward and listed to port so that the plank sluice was about four feet under water." Thus the captain ordered the vessel backed off the rocks which had ripped open the ship's bottom, and she sank at once.[3]

The *City of Columbus* crashed on the ledge at 3:45 that morning, and by ten minutes past four most of the men, women, and children on the liner had perished. Number six lifeboat was launched but capsized at once. The crew lowered another boat which was crushed against the side of the ship. Four men later reached shore in it, however. Some of the men managed to set adrift one of the life rafts, but all aboard were swept off and drowned. Although a few survivors reached shore holding spars or woodwork, most of the others sank to their death in the icy waters.

The remaining twenty or so persons in the rigging suffered all the tortures that living people could endure. Frozen onto the shrouds because of the surf which lashed around them, and numbed by the zero wind which swept through their thin garments, the survivors, all men, waited for daylight. An hour after dawn the sufferers were gladdened when they saw smoke from a steamer which appeared around the west end of Cuttyhunk Island, dead to the windward of them. Four miles away, the ship was within easy view, and the watchers in the rigging counted the minutes before the vessel could arrive to save them. But their hopes were in vain. To their dismay, the steamer continued on her regular run up the coast, ignoring the now thoroughly discouraged victims. The ship had been the steamer *Glaucus*, commanded by Captain Bearse.

The keepers of the Gay Head Lighthouse had noticed a light out near the end of the Devil's Bridge and were organizing a crew to go to the wreck. Head Lighthouse Keeper Horace N. Pease had been called by his assistant at six that morning. Realizing that a shipwreck had taken place, Pease ordered Assistant Keeper Frederick Poole to make up a crew to row out to the scene. By dawn the attempt was begun. Poole had recruited lifesavers from the Gay Head Indians. Despite the heavy surf the lifeboat was launched into the breakers, but it soon overturned. All men reached the beach safely. Now soaking wet, their clothing was beginning to freeze. Poole ordered the men to remove their shoes and start out again in their stockings so their feet would not freeze. This time the lifeboat was successfully launched, and the dangerous waves were conquered. After an hour's struggle with the oars, the volunteers reached the scene of the wreck. Since the lifeboat would have capsized had it approached too close to the mast, the survivors, still clinging to the rigging, were told to jump into the water, where they would be picked up.

One by one the men in the shrouds jumped into the icy waves, and each one was quickly rescued by the lifesavers. The overcrowded lifeboat now started for land, but another danger awaited the survivors. As the boat neared the shore, a breaking wave swamped the craft, and she capsized just off the beach. No one was drowned because of the quick work of the Gay Head Indians, who pulled the shipwrecked victims out of the surf.

Meanwhile Keeper Pease had notified the residents of the adjoining village of Squibnocket that a shipwreck had taken place, and soon their volunteer lifesaving crew was on the way to the wreck. They reached the scene and had rescued several persons when a whistle in the distance drew their attention to the revenue cutter *Dexter* steaming toward them under forced draft. The Squibnocket lifeboat started for shore with its load of humanity, leaving nineteen forms clinging to the rigging.

When two boats were sent over to the wreck from the revenue cutter, seventeen more survivors dropped into the sea and were saved.[4] Only two persons could now be seen clinging to the rigging. As it appeared that they were afraid to leave the wreck, young Lieutenant Rhodes of the *Dexter* volunteered to swim over to the *Columbus* to rescue the men. With a rope around his waist, Rhodes jumped into the January seas. Swimming through the water, he was hit by some floating wreckage and had to be hauled back to the *Dexter*. Shortly afterwards the wind went down, and Lieutenant Rhodes made a second attempt, this time using the dingy. After trying unsuccessfully several times, Rhodes made the dingy fast to the rigging, and began to climb the futtock shrouds. When he reached the two men, he found that both had frozen to death in the ratlines. Cutting the bodies down, Rhodes dropped them into the water, later rowing back to the revenue cutter with them. He left the wreck alone in the sea, with its icy rigging glistening in the sun and the bow of the *City of Columbus* barely showing above the waves. One hundred lives had been sacrificed to carelessness.[5]

Several of the men who were active either on the wreck or ashore have left their personal testimony of the disaster. One of these individuals was Quartermaster Roderick A. MacDonald, the man at the helm when the vessel struck. His testimony follows:

"I went on duty at midnight. Heavy winds, clear, could see lights plainly, a little hazy on land. Wind a little on starboard bow. The usual course on passing Tarpaulin Light on Naushon is southwest by west, which should take us clear of the Sow and Pigs Lightship. We generally intend to steer in midchannel. The captain went below about three-quarters of an hour before the vessel struck, and gave me the course a quarter or half an hour before he went below. It was southwest by west. The second mate was in the pilot house when the course was given. The second mate told me a short time before she struck not to go to leeward of that course. . . . The light shone out plain enough but you could not judge the distance from the light. It appeared closer than usual but I was not in command of the ship. That is the course I always steer through there."

Quartermaster MacDonald, after the crash, was successful in swimming to the lifeboat which had floated some distance from the wreck, and took charge of operations to reach the island. Time after time the crew tried to row directly for the shore, where they would have drowned in the great breakers, but MacDonald prevailed upon them to keep off until the calmer waters of Menemsha Bight were reached. By this time one of the passengers in the lifeboat had died of exposure, but the craft was landed safely near the home of an Indian named Ryan, where the survivors were given the best of care.

The aftermath of the shipwreck ˙of the *City of Columbus* included many touching scenes. Among the bodies found was that of a young woman with a tiny pair of shoes frozen to her breast, her child having been separated from her in the terrifying moments after the crash.[6]

Captain Bearse of the *Glaucus* was later called before the investigation committee and asked why he had not bothered to sail over closer to the wreck of the *City of Columbus*. He admitted that he recognized the ship on the Devil's Bridge as the *City of Columbus*, but since he knew she had been supposed to pass that particular point hours before, he figured all the survivors had been removed from the ship. He said at the investigation that he looked through his telescope at the wreck and could see no movement of any kind. Although the United States Marine Inspectors exonerated Captain Bearse, Robert Bennet Forbes condemned their action as "lame and impotent." Captain Forbes said that it was because of a deplorable dullness of mind and vision that Bearse did not sail close enough to see the men in the rigging, where he could have saved the lives of many who subsequently perished.

Captain S. C. Wright, the master of the *Columbus*, was deprived of his license as pilot and his certificate as shipmaster. Many years later a prominent Boston sea captain was ashore at Savannah, Georgia. As he walked up the pier, stepping between bales of cotton and other cargo piled up ready for shipment, he heard a voice hailing him. Stepping closer, the Boston mariner recognized the former master of the *City of Columbus* working as a stevedore on the wharves at Savannah.

A NANTUCKET RESCUE

THE evening of January 19, 1892, was a typical wintry night on the Nantucket coast. The sky was dull and overcast, with an occasional squall to vary the monotony. The weather was nearer zero than the freezing point, and the northerly winds were biting across the sand dunes around the Coskata Life Saving Station. The regular patrols departed and returned; Keeper Walter N. Chase took a final glance along the coast as darkness descended, but there was no vessel in distress near his station.

A short time later, however, the three-masted schooner *H. P. Kirkham* struck far off the shore on the Rose and Crown Shoal. The vessel commanded by Captain Mc-Cloud of Liverpool, Nova Scotia, settled into the sand, forcing the men to take to the rigging. The location is not visible from the Coskata Station, which is on the inner or western side of Coskata Beach. At daylight Keeper Chase received a telephone call from the keeper of Sankaty Head Light, who said that he had seen rockets from the vicinity of the Rose and Crown Shoal, and at dawn could make out a vessel's masts on the Bass Rip, ten miles away.[1]

Keeper Chase called his crew at once, and they hauled the lifeboat across the sands to the outside of Great Point where they successfully launched the craft into the foaming breakers. Meanwhile Keeper Remsen at Sankaty Head Lighthouse telephoned Vineyard Haven for a tug to proceed to the scene of the shipwreck. The lifeboat sailed the long distance to the *H. P. Kirkham* without incident, finding it five miles farther out than on the Bass Rips as reported by Keeper Remsen. Since the starboard rail of the *Kirkham* was submerged, the men would have to be removed from that side. The lifeboat was then anchored with a long scope and the hawser was taken over the weather bow. The boat dropped down with the current, carefully aided by skillful handling of the oars, and after several attempts the heaving stick was thrown into the rigging of the schooner.

The keeper shouted across to the sailors to bend a line to the heaving stick; this was done at once, and the end of a topsail clewline was taken aboard. The boat was slowly hauled toward the schooner. The frenzied sailors, anxious to leave their sinking ship, tried to haul in on their end of the line, but Keeper Chase passed his boat knife forward to the stroke oarsman, telling the schooner's sailors: "Pull that boat one foot nearer and we cut the line." Chase was six feet four, and very impressive; the sailors obeyed him instantly, letting go the hawser.

The end of a line tied with a bowline was thrown to the wreck. The first sailor to reach it put his leg through the loop, and Keeper Chase ordered him to jump overboard and hang on. Cautiously he followed directions. He jumped and was hauled aboard as the boat slacked away. Then the lifeboat was brought in for the next man, and continued until every one of the seven men, who had been on the wreck for fifteen hours by this time, was in the boat.

The troubles of the lifeboat crew and the sailors they had rescued were not over, however. No land could be seen, but when on the crest of the waves, the men could barely make out the top of Sankaty Head Lighthouse. They weighed anchor and threw overboard the mast and sail as they would be of no further use in the long journey home against wind and tide. Three hours of hard rowing brought the lifeboat across the shoal, and the boat was then anchored to await the southern tide, which would set them toward land. At sunset they began rowing again, but six hours after leaving the wreck they had actually covered less than a mile. The location of the wreck was now nothing but sea and waves; the *Kirkham* had vanished.

The situation was very grave. They watched, hopefully at first and then in despair, for the Vineyard Haven tug, but it never came. Every few minutes they would ship a sea, after which frantic bailing would keep the lifeboat from swamping. At nine p.m. the southern tide was done, and they had not landed. There was nothing left to do but to anchor again, as the northern tide would carry them out to sea again.

The men said afterwards that the period from nine until three the next morning was the longest in their lives. Terrible scenes were enacted in the overcrowded lifeboat. The cross sea made the men violently seasick, while the waves threatened every minute to swamp them. When the tide changed, the wind went down and the men were visibly encouraged. The snow squalls ended and the sun came out. With the moderating weather and the favorable tide the men rowed for Siasconset, where they landed at ten in the morning, having spent twenty-six hours at sea.

During the long night when the men did not come home, Keeper Chase's wife kept the watch at the station. Her thoughts during the period when the lifeboat failed to return can only be imagined. The crew had actually

THE CITY OF COLUMBUS ON THE ROCKS AT GAY HEAD, JANUARY 18, 1884

WRECK OF THE CITY OF COLUMBUS AT MARTHA'S VINEYARD
GAY HEAD LIGHT AND DEVIL'S DEN IN BACKGROUND.

LOVER'S ROCK, LOVELL'S ISLAND, BOSTON HARBOR

A GROUP INGLUDING TWO LOVERS FROZE TO DEATH HERE DURING THE
GREAT DECEMBER SNOWSTORM OF 1786.

THE STEAMER LARCHMONT WHICH SANK AFTER A COLLISION NEAR BLOCK ISLAND, FEBRUARY 11, 1907

THE STEAMER FAIRFAX WHICH COLLIDED WITH THE
PINTHIS, JUNE 10, 1930.

COURTESY THE BOSTON POST

SMOKE FROM THE BURNING OIL ONE WEEK AFTER THE
FAIRFAX-PINTHIS DISASTER.
THE OIL IS COMING UP TO THE SURFACE FROM THE PINTHIS, WHICH SANK
FATHOMS DEEP TO THE BOTTOM OFF THE MASSACHUSETTS COAST.

been given up for lost by friends along the shore who could not sight the small dory from any vantage point on the island. Dawn enabled the discouraged onlookers to sweep the ocean with their telescopes, and the lifeboat was finally sighted. This rescue and subsequent fight against a head-on sea brought acclamation from all New England, praise which the heroic rescuers deserved. The crew members under Keeper Chase were Jesse H. Eldredge, John Lyman, Charles B. Cathcart, Josiah B. Gould, George H. Flood, and Roland H. Perkins. It had been an epic rescue of the sea.[2]

In the month of January 1893, the keeper and his associates were presented with medals awarded them by the government, the presentations being made in the Unitarian Church. There was one sad note to the occasion, however. Surfman Roland H. Perkins, who had suffered severely from exposure during the long night out at sea, steadily grew worse after his return. Failing to rally, he died as a result of his part in the successful efforts to save the lives of those aboard the *H. P. Kirkham*, and his medal was given to representatives of his family, who were present at the church.[3]

THE BAD LUCK OF THE JASON

IN many cases it seems that ships are like people. Some persons are born lucky while others are always having accidents from time to time. There have been barks, brigantines, or full-rigged ships which appear to have had their share of ill-fortune. Sailors would fall from the rigging, or the vessels would strand while coming into the harbor, and if there happened to be any blow worth mentioning, there would be this particular ship right in the middle of it.[1]

When accident after accident occurs in the lives of certain people, they are said to have bad luck. And so it is with ships of the sea. The story of the *Jason* is hard luck and bad luck from the start of its voyage to the finish. Even the sole survivor of the wreck died a short time later.

The ship *Jason* sailed from Barry, England, in February 1892, with a load of coal for Zanzibar. Three days out a great black object loomed across the bow of the *Jason*, crashing into the coal ship with terrific force. It was the steamer *Trilawie* from St. Ives. Temporary repairs were made after which the *Jason* was placed in drydock at Queenstown. Another start was then made for Zanzibar.

While rounding the Cape of Good Hope, the ship encountered a terrific gale during which one of the men furling sail lost his hold and fell overboard. The *Jason* reached Zanzibar, discharged her cargo, and began a voyage for Calcutta. In the harbor of Calcutta one of the crew fell from a Hindoo craft and was drowned.

After loading a great cargo of jute at the Calcutta port, the *Jason* sailed for Boston. For once conditions seemed to favor the ship, with fair winds and pleasant weather. But the fair winds gave way to strong gales, which in turn developed into a hurricane. At the height of the storm the ship was laid over on her beam ends, all masts went by the board, and the vessel became a hopeless mass of wreckage. In the midst of the confusion the captain of the ship broke his leg.

After three days the storm went down. With a jury mast rigged, the *Jason* sailed for the nearest port, Mauritius, where she arrived ten days later. Six months were needed this time to repair the *Jason* and give her a new cabin. Almost everything was made over except the hull itself, which they decided had come through pretty well. They later found out how weakened the hull actually was.

The captain, with his broken leg, was sent back to England with his wife. There are those who say a woman should not be aboard a ship as she brings bad luck, but the worst luck aboard the *Jason* occurred after the lady had left for England with her husband.

Again the *Jason* attempted an Atlantic crossing, this time with a new captain. Hardly had they left port when another sailor fell out of the rigging and was killed. The jute cargo below decks swelled so much that the ship had to return and leave some of it behind. This caused a further substantial delay, but finally a start was made for America.

The new captain, McMillan by name, arrived with his ship off the New England coast the first day of December, 1893, almost two years after the *Jason* had left England.

Thick weather prevailed, with the captain uncertain as to his exact location. Falling in with a New York pilot boat, he was given his bearings, and shaped his course accordingly. Although he did not realize it, he was then approaching Cape Cod in such a way that he was doomed should an easterly set in. Cape Cod has a natural trap for sailing vessels from which very few escape. It is a triangular area made up of Pollock Rip Shoal, Chatham, and Highland Light. Once inside this area with a strong northeast breeze, the ship's doom is sealed, for there is not room enough to wear around and avoid the shoals to leeward or weather the Cape hard on the starboard tack.

A driving rain now began with the wind from the northeast, and the rain shortly turned to sleet and snow. Nauset Three Lights was the first landfall the *Jason* made, late in the afternoon of the 5th of December. The ship was on a lee shore and the captain realized there was no hope. The men worked hard to get out their boats and prepare for the disaster which they knew was coming.

Back on shore the vessel had been under close observation for hours. The telephone which runs from one Cape Cod life saving station to another was constantly ringing that afternoon as the *Jason* made her way up the coast. Captain Charles first reported the ship off his Orleans station. Every station crew from Nauset Beach to Race Point hauled out their boat and gear and awaited the inevitable.

Down at Chatham, Captain Hezekiah F. Doane at Old Harbor Station was the first to report. "She's gone by me," said Doane.

The next to be heard from was Captain Charles at Orleans. "I've missed her," he said as he watched the

Jason edge on up the coast.

Captain Daniel Cole at Cahoon's Hollow came through later with "She's got by our station."

Finally came the last report. "I've got her," shouted Captain David Rich from Pamet River[2] over the wire. "She's stranded off the beach."

The crew of the Pamet River Station rushed the beach cart to the scene. By this time the shore was piled high with wreckage, and the slatting of the *Jason's* sails could be heard even above the storm. Unable to launch a lifeboat into the sea, the men fired their gun out to the vessel, but there was no response. Unknown to them, most of the sailors on the *Jason* had already perished when the mizzenmast fell into the sea. The ship, presumably weakened from her previous encounters, broke in two almost as soon as she struck. One person, a young man named Samuel Evans, had been too late to climb the mizzenmast with the others, and a great sea swept him overboard. His lifebelt secure, he swam to a nearby bale of yellow jute, grasped it, and knew no more until the men picked him up on the shore.[3]

"Be I saved?" asked the lad, as he came to.

"Yes," was the answer, "but you're the only one." Twenty-six others had been engulfed by the storm. The great jute cargo littered the beach for miles, with many of the residents reaping a rich harvest because of the disaster. The foremast of the *Jason* continued to show out of water day after day, prompting the observation that if the crew had chosen the right mast, many of them would have been saved. In the clear weather which followed scores of pictures were taken of the broken ship, her stern showing out of water many yards from the bow. The broken rigging and tattered sails of the *Jason* presented a fascinating but awesome sight to the thousands who viewed her from the shelter of the mainland. It is said by some that part of the *Jason* can still be seen at low water off the shore, but not for many years has any of her cargo washed up on the beach.

Samuel Evans, the sole survivor, returned to England with the memory of the strange voyage of the *Jason* in his thoughts. When he sailed again shortly afterwards, it is said that he fell from his bunk and was killed. There are those who believe that every man aboard the *Jason* when she left England was doomed the moment the vessel sailed out of the harbor and Evans' death was delayed only a short time longer than the others.

Without question some shipwrecks are recalled more frequently than others as the years go by. The *Jason* is one of them. From time to time grizzled old sea captains, talking of the ways of the ocean, have mentioned the *Jason* among the shipwrecks they easily recall. This sad tale of the bad luck and subsequent disaster of the *Jason* holds an unusual place in the minds of the people of Cape Cod.

THE MONOMOY DISASTER

A N event which excited much popular sympathy over the entire country in the year 1902 was the disaster which befell the Monomoy life saving boat as she neared the beach at Monomoy Point, south of Chatham, Massachusetts, on the morning of March 17. Together with the subsequent rescue of the sole survivor, Surfman Ellis, by Captain Elmer Mayo, the event created an unusual amount of interest, especially around New England.[1]

Two coal barges, the *Wadena* and the *Fitzpatrick*, had been stranded several days before on the Shovelful Shoal off Monomoy Point, and several men were rescued by the Monomoy Life Saving Crew. The weather moderated, allowing wreckers to go aboard and plan the task of lightering the vessels. On the evening of March 16 the weather grew heavy, so that all but a few of the men were taken ashore by the tug *Peter Smith*.

The next morning when the barge *Wadena* flew a distress signal, Captain Eldridge organized a lifeboat crew to reach the craft. At several places on the shoals the seas were extremely rough, but the surfboat reached the lee of the barge without further incident. With a line made fast, plans were formed for the return journey. Five men were on the barge, all of whom excitedly asked to be taken ashore. It is believed that the workers on the *Wadena* were in a partial state of panic and fright from their perilous position.

Four of the five men lowered themselves into the boat successfully, but the captain of the barge, who was a heavy man, let go his hold when he was a few feet above the lifeboat, and fell breaking the after thwart. The painter or rope was cut as soon as the five men had been placed in position in the lifeboat, and the trip to safety began. Getting out from the lee of the *Wadena,* the lifeboat was hit by a great wave which partly filled the craft. This made the bargemen frantic, and they leaped to their feet in the lifeboat throwing their arms about the bodies of the surfmen. One after another the seas struck the little lifeboat, until it finally filled and capsized with its thirteen occupants. Twice the lifeboat was righted by the surfmen in the water, but each time the seas overturned her.

The five bargemen were the first to drown since they could not get back to the overturned craft. The surfmen clung desperately to the bottom of the boat, but soon their strength began to fail. Surfman Chase was the first to perish, and then Nickerson and Small disappeared. Only five remained. Ellis, who was the sole survivor, later wrote down his experience.[2] We quote now from his journal:

"Captain Eldredge, Surfmen Kendrick, Foye and Rogers and myself still managed to hold to the boat. Every sea which struck the boat swept completely over us, almost smothering us. Kendrick was the next one of our crew to perish, and poor Foye soon followed him. Captain Eldridge and Surfman Rogers and myself were the only ones left and we expected that we, too, would soon share the fate of our comrades.

"Rogers was clinging to the boat about amidships, while Captain Eldridge and myself were holding on near the stern. Captain Eldridge called to me to help him get a better hold, and I managed to pull him on to the bottom of the boat, when a sea struck us and washed us both off. I managed to regain a hold on the bottom of the boat, and looking around for Captain Eldridge, I saw that he was holding on to the spar and sail which had drifted from underneath the boat, but was still fast to it. The seas were washing me off the boat continually at this time, and when I last saw our brave captain, he was drifting away from the boat holding on to the spar and the sail.

"My strength was fast going, and when poor Rogers begged me to help him climb further up onto the boat, the only thing I could do was to tell him that we were drifting toward the beach, and that help would soon be at hand and to hang on.

"Rogers had lost his strength, however, and failing to get more secure place on the bottom of the boat, feebly moaning, 'I have got to go,' he fell off the boat and sank beneath the waters.

"I was now alone on the bottom of the boat, and seeing that the center board had slipped part way out, I managed to get hold of it, and holding it with one hand had succeeded in getting my oil clothes, undercoat, vest, and boots off.

"By that time the overturned boat had drifted down over the shoals in the direction of the barge *Fitzpatrick*, which was also stranded on the shoals, and when I sighted the craft I waved my hand as a signal for help. I soon saw those on the barge fling a dory over the side into the water, but could see nothing more of the dory after that until it hove in sight with a man in it rowing towards me."

The man in the dory was Captain Elmer F. Mayo, who at the time of the Monomoy disaster, was aboard the barge *Fitzpatrick* in company with Captain Mallows of Chatham and the barge captain. There had been a fourteen-foot dory alongside the barge, which was hauled on deck the night before. The only oars aboard were too long for the dory, so Mayo cut them down.

Mayo knew nothing of the tragedy until he noticed Surfman Ellis drifting along, clinging to the overturned lifeboat. Realizing that a terrible catastrophe had occurred, Mayo stripped down to his underwear, let over the dory, and climbed down a rope into the little craft.

With improvised thole pins and oars so large he could hardly hold them, Mayo fought his way toward the lifeboat. Surfman Ellis saw the dory just as it reached him. It was a difficult feat to take Ellis from the water, but as both men were experts at the task of lifesaving, it was successfully accomplished. Mayo realized that Ellis could not stand the exposure much longer, and headed the dory for shore at once. Only his expert knowledge of the shoals and rips around Monomoy allowed Mayo to reach the shore where Surfman Walter Bloomer rushed into the breakers to assist in beaching the dory. The two men were quickly cared for.

Mayo's feat had been one of outstanding heroism earning for him the title "Hero of Monomoy." Both the

United States and the Massachusetts Humane Society recognized Mayo's gallantry, awarding him medals for his
rescue.[3]

The people of New England quickly responded to a
call for help for the widows of the Monomoy life savers.
William U. Swan, then of the Associated Press, publicized
the story throughout the nation, and a benefit meeting was
held at the Tremont Theatre, Boston, where Ellis, Mayo,
and the Mayo's dory were on view.   In a comparatively
short time a fund of several thousand dollars was raised
for the widows of the men who sacrificed their lives that
wintry morning off Cape Cod.[4]

THE LARCHMONT DISASTER

O FTEN we find that history teaches but man disregards the lesson. It is the same way with marine disasters. When the *Portland* sank in 1898 carrying the only passenger list, tremendous agitation developed for requiring an extra list to be left ashore whenever a passenger vessel sailed from port. Yet in 1907, more than eight years after the *Portland* storm, the Joy liner *Larchmont* left her pier in Providence, Rhode Island, with the only passenger list available. Evidently the steamship lines of that period had learned nothing from bitter experience, continuing a policy which had caused such indignation with the general public. But the period of which we write has gone; today maritime regulations are better than in any other period in the nation's history.

It was at seven o'clock on February 11, 1907, that the *Larchmont* left Providence, about half an hour behind her regular schedule. The wind was about northwest, blowing almost forty miles an hour, when Captain G. W. McVey took the steamer down the river. As the *Larchmont* approached Sabine Point, McVey gave charge of the wheel to Quartermaster Staples, under the supervision of Mr. Anson, the First Pilot.[1]

Captain McVey now proceeded on his usual tour of the ship, after which he called on the ship's purser. At about quarter of eleven he passed through the pilot house, where he conversed briefly with the man at the wheel. The pilot was in command of the course to be steered.

The steamer's headlight, masthead light, and sidelights were all burning brightly and everything was in satisfactory order.

Shortly before eleven-fifty when Watch Hill Light bore four miles northwest, Quartermaster Staples, at the wheel, saw the lights of a schooner ahead. The vessel was yawing and luffing, making it hard to figure her course. As she appeared on the port side of the *Larchmont*, Staples swung his wheel hard-a-port, but evidently the schooner, later identified as the *Harry Knowlton*, luffed just at that time, for the schooner's red lights disappeared completely. The *Knowlton* was even then headed directly for the doomed *Larchmont*, crashing a moment later into the steamer's port side just forward of amidships.

As the schooner bore down on the steamer, several short, rapid blasts of the steam whistle were sounded from the wheel house of the *Larchmont*, bringing Captain McVey from his cabin into the pilot house just as the schooner loomed up and smashed against the steamer. Captain McVey's own story follows:

"Realizing that this was a severe blow, I at once rang the bell to call the engineer so as to have him report to me the conditions of affairs below. Failing to get any response, I at once sent Mr. Wyman, who had appeared on the scene, and Mr. Staples, the quartermaster, to get the desired information.

"At this time the boat became enveloped in steam, and everybody appeared panic-stricken except the crew. I at once from my station in the pilot house ordered everybody to their stations as I realized by the starboard list of the boat that she must be in a sinking condition.

"Almost immediately after this Mr. Wyman and the quartermaster reported to me that the *Larchmont* was in a sinking condition and I think told me that it was the request of the chief engineer that I should beach the boat as soon as possible.

"I at once proceeded to the pilot house, rang the necessary bells to start the engines ahead, but could receive no response and I turned again to the deck to superintend the clearing away of the boats.

"At this time the *Larchmont* had a very heavy starboard list, in fact, I think her freight deck was under water which brought my own boat which was the forward starboard boat quite near the water.

"At this time there were no passengers in the vicinity of my boat, and knowing that the only way to save lives in the proper manner was to lower my boat and go around to the other side of the *Larchmont*, I proceeded at once to have my boat lowered into the water and at this time the ones who got into my boat were the only ones that were on my side of the ship, unless some one might have been aft, hidden by the starboard paddlebox. . . . We at once proceeded around the bow of the sinking Larchmont to get on her port side to be in a position to save life."

The wind and sea, however, prevented Captain Mc-Vey's boat from helping those still aboard the *Larchmont*. In fact, it is doubtful if there were many on the *Larchmont* who could be helped by that time. When the captain had launched his lifeboat into the bitterly cold waters of Long Island Sound, five other lifeboats and two life rafts had already left the ship. It is true that one or two shady forms could be discerned through the steam and spray still standing on the deck, but they made no efforts to jump into the boat. All this time the *Larchmont* had been steadily settling in the water; she soon started her final plunge and disappeared into the icy February seas, carrying with her an unknown number of victims. Since it was then two minutes past eleven o'clock, the entire incident covered a period of twelve minutes.[2]

The six lifeboats and the two rafts were now left floating in the rough seas. As the night wore on, the survivors noticed the gleam of a lighthouse beacon far in the distance, and rowed for the welcome flash. The icy waves, driven by a wind which at times reached fifty miles an hour, swept over the boats and rafts until every person was coated with freezing spray. As it was practically impossible to do anything toward reaching land except drift before the wind, the passengers and crew still alive did what they could to face the icy gale.

Block Island was in the direct path of the survivors. Keeper Elam P. Littlefield of the Sandy Point Lighthouse had been aroused by the barking of his dog Leo. Getting up to quiet the animal, Littlefield was startled by a knock against the window pane, and pulled open the door. A boy fell across the threshold, muttering, "More coming, more coming."

It was then five minutes of six in the morning of February 12. Keeper Littlefield aroused his wife and five children, after which he telephoned the New Shoreham

Life Saving Station. Two guests at the lighthouse volunteered to help, and the first trip down to the beach was
made. Purser Young of the *Larchmont* was brought back.
"The *Larchmont* has gone down, 200 have perished,"
Young gasped, as oil was applied to his face. His body
was completely encased in ice. One after another the
survivors were brought into the old Sandy Point Lighthouse, until it resembled a hospital. Bed spreads were
torn into strips for bandages to be used on frozen arms
and legs. The keeper's eldest daughter, Addie Littlefield,
took charge of the newcomers. It was a race with death
to keep many of the sufferers alive, but only one man, the
Turkish fireman of the wrecked vessel, succumbed. The
work of the keeper was made easier by the arrival of the
New Shoreham Life Savers. Keeper Littlefield drove
along the beach with his team, stopping here and there,
while the victims were placed aboard and rushed to the
lighthouse.[3]

A lifeboat came through the breakers with one live
man who jumped ashore. Left in the boat were ten dead
men, all but one of whom had slowly frozen to death.
This man had cut his own throat to end his agony. The
survivor was quickly taken to the impromptu hospital and
cared for. After the living had been attended to, thirty-
eight bodies were brought to the station. The young boy
who had first arrived at the lighthouse, Fred Heirgsell,
now began to tell his story of the disaster, and it chilled
the hearts of the keeper and his family. He described
how the others had frozen to death. According to his
account, he too was about to fall asleep when the lifeboat
grated on the shore. He was barely able to reach the
lighthouse when he was encouraged by the barking of a

dog, whose commotion had already aroused the lighthouse keeper. Summoning his remaining strength, Fred Heirgsell rapped on the window pane, and the last he remembered was falling across the open doorway. Others told equally harrowing tales of exposure and suffering.[4]

Captain McVey landed at Block Island around six-thirty that morning, with his hands and feet terribly frozen. He was later taken home to Providence, where he was placed under a doctor's care. Although it had been a bitter experience, he had been subjected to much criticism for his actions. But it is always easy to criticise in times of extreme trouble and danger, and the majority of sea captains with whom I have talked have believed he did what they would have done.

The schooner *Harry Knowlton,* after striking the *Larchmont,* was abandoned by her captain, Frank T. Haley, and his crew three miles from Block Island. They rowed to safety at the Life Saving Station of Weekahaug. A prominent Rockland sea captain expressed his opinion on the cause of the disaster as follows:

"I have talked with both captains, and feel that it was a case of stubbornness on the part of the schooner's captain. According to his sworn testimony Captain Haley saw the steamer's red lights less than one hundred yards away from him, but he told his helmsman to keep her on her course. Technically he was right, as a schooner does have the right of way, but it was a case of bull headedness, as the *Knowlton* was yawing considerably." The disaster which befell the *Larchmont* was the last major marine calamity in the vicinity.

THE FAIRFAX-PINTHIS DISASTER

AT five o'clock in the evening of June 10, 1930, the Merchants and Miners passenger liner *Fairfax* sailed from Boston Harbor on her regular run down the coast. A heavy fog soon settled over Massachusetts Bay, so Captain A. H. Brooks ordered the ship to proceed at a moderate rate of speed, from ten to twelve knots.

At 6:58 that night the Shell Oil tanker *Pinthis* hove in view half a point on the *Fairfax's* starboard bow. Captain Brooks, hearing one blast of the whistle, ordered the helm hard-aport and backed away full speed. The *Fairfax* quivered from stem to stern as the engines changed their direction, but it was too late. The two ships came together with a sickening crash, and the *Pinthis* caught fire. Eleven thousand barrels of oil spouted high into the air to come down on the two steamers. Locked with the *Pinthis*, the *Fairfax*[1] also broke out in flames, her decks soon a mass of roaring fire.

The *Pinthis* started to sink at once, pulling away from the *Fairfax* as she began her final plunge into the foggy sea. Captain Brooks now cleverly maneuvered the *Fairfax* in order to get the fire on her decks into the lee, thus preventing it from spreading. The crew showed their splendid discipline by rushing to the scene with the fire apparatus, extinguishing the blaze with quickness and dispatch. Several marines and sailors who were passengers helped the ship's company in beating out the flames and maintaining general order.

Immediately after the collision the captain ordered an S.O.S. radioed. The radio operator later testified that although he had directions to send the S.O.S., he found the calls were not going out and cancelled the appeal on his own responsibility. Later, when the radio worked properly, he did not again send the S.O.S., but radioed many personal and private messages. The reason for the radio operator's inexcusable behavior has never been clearly explained.

Shortly afterwards the captain anchored the *Fairfax*. Blazing oil from the tanker lighted up the sea for miles around. The Coast Guard Cutter *Tampa* was a short distance away, but Captain Brooks said that he did not request her aid because with the sea on fire the cutter was unable to approach.

To escape the flames two boys, John V. Eubank, 19-year-old quartermaster, and Joseph Poco, negro pantry boy, dived through the burning oil, swam under water until they reached a clear area, dived again and again until they arrived at the edge of the flames. Locating one of the *Pinthis* lifeboats so wrenched and broken as to be almost sinking, they made it serviceable by stuffing the largest holes with clothing which they tore from their bodies. Having bailed the boat dry, the two boys drifted along until picked up by the two-master *Dacia*, which took them into Boston.[2]

One of the woman passengers on the *Fairfax* who was terribly injured and had been told that she could not live, kept repeating over and over the words, "Tell Ellsworth that I love him. Tell Ellsworth that I love him." She died shortly afterwards.

There was much criticism of the handling of information in connection with the collision. In spite of the relative nearness of Boston to the scene of the catastrophe, the entire incident was shrouded in mystery for several hours. Hundreds of relatives and friends of those aboard the *Fairfax* crowded around the Boston pier of the steamship company, anxious for information of their loved ones. Ambulances waited in vain. Even at 2 a.m. the Scituate Coast Guard had not been notified of the disaster a few miles off their station. It is said that the *Tampa* radioed to the *Fairfax* asking what was wrong and received a reply that all was well.

Meanwhile the *Fairfax* had contacted her sister ship, the *Gloucester*, which proceeded to the scene of the collision. Fifty-six passengers transferred to the rescue ship were later safely landed ashore. There were forty-seven lives lost in the disaster, including those who perished from both ships.[3]

For days after the accident the waters off Scituate were the scene of a spectacular phenomenon. An enormous cloud of fire and smoke billowed high into the heavens day and night, unceasingly raising its gigantic signal message of warning so all might notice. The cloud of smoke gave a strange sensation to those who witnessed it. Even stranger, however, must have been the feelings of those who stood on the deck of the *Fairfax* that June evening when they watched the huge unwielding bulk of the *Pinthis* bear down at them out of the fog.

THE NEW ENGLAND HURRICANE

NEW ENGLAND'S 1938 hurricane was unparalleled in the entire history of the United States in the widespread destruction which it created, the gale of September 21 causing more property damage than had ever occurred before in a single storm anywhere in the world. Although the exact number can never be known, there were from 682 to 700 persons who lost their lives in the tempest which swept over the New England shores and countryside.[1]

Residents of every part of New England thought that their section was the hardest hit, but without question Rhode Island has that unfortunate distinction. Providence, as in the 1815 hurricane, suffered more comparatively than any other city its size. Since Rhode Island was directly in the path of the terrific upheaval of the elements, more than 300 men, women, and children in this state died before nightfall on that memorable day. Entire beach settlements were obliterated, the actual contours of the state's geographical boundaries changed radically, and downtown Providence, the metropolis of Rhode Island, was inundated to a depth of ten feet!

The Providence Weather Bureau early that afternoon reported winds of forty miles an hour, and hurricane warnings were received by the *Providence Journal* at 3:10 p.m. Forty-mile winds, however, were not too uncommon for the autumnal season, so the people paid little heed to reports of trouble ahead. Only the historians remembered

the terrible 1815 disaster. Later that September afternoon, however, when slates began to fly from the roofs,
knifing down into the streets below, and when windows
started to crash inward and church steeples to sway back
and forth, the nonchalant attitude of the average by-
stander changed first to one of extreme concern and then
to utmost horror. By this time the gale had begun an
ominous vibrating whine of warning and danger. Shortly
after five o'clock the Providence Weather Bureau gauge
registered 87 miles an hour.[2]

The newspapers were among the first to feel the
effects of the storm. The *Evening Bulletin* never reached
the streets with its hurricane extra because all power failed
at 5:16 p.m. Just as the edition was about to be printed,
the news room lights faded and went out, and the workers
were forced to give up their efforts.[3]

Narragansett Bay was then being subjected to a 121-
mile an hour gale which was pushing the waters of the
Atlantic toward Providence. Reaching the center of the
city around five o'clock, the gale within a half hour filled
Union Street in the business section of Providence with
six feet of water, marooning thousands on upper floors of
the banking and industrial buildings. Hundreds of automobiles sank out of sight in the deep water of the Providence streets. People struggled for their lives as they
fled from street cars, busses, and autos. Chimneys fell on
three different cars in separate parts of the city, killing a
person in each case. Four men were drowned in the city
itself. At the height of the tide the water rose to a point
13 feet 9 inches above mean high water, as compared with
the mark of 11 feet $9\frac{1}{4}$ inches in the 1815 hurricane.[4]

Outside of the city, in Charlestown Beach, Watch

Hill, Mataunuck, and other locations, scores of people were drowned. Great waves thirty feet high with breaking crests came roaring through the villages, sweeping all before them, and leaving death and desolation in their wake.

At the amusement center on Rocky Point the roller coaster was shattered and the large dining hall and bath houses became a mass of wreckage. At Misquamicut ten women attending a church social were swept out to sea when the building collapsed, and were never seen again.

At about 7:30 in the evening the tide in Providence began to go down, but Rhode Island had been laid in ruin. The state had lost its electricity and its transportation, while telephone connections were broken, and even water was at a premium. A few days later the Department of Commerce issued warnings that all coastal charts were worthless because of the great changes the hurricane had caused. Without question no living person had ever seen disaster to equal this Rhode Island destruction.

Every storm or hurricane has its ridiculous story, and the 1938 storm was no exception. At the height of the gale, when hundreds were fighting for their lives as the rising tide swept through the state, the phone in the *Providence Journal* offices rang vigorously. A woman wished to register a complaint with the paper because a tree had fallen across her property, and the forestry department had refused to do anything about it!

The *Boston Post* published the *Providence Evening Bulletin* for nine emergency editions, the fine work done by this Massachusetts daily paper creating considerable favorable comment. In addition to the *Bulletin*, the *Post* printed an issue of the *Fall River Herald*. The *Providence*

Evening Bulletin resumed its regular edition on October 3, 1938.[5]

Devastation in New Bedford was considerable. The New Bedford Yacht Club was smashed to kindling wood, while out in the harbor the wife of Keeper Arthur Small of the Palmer Island Light was drowned. She had tried to row over to help her husband when the gale hit, and her rowboat overturned. Although Mrs. Small was lost, Keeper Small survived the gale.

Lighthouses themselves, ancient guardians of the deep, could not stand against the hurricane. The Whale Rock Lighthouse fell into the sea, taking the keeper to his death. This iron-plated beacon located at the entrance to Narragansett Bay had survived hundreds of ordinary storms and gales since its erection in 1822, only to crash in the hurricane of 1938.

Five persons were carried to their death from the keeper's dwelling at Sand Point Light on Prudence Island. The keeper himself survived as he was on another part of the island at the time, but his wife and son perished.[6]

A priest, the Reverend Mr. T. F. McKitchen, was trapped with his mother by the gale at Conimicut Point. Escaping in a small skiff, Father McKitchen realized that his dory was being swept away from land in the gathering dusk, and was about to administer the last rites of the church to his mother when the current shifted, and the skiff soon grounded at Anawamscutt Beach in Barrington. A little girl at Conimicut Point rode through the storm on a kapok mattress, finally coming ashore after four hours at Narragansett Terrace. Both her parents had perished.

At Mackerel Cove on Conanicut Island, seven small children, four in one family, were drowned when their bus was caught by the ocean. The driver was trying to move the frightened youngsters to safety when three enormous waves swept the road, engulfing everything in their path.

The noted Herreshoff shipyards were destroyed. The only possession of the Bristol Yacht Club after the gale went down was a flagpole as the club and all its other possessions were swept out to sea. Bailey's Beach at Newport was wiped off the map by the giant hand of the storm, and Newport Beach suffered the same fate.

The state of Connecticut was in the direct path of the storm. Hartford experienced heavy damage around the State Capitol. The Park River overflowed into the business district, while the Connecticut River at midnight had risen to almost twenty-five feet. 7,000 people were forced to evacuate their residences in the city.[7]

At Stonington, Connecticut, the passenger train *Bostonian* encountered first a cabin cruiser on the tracks, and then a house. The track ahead had washed out, and so all the passengers were placed in a coach and diner for the night. As the night wore on, the passengers ate food from the diner and seemed to enjoy their unusual experience. They were cut off from the world for almost twenty hours.

In Bridgeport, thirty passengers and the crew of the ferryboat *Park City*, which ran to Jefferson City, encountered the gale fifteen miles from land. With her engines dead she drifted helplessly until the storm went down. She was later towed back into Bridgeport by the *Galatea*, a coast guard patrol boat.

New London experienced the brunt of the hurricane. The spectacular sight of the barkentine *Marsala*, a training ship, tossed against a railroad trestle was matched by the lighthouse tender *Tulip* which reposed on the railroad tracks when the gale went down. Barges, tenders, yachts, and motorboats were jammed in helpless confusion into the New London streets. Whole sections of the city were devastated. Fires broke out threatening to destroy the entire city, but the wind shifted so that the flames were put under control.

As in the 1635, 1723, and 1815 gales, Massachusetts was hard hit by the 1938 hurricane.[8] The people of the state, however, fell to work and with unyielding enthusiasm soon were able to overcome the worst effects of the storm. Provincetown, Massachusetts, was prepared for the worst, but aside from a schooner which parted from its moorings, the majority of the fishing fleet rode out the storm. Fear as to what might happen at high tide, 10 p.m., was dispelled when the gale diminished before that time.

Marion, Massachusetts, lost its Beverly Yacht Club. Tabor Academy was flooded to its second floor; the schooner *Tabor Boy*, however, rode out the storm without too much damage. The entire personnel at the school helped the townspeople to save their belongings. Fairhaven suffered severely. Seven deaths were reported in this area, and five boat yards at the waterfront were put out of business. Many vessels were left stranded on the Fairhaven-New Bedford bridge when the tide went down leaving them high and dry.[9]

Twelve residents of suburban Fall River died. The City Hall roof was blown off and the sides of the water tower were blown in. The Shell oil tanker *Phoenix* was torn from her moorings at Fall River and was pushed by the gale to Somerset, disrupting telephone service when her dragging anchor broke a cable.

The Boston and Albany tracks were undermined in Adams, Massachusetts, and when the street caved in at Mc-Kinley Square in that town, two automobiles were cata-pulted into the excavation.

With all trains at a standstill and all wires down be-tween Boston and New York, unusual methods were re-sorted to for necessary transportation and communication. Boston talked with New York via London. In eight days air lines between Boston and New York carried 8,000 pas-sengers. One of Uncle Sam's giant battleships carried mail between the two cities. On October 1, train service was resumed.

The hurricane force lasted two hours at high inten-sity around Boston; the peak of the storm was about 6:47 p.m. Boston Common was greatly damaged as was the famed Arnold Arboretum. Churches were hard hit in Greater Boston, with over a score suffering substantial damage. The anemometer at the Blue Hills Observatory registered 180 miles an hour before blowing away.[10]

City Point seemed to draw the gale's worst blasts around Boston. A million dollars' worth of sailboats, motor yachts, expensive pleasure cruisers, and excursion steamers were in the path of the storm. Three great yacht clubs, the Columbia, South Boston, and Boston Yacht Clubs all had their fleets anchored in the area between Thompson's Island and the mainland, but when the gale had gone down around midnight on September 21 only a handful had ridden out the storm. The rest were battered into hopeless masses of unidentifiable wreckage, and were heaped up in a jumbled pile against the City Point Public Landing and the Columbia Road Breakwater—hundreds of thousands of dollars worth of vessels gone forever.

One of the epic stories of the storm is the fight which Captain Fred Esterhill and his younger brother Eddie put up against the gale. Realizing that the hurricane was coming, they went down to the landing pier just in time to watch their 60-foot excursion motorship *Francis* break loose from her moorings and start toward them. As luck would have it, the *Francis* ended her dash from her moorings by hitting the end of the pier, whereupon the two courageous brothers jumped aboard the vessel, Fred rushing to the pilot house and Eddie taking charge of the engine room. They soon had the *Francis* under way and ran her across the harbor, keeping the motorship headed into the wind, which at one point registered 100 miles an hour. The brothers won their fight with the gale, and the *Francis* was one of the few vessels in the vicinity to ride out the hurricane of 1938.

Captain Lawrence H. Dunn of the Boston Harbor Police and the crew of the police boat, *Michael H. Crowley*, risked almost certain death when, at the height of the worst hurricane in at least one hundred years, they attempted the rescue of eight men caught at the end of a piling jetty near the Boston Fish Pier. Running the *Crowley* into the teeth of the gale, Captain Dunn edged the sturdy vessel up to the men who were clinging desperately to the piles. Watching their chances, the crew maneuvered the motorboat at opportune moments between the waves, and the men were saved from death. Only an expert mariner could have accomplished this feat.[11]

The state of Vermont had never before seen such a wind as swept up in the Green Hills that evening, and even the most secluded villages and towns nestling in the comparative security of the deep valleys were ravaged. Maple sugar groves and almost the entire apple crop suffered terrific losses, but there were only seven deaths because of the gale.[12]

The White Mountains of New Hampshire, as well as the seacoast, received some damage, but the force of the gale did not approach that of the southern New England states. Apple crops, bridges, and highways were considerably affected.[13]

Maine was able to escape the worst effects of the hurricane, as the storm veered off inland. However, the forests of Maine had their thousands of trees blown down, and for many years afterwards the fire hazard there was great.[14]

The beautiful trees of New England suffered irreparable damage in the hurricane. Millions crashed to earth. Many of the historic trees were damaged, including the Governor Winthrop willow in Winthrop, Massachusetts. It has been estimated that it will be more than half a century before New England's forests can recover from the 1938 storm.

Of course in damage created, the 1938 hurricane, as compared with the 1635, 1723, or 1815 storms, caused far greater damage. But the writer believes that the three other storms, had they occurred today, would have created devastation almost equal to New England's worst hurricane, that of September 21, 1938.

MAINE AND NEW HAMPSHIRE

FOR centuries the men of Maine have sailed the seven seas. During the period from 1790 to 1850, three out of every five sailors in New England drowned at sea, and the men in Maine were no exception. Wrecks have occurred by the hundreds along the Maine coast, and the shipwreck list at the back of this volume includes most of the outstanding disasters. The loss of the *Royal Tar* and the *Portland*, as well as many other ships which either hailed from Maine ports, or had Maine sailors aboard, are mentioned elsewhere in the book.

New Hampshire, although having a short coastline, has been the scene of many great shipwrecks, while nearby Boon Island and the Isles of Shoals have had harrowing experiences.

THE PLYMOUTH PINNACE

One of the earliest shipwrecks of which we have definite knowledge is that of a pinnace from the Plymouth Colony, which was wrecked at Damariscove over three centuries ago. The sequel to the story of the shipwreck is of interest.

Governor William Bradford tells us[1] that in March of 1624 the Pilgrims went to quite a little trouble having "new-masted and rigged their pinass", sending the vessel on a fishing trip to Damariscove. Here she was "well-harbored in a place where ships used to ride, there being also some ships already arrived out of England." Shortly after this a violent storm hit the Maine coast, and the pinnace was driven against the rocks, "which beat such a hole in her bulke, as a horse and carte might have gone in, and after drive her into deep water, wher she lay sunke. The master was drowned, the rest of the men, all save one, with much adoe; all her provision, salt, and what els was in her, was lost." [2]

As it was a sturdy vessel the Pilgrims agreed to have the Plymouth pinnace repaired and refitted. Casks were placed around the ship at low water and she was floated to a cove where carpenters and coopers worked on her for some time. Finally she was ready to leave and after a substantial amount was paid, the craft sailed for Plymouth, at which port she eventually arrived. Bradford, however, was not reconciled to the expenses presented by the first Maine wreckers in history, and ends his comments on her as follows:

"But she cost a great deale of money, in thus recovering her, and buying riging and seails for her, both now and when before she lost her mast; so as she proved a chargable vessell to the poor plantation."

THE INDUSTRY

One of the wrecks recounted around the firesides during the last century was that of the *Industry*, built at Packard's Rock, in what is now Cushing, Maine. She was commanded by David Patterson, 2nd, who had previously coasted for some time with Reuben Hall.

No one ever learned what happened to the *Industry*. She was launched late in the fall, and sailed for Boston on her first trip in November 1770. Wreckage began to come ashore along Cape Ann some time later, but no one from the *Industry* was ever seen again. Those on board included Major Fales and his son from Massachusetts, George Briggs, John Porterfield, Robert Gamble, John Mastick, David Malcolm, Alexander Baird, Samuel Watson, Mrs. Benjamin Packard and her child, and Abagail Patterson. The captain's brother had been lost two years before at Mosquito Harbor with seventeen persons, all perishing.

THE ALBANY

The British sloop-of-war *Albany* was wrecked on the Northern Triangles, between Mussel Ridges and Green Island, just before the close of the American Revolution. Joshua Thorndyke, who previously had been a prisoner on the *Albany*, heard of the shipwreck and sailed out to the scene with two friends, Mr. Elwell and Isaac Orbeton. There they found that all of the cannon aboard had gone down through the broken bottom of the vessel to rest on the rocky ledge, where they remained for many years visible at low tide. Even today, it is said, cannon can be retrieved from the Triangle Ledges off the Maine coast.[1]

When the crew of the *Albany* abandoned ship, they rowed away in an open boat for Castine, but became lost in the "vapor," necessitating a landing at Matinicus.[2] Three of the men froze to death before the boat reached shore, and the others were in a pitiful condition. Taken into the homes of the island inhabitants, the men of the enemy were given the best of attention. While dressing the frozen hand of one of the British sailors, Aunt Susan, one of the interesting personalities on the island, noticed tears coming from the young man's eyes. He admitted that he had been one of a party of raiders who shot and

WRECKAGE FROM THE 1938 HURRICANE AT CITY POINT, BOSTON
THE FAMED HEAD HOUSE SHOWS IN THE BACKGROUND WITH
THE CITY POINT PUBLIC LANDING ON THE RIGHT.

THE TWO TABLETS TO PROVIDENCE'S TWO GREAT DISASTERS
EDWARD ROWE SNOW STANDING BESIDE THE OLD MARKET HOUSE
IN MARKET SQUARE, PROVIDENCE.

THE NORTHERN SWORD OFF THE WINTHROP WATER TOWER.
IN THE RIGHT FOREGROUND WINTHROP BAR IS SEEN.

WINTHROP'S SHORE DRIVE
SHOWING TERRIFIC DAMAGE CAUSED BY AN OCEAN STORM. SEAWALL, RAIL-
ING, SIDEWALK, AND STREET HAVE ALL BEEN WASHED AWAY BY THE WAVES.

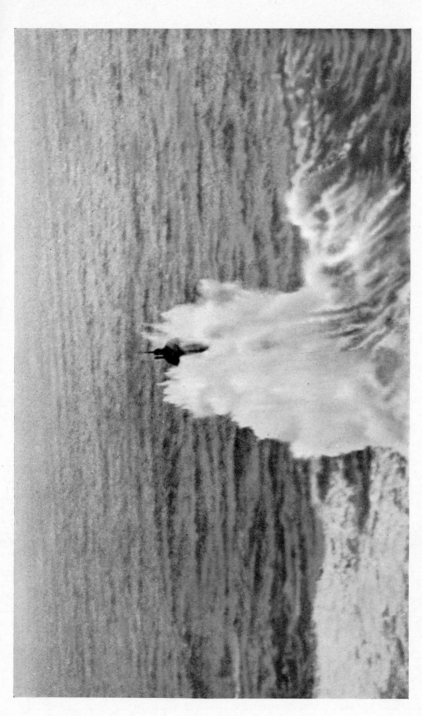

A SPECTACULAR 120 FOOT WAVE ALMOST COMPLETELY COVERS MINOT'S LIGHT—JANUARY 12, 1941

THE ROYAL TAR ABLAZE OFF FOX ISLAND THOROUGHFARE
THE ELEPHANT IS SEEN SWIMMING FROM THE BURNING SHIP,
WHILE IN THE DISTANCE THE REVENUE CUTTER VETO CAN BE
SEEN, WITH THE ISLE OF HAUT IN THE BACKGROUND.

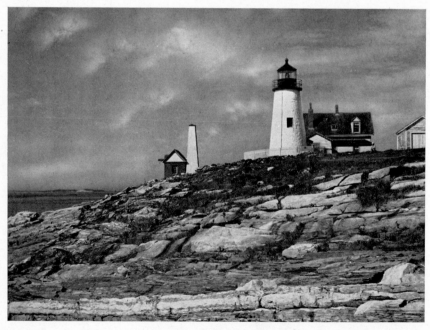

PEMAQUID POINT, MAINE
WHERE THE ANGEL GABRIEL HIT IN 1635 AND THE EDMUNDS
STRUCK IN 1903.

killed her heifer on the island some months before. On Matinicus Island today there are many coins taken from the clothing of the bodies of the British sailors frozen to death and buried there.[3]

THE ADAMS

In the month of August 1814, the United States frigate *Adams* ran upon a ledge near the Isle of Haut. A tent was erected for the accommodation of sailors ill with scurvy, while the guns and other articles were brought ashore. British prisoners were aboard, and Captain Morris arranged to have Robert Knowlton and his brother of Deer Isle, Maine, transport them to Thomaston. While on the way the prisoners rebelled, but the two men soon quelled the uprising, landing the prisoners a short time later at that part of Thomaston now known as Rockland.[1]

Later the frigate was floated off the rocks, and proceeded up the river to Hampden.[2] While she was in port there, word came of the capture of Castine by the British, whereupon the gallant Captain Morris blew up his vessel to prevent the *Adams* from falling into the hands of the enemy. All the sailors aboard were successful in reaching the American lines.

THE NEW YORK

The steam brig *New York* commanded by Captain Harrold, left Portland, Maine, August 22, 1826. On the following Thursday evening at nine o'clock the brig caught fire while eight miles off Petit Manan Light,[1] and Captain Harrold soon saw that he would have to abandon ship. There were aboard fourteen passengers and a crew of eighteen, all of whom took to the boats, reaching Petit

Manan about eleven o'clock that night. The *New York* was entirely consumed by flames.

A Miss Sarah Tucker of Kennebunk was among those on board. When interviewed later she said, "I lost everything except what I had on, which was the meanest I had, my habit, my shawl, and bonnet."

THE SARAH

In the year 1835 the packet *Sarah* sailed from Boston to Eastport, Maine, on its regular run, but the master, Captain Pierce, mistook Mount Desert Rock for the gleam of Moosepeak Reach Light wrecking the vessel on one of the islands off Jonesport.

Daniel Goulden, one of the young passengers, could not swim. A capable negro woman volunteered to get him ashore, and told the boy to climb on her shoulders after she jumped into the water. Goulden jumped and clung to her as she swam toward the beach. They both reached shore safely, but sixteen of the others were lost.[1]

Some time later the ballad, *The Loss of the Sarah*, appeared, which had a substantial sale in Eastern Maine.

In Fannie Eckstrom and Mary Smyth's fine collection *Minstrelsy of Maine*, the *Loss of the Sarah* is quoted in full. We reproduce two of the verses:

> *Ye landsmen all, now pray draw near,*
>
> > *A lamentation ye shall hear;*
>
> *A ship was lost on the sea,*
>
> > *It was the Sarah's lot to be.*

*   *   *   *

Thirty and two were the Sarah's crew

And landsmen were all counted too;

Sixteen survived to reach the shore,

Sixteen are lost, they are no more.

THE BOHEMIAN

The steamer *Bohemian* sailed from Liverpool on February 4, 1864, with a passenger list of 218 and a crew of ninety-nine. Captain Borland made a brief stop at Londonderry before starting out across the ocean. Stormy weather delayed the vessel several days, and so it was late on the afternoon of February 22 that she made Cape Elizabeth, Maine.

A peculiar condition of haze confused Captain Borland into believing that he was quite a distance off the shores of Cape Elizabeth, but actually he was approaching Alden's Rock. Realizing that he needed help, he sent up rockets and blue lights to attract the attention of a pilot, also slowing his speed to a knot and a half. The ship's gun was fired.

Suddenly, without warning, the *Bohemian* crashed against Alden's Rock,[1] and slid over. A hasty examination revealed that the engine compartment had sprung a bad leak, and so the captain headed the *Bohemian* for land, at the same time ordering all lifeboats over. The crew took their stations in orderly fashion, but the passengers became excited, milling around the boats in confusion. When the number 2 lifeboat had been loaded, the pin broke, dropping everyone into the sea. This particular accident caused the greatest loss of life.

The other lifeboats were successfully launched, although only partially filled with passengers. Captain Borland ordered the rowers to return to the ship, as there were more than eighty still aboard. They refused, heading at once for shore, where they all landed safely. Three hours later, however, others brought the lifeboats back to the *Bohemian*, and the remaining survivors were taken ashore without accident.

The fact that it was Washington's birthday caused an unfortunate interpretation of the ship's distress rockets and the firing of the ship's gun. Several pilots had heard the cannon's firing, and had seen the rockets in the air, but concluded that some patriotic festivities were being celebrated in honor of George Washington. They gave the matter no further thought.

Later Captain Borland testified that the peculiar haze made the land look many miles farther away than was actually the case. He had two lookouts on the forecastle and one aloft. He had tried to reach shore, but the fires in the engine room were drowned within ten minutes, and his proud ship, the *Bohemian*, went down near Richmond's Island within ninety minutes after the accident.[2]

There had been considerable mail aboard, and divers were sent down to recover it. Every sack except a mail-bag destined to Philadelphia was eventually brought to the surface.

A tradition has it that John F. Fitzgerald, famous Boston mayor, was aboard the *Bohemian*. When the writer asked Mr. Fitzgerald for details of the wreck, the eminent Bostonian replied that he was not the Fitzgerald in question. A John Fitzgerald of New York was the person aboard the *Bohemian*.[3]

THE ANNIE C. MAGUIRE

Thousands who journey down to Portland Head's historic lighthouse look out on the dangerous ledge which juts out into the Atlantic there, and read the inscription painted on the natural rock: "In memory of the ship Annie C. Maguire wrecked here, Dec. 24, 1886."

Captain Thomas O'Neil had lost his bearings, and the vessel crashed on the ledge off Portland Head on Christmas Eve. Fifteen members of the crew, together with the captain, his wife and son, were brought ashore in a boatswain's chair by young Joseph Strout, son of the keeper of Portland Head Light. The *Annie C. Maguire* stayed on the ledge until a snowstorm swept the coast a few days later, when she broke up and went to pieces.

THE GALE OF 1888

In the Rockland, Maine, *Courier-Gazette* for Tuesday, November 27, 1888, appears a telegram addressed to S. M. Bird:

> Hingham, Mass., Nov. 26
> Sch. H. C. Higginson ashore on Nantasket Beach. Will be total loss. Captain and two men lost. Wire instructions.
>
> E. C. ROAD, Mate

There were many similar messages sent from scores of coastal points along the Atlantic Coast after the great November gale of 1888 had run its course. There are still old men living who witnessed both the 1888 and 1898 blows who claim the 1888 was the more severe of the two storms. Regardless of which was the greater storm, the 1888 gale was particularly hard on Maine ships.[1]

The *Higginson* had sailed from Hillsboro, Nova Scotia, for Newburg, New York, but adverse winds had driven her off her course. Captain A. N. Fales had gone out with his summer sails on because his winter canvas was in the hands of the sailmaker. The two sailors lost with him were strangers who had signed on just before the schooner sailed. Four others besides the mate were saved.

During the storm a hay schooner was abandoned at Webster's Head on the northern part of North Haven, while the schooner *Mountain Fawn* went ashore at Naskeag Harbor. The Gouldsboro *Golden Eagle* crashed at Owl's Head and went to pieces, a total loss. The *Maud S.* of Ellsworth smashed against the rocks nearby, but was later pulled off and repaired. In Rockland Harbor the *William McLoon* broke from its moorings and hit the end of Atlantic Wharf, finally becoming a complete wreck.[2]

A Maine schooner, the *G. W. Rawley* went ashore at Edgartown, and was condemned and stripped. The *Robert Ripley* with 500 bushels of corn and flour went ashore in the storm at Dolliver's Neck.

THE PORTLAND GALE

Rockland suffered greatly during the *Portland* storm. At the height of the gale one could not see across Rockland Harbor. Over twenty vessels met trouble. The schooner *S. F. Mayer* and the *Fannie May*, a lobster boat, were wrecked in the harbor. The schooner *Georgietta* was ashore at Spruce Head; the *Alida* was on Ash Island Bar. Captain Leslie Blake's *Anna W. Barker* was ashore at Southern Island. A twenty-ton schooner hit the beach at Martinsville, soon breaking up. *Carrie C. Miles* was damaged at Northport. The *Woodruff* was also there in distress. The *Ella F. Crowell*, the *James A. Brown* and the *E. G. Willard* were all at Vineyard Haven. The *Bertha E. Glover* of Owl's Head was at Vineyard Haven. The *Idella Small* was ashore at Bay View, Massachusetts.[1]

The steamer *Hurricane* went to pieces in a short time when caught in Rockland Harbor. Mrs. H. A. Bain, now of Riverside, California, observed that it was astonishing to see how quickly the steamer broke up into kindling wood.[2]

THE PEMAQUID SHIPWRECKS

A gale which caused great damage all along the Eastern seaboard hit New England September 17, 1903. Two shipwrecks occurred at Pemaquid Point, Maine, both of them resulting in loss of life. The *George F. Edmunds* of Gloucester hit on the east side of the rocks. Her captain, Willard F. Poole, was master and owner. The schooner had left Gloucester seven weeks before, but ran into bad luck, catching less than a barrel of mackerel. Finally deciding to return home, Captain Poole sailed by Monhegan and was headed for Boothbay Harbor. He missed the way in the gale, however, crashing on the ledges of Pemaquid. He and thirteen of his men were lost, only two of the sailors being rescued.[1]

The other vessel was the little two-masted coaster, *Sadie and Lillie*, which hit close by. Weston Curtis of Pemaquid, who saw the wreck, managed to get a line out to the schooner, and two men made their way safely to shore. The last to leave his ship, Captain William S. Harding, of Prospect, Maine, began the hazardous trip in over the lines. Just as the captain was buried in the swirling seas halfway to shore, the lines snarked and jammed, and Captain Harding drowned before the eyes of the helpless watchers ashore.[2]

THE CATAWAMTEAK

One of the outstanding schooners along the Maine coast was the *Catawamteak,* on which many fine Maine captains and seamen have sailed. The writer's grandfather, Captain Joshua N. Rowe,[1] was among those who considered it a privilege to command her under sail. The schooner was wrecked on Cape Cod, July 28, 1911. Floated off successfully, the *Catawamteak* continued on her sailing career for many years. George M. Cook of Friendship, Maine, saw the *Catawamteak,* loaded with stone, sink after a gale about three miles west of Monhegan Island.[2]

THE FLORA D. THOMPSON

An unusual rescue story involving one of America's destroyers and a schooner was enacted in Maine waters in 1915.

On the evening of December 9, 1915, the sloop *Flora D. Thompson,* with seven men aboard, anchored off the Kennebec River near the Seguin Island Lighthouse. Before morning a gale came up, and the *Thompson* parted her cable, beginning to drift out to sea.

Discovered by watchers from the Hunniwells Beach Life Saving Station at daylight on December 10, the *Flora D. Thompson* was then slowly drifting farther away, the only deterrent being a sea anchor made of the cookstove taken from the galley and thrown overboard. A surfboat was quickly dispatched to the scene, many miles at sea, and on the journey the lifesavers fell in with the new destroyer *Conyngham* on the way to undergo her trial runs on the course off Rockland, Maine. The captain of the *Conyngham* agreed to help, so proceeded to the scene and threw a line aboard.

The *Conyngham* now began the tow toward shore. Approaching Seguin Island, the *Flora D. Thompson* started to settle in the water, so all hands, including four women and children, were removed as the *Thompson* went down. They all were shortly afterwards transferred to the tug *Cumberland*, which had appeared on the scene.

THE GOAT ISLAND SHIPWRECKS

The double shipwreck of January 7, 1920 at Goat Island, Cape Porpoise, was one of the unusual occurrences along the coast that year. The *Charles H. Tuckey* came in on the wrong side of the spindle striking the ledge, and the *Mary E. Olys* tried to pass to starboard of the *Tuckey*. The *Olys* also went aground, but hit much more heavily than the *Tuckey*, for within five minutes she had broken to pieces. The *Tuckey* was later floated, but only kindling wood remained of the other vessel.[1]

THE WANDBY

One of the mysterious ships of the early 1920s was the British steamer *Wandby*. She had gone on a long voyage to the White Sea, where the *Wandby* completely disappeared from contact with the outside world. Sailing as far north as latitude 71 degrees, she returned to civilization to find the insurance agents had paid off on the vessel, and every member of the crew had been mourned as lost, many of them discovering that funeral services had been held in their memory.[1]

After this unusual experience the *Wandby* sailed to American waters. Around the year 1921 she was off the coast of Maine. Sailing from Portland one day, she headed for what the captain believed to be Cash's Ledge,[2] but it was actually Cape Porpoise where the *Wandby* ran aground.

THE CITY OF ROCKLAND

On September 2, 1923, the steamer *City of Rockland* ran up on the reef off Parker's Head on Dix's Island in the Kennebec River. The popular steamer had sailed with 300 passengers from Bath at 7:30 in a dense fog, going ashore a half hour later. Attention of those on land was attracted by long, repeated blasts of the steamer's whistle, and soon surf boats from the Popham Beach Coast Guard Station arrived.

As they jumped from the lower deck, the passengers were caught by the coast guardsmen and placed in the surf boats and lifeboats from the *City of Rockland* for the short trip to Dix's Island. Most of the passengers crowded around a gigantic bonfire which had been built on the beach. Blankets and food were brought ashore from the ship. The castaways were good natured and made the best of it. The children, while sliding down the sloping sides of the steamer into the boats, enlived the proceedings by their songs, singing at the top of their voices, *Yes, We Have No Bananas,* or *Barney Google,* the favorites of the period.[1]

Later the *City of Rockland* was floated off and taken to Salem by Captain Betts. She was burned for her fittings between Little and Great Misery Island in Outer Salem Harbor, October 29, 1924.[2]

THE CASTINE

On the morning of June 8, 1935, the steamer *Castine* went ashore on the Bay Ledges near Vinalhaven. Since Captain Leighton Coombs had his engines stopped at the time because of the dense fog, the situation was not regarded as too serious until the vessel began to careen at an alarming angle. When she reached an angle of 45 degrees more than a score of passengers were thrown into the waters of the Penobscot. Four of them drowned.

Many vessels responded to the distress signal which Captain Coombs sounded, among them the steamer *North Haven* and several lobster fishermen. Aboard the *Castine* were seventy-five members of the Limerock Valley Pomona Grange.

The steamer *Castine* quickly broke in two, and proved to be a total loss. The forward part of her hull, however, was used in the building of an unusual cottage on the shore at Treasure Island, Vinalhaven.

THE ISLES OF SHOALS

Crashing against the ledges of Smuttynose Island, one of the Isles of Shoals, in January 1813, a Spanish ship went to her doom. At the height of a blinding snowstorm the richly laden craft struck, leaving no living soul to tell the story of the ship. She was believed by some to be named the *Sagunto*,[1] while others claimed that her name was not known. Several sailors did reach shore, but were unable to get to the home of Captain Sam Haley, who always kept a light burning in his window during a storm. It seems even more tragic when it is realized that the men who had escaped from the wreck walked some of the distance toward the house when their strength gave out and they fell exhausted to the ground. Their bodies were found after the storm. Two of them actually reached the stone wall in front of Haley's house but they could not climb over the wall.

The surf brought ashore many boxes of raisins and almonds. A silver watch was later found, having stopped at four o'clock, possibly the time its owner was lost. On the back of the watch were the initials *P. S.*

Fourteen bodies from the wreck were found and buried in a little plot of land on the island where the rude stones may still be seen. Celia Thaxter often visited the graves of the Spanish sailors at Smuttynose Island, and part of her poem[2] is quoted here:

O sailors did sweet eyes look after you
   The day you sailed away from sunny Spain?
Bright eyes that followed fading ship and crew,
   Melting in tender rain?

   .   .   .   .

O Spanish women, over the far seas,
   Could I but show you where your dead repose!
Could I send tidings on this northern breeze
   That strong and steady blows!

Lonely, unknown, deserted, but for me,
   And the wild birds that flit with mournful cry,
And sadder winds, and voices of the sea
   That moans perpetually.

Dear dark-eyed sisters, you remember yet

These you have lost, but you can never know

One stands at their bleak graves whose eyes are wet

With thinking of your woe.

The writer, while flying over the Isles of Shoals at Christmas time dropping packages[3] on New England lighthouses, has often looked down at Smuttynose Island and thought of the Spaniards buried there and of the women who waited in vain for their men to return. Celia Thaxter's words always came back as the plane roared across the island. In January 1942, 129 years after the wreck, as an officer in the Army Air Corps, the writer was convalescing in a hospital in Oran, North Africa. One of the ladies who attended him was from Malaga, Spain, sixty miles up the Mediterranean from Gibraltar. She was a Spanish refugee from Franco's government. Of a historical frame of mind, the lady had remembered the ship, with some of her ancestors aboard, which had never returned to port in 1813, and the writer thus became the first one to tell her (in doubtful French) of the story of the Spaniard's shipwreck at the Isles of Shoals.

THE KATAHDIN

The experience of the paddle-steamer *Katahdin*[1] during the blizzard of January 1886, on the route from Bangor to Boston, gives an idea of what the *Portland* must have gone through before she foundered in the 1898 gale.

On January 9, 1886, the *Katahdin* left Bangor for Boston. Running into a heavy gale off Cape Porpoise, her master, Captain Homer, decided to take no chances and ran to sea. Reaching the vicinity of Boone Island, he tried for its shelter and failed. All night long the terrific blast from the northeast continued and the *Katahdin* kept her head into the wind. The fuel was entirely consumed, however, and a shipment of spoolwood, excellent for fuel, was also used. Finally the ship was driven to a position near the Isles of Shoals. By this time all the spare fixtures had been thrown into the fires and the dismantling of staterooms began.

Frank A. Garnsey of Bangor was the freight clerk. "I never expected to see land again. I was going down to the engine room and met Captain Pierce. I asked him how long we'd stay up and he said:

"'The old *Katahdin* won't last another hour.' When we began to fill, a list of the passengers and crew was made out and placed in a bottle. I was pulling down stateroom doors when land was sighted; everything else had been consumed."

The *Katahdin* had sighted Portsmouth harbor; a short time later, visibly battered and bruised, her houses wrecked, her cargo burned, and her bulkheads smashed in, she limped into a safe harbor. Captain Pierce said that it had been a dreadful experience. "I never expected to see shore again. The only thing that saved us was a shift in the wind which beat down the seas and gave us a chance to get into Portsmouth." [2]

THE OLIVER DYER

At one-thirty in the morning of November 25, 1888, the schooner *Oliver Dyer* anchored in the harbor at Portsmouth, New Hampshire. The wind began to breeze up at sunrise, continued throughout the day, and by evening a howling gale from the northeast had set in, bringing thick snow and tremendous surf.

At sunset Keeper Silas H. Harding of the Jerry's Point Life Saving Station displayed the international code signal *M T*, informing the *Dyer* that a lookout would be on the beach all night. When the *Dyer* began to drag anchor at 5:45 the morning of November 26, Surfman Robinson, then on the beach, fired his Coston signal, giving the alarm. Keeper Harding called out the crew and went over opposite the ledge east of the station. A tremendous sea caught the *Dyer*, throwing her fifty feet nearer shore. The seas now made breaches over the schooner, washing a man from the rigging forty feet up.[1]

One of the vessel's crew jumped into the water and swam for the rocks. Surfman Hall dashed into the surf to save him and, although both were terribly cut by the rocky ledges, they managed to climb up on the beach. The schooner's cook then leaped into the sea, and Surfman Randall grabbed him just as the undertow was pulling him down. The last two men aboard were saved by a heaving line. Keeper Harding and his brave men received medals for their outstanding heroism.[2]

SOUTHERN NEW ENGLAND

A T twenty minutes of four on the morning of August 30, 1872, the schooner *Nettie Cushing* collided with the steamer *Metis* off Watch Hill, Rhode Island. The captain of the *Metis*, Charles L. Burton, sailing the steamer from New York City to Providence, had encountered rough seas while passing through Long Island Sound. When the vessels came together, the schooner hit the steamer about forty feet abaft the bow abeam of the pilot house.[1]

It was believed at first that the damage was slight, and many passengers who came crowding out on deck were told to go back to bed as there was nothing to worry about. Shortly after this the engineer discovered that the ship was leaking badly, and so all persons were told to get up and dress. Before the *Metis* could be beached, however, she sank in the waters of Long Island Sound. The hurricane deck, crowded with passengers, soon floated free. A lifeboat and a life raft were quickly filled to capacity and pushed off from the wreck. As daylight came, the superstructure of the *Metis* was drifting toward the shores of Watch Hill.

Back on the Connecticut shore, the residents of Watch Hill had heard of the tragedy. Some of them rushed down to the shore scantily clad, others hastily donned more suitable garments, while still others waited to dress in their usual manner. As dawn lighted up the sea, the beach was thronged with people all shouting in their excitement.

The deck of the steamer was less than a mile away by seven o'clock, while the lifeboat and the life raft were just off the beach. The boat soon entered the breakers, and all except three passengers who perished in the undertow were saved. Then the life raft caught itself in the relentless surging of the waves and dashed against the shore. All but one or two on the raft were quickly grabbed by the people of Watch Hill.

Now the superstructure of the *Metis* was just off the beach. Those on shore, preparing for the inevitable, formed two chain gangs of a dozen or so each, the end man securely anchored high and dry above the pull of the under-tow, and the lower man waist deep in the dangerous surf. With a great shout from those on shore, the hurricane deck caught in a giant comber and started for the beach. Smash-ing and grinding itself into the sands of Watch Hill, the deck rapidly went to pieces, but not before the human chain had done its duty well. Most of the men were pulled out of the foam, although several of the women who were not so fortunate perished in the breakers.[2]

Some of the personal experiences of the survivors have been recorded. Colonel A. S. Gallop, awakened by the crash, later went back to bed, and then was told to dress. He jumped into a lifeboat which capsized and was righted again. After rowing for a short time, he had to bail the boat with his shoe. Before long his craft was picked up by a fishing smack. Mr. P. F. Brown, who was also awakened by the collision, was sent back to his room where he stayed a short time. According to Brown the captain ordered all hands to don life belts and jump into the raging sea. Many jumped and were lost. Several women on the upper deck were washed off. Two, however, clung to Brown, all three being saved when the deck hit the beach.

After the deck went to pieces, a man wrapped in a blanket was seen sitting on a rock gazing intently at the breakers. He and his wife had clung to a cotton bale until within a few feet of the shore, but a great wave separated them just off the beach, and she disappeared. He was unhurt, but he sat there watching each returning wave hoping it would reveal the body of the woman he loved.

At first it was feared that over one hundred lives had been lost, but one by one the missing persons were located alive and well, so that the final total of victims was around twenty-five. Many of these were in the lower part of the *Metis* and their names were never known.

By the spring of 1880 the competition for passengers had become so great among Long Island Sound steamers that the price of tickets between Boston and New York had been reduced to $1. This ridiculously low fare brought hundreds of people daily to board the Sound steamers. Bitter races sometimes resulted from the efforts of rival ship captains to better their opponents, with chances being taken in the heat of the contest which, in saner moments, would never have been attempted.

Running at a twelve-knot speed through a dense fog, the steamer *Narragansett* collided with the steamer *Stonington* near midnight on July 11, 1880. Efforts had been made to avoid the crash, but it was too late. The helm of the *Narragansett* was thrown sharply around when the other steamer came out of the fog at her, so that the *Narragansett* was broadside when the *Stonington* smashed into her forward of the wheel on the starboard side. It was a terrific shock, throwing all the sleeping passengers out of their berths. There was an immense hole ripped in the steamer's bow, all the lights aboard the *Narragansett* went out, and she caught fire. The *Stonington* had veered off into the night after the collision, and did not return, evidently becoming lost in the fog again.[1]

The captain ran the *Narragansett* into shallow water, where she settled until she rested on the bottom. The flames gained rapidly, forcing many people to leap into the sea. All the lifeboats to leeward were caught by the flames, but windward boats were launched with one exception. Two life rafts saved many of those forced to jump overboard. About this time the steamer *City of New York* arrived on the scene in time to rescue many from the water. Afire from stem to stern, the *Narragansett* half an hour later had burned to the water's edge.

Miss Elizabeth Peall of Philadelphia had left New York for Boston on the *Narragansett*. Sick nearly all that day, she retired early. When the crash came, she quickly dressed. Her story[2] follows:

"Most of the ladies had time to slip on their skirts. Oh! Such screaming. Mrs. Branyan of Boston Highlands was with me and her little girl. We stood on the main deck and screamed as loud as we could. . . . I asked a man to save me. He pushed me away, and said he had enough to do to save himself. By this time the boat was sinking. The water was up to my knees on the main deck."

Reaching a lifeboat, Miss Peall was placed in it by the *Narragansett's* captain himself, and the lifeboat was pushed away from the ship.

"A lady and her baby, not more than eight months old, were left on the deck. She begged us to let her in, but the boat had floated away from the steamer, and we had no oars. . . . The last I saw of her she had her hands raised crying for us to come. . . . There was only one little spot left, where the fire had not reached, and she was standing there, crying out. Another lifeboat came up and gave us oars. We rowed up to the City of New York and she took us in. . . . I found on the City of New York a good many rescued persons. . . . A lady said she had lost three children. She was weeping so hard!"

No accurate list of the *Narragansett's* dead was ever made, but the writer believes, after comparing various estimates and accounts, that from fifty-five to seventy met their death as a result of the collision. Captain Nye[3] of the other steamer, the *Stonington*, continued his trip to the mainland, where he reported the accident on his arrival.

BLOCK ISLAND

Block Island is known as "the island of a thousand shipwrecks" for good reason. Probably far more than that number of vessels have been wrecked around or off the shores of this beautiful land, but of course no accurate survey is possible. Only the most outstanding disasters can be included in this volume.

The ship *Princess Augusta*, commanded by Captain Andrew Brook, sailed from Rotterdam for Philadelphia with a cargo of Palatinate[1] prisoners about the year 1720. The stories told of this ship and the people aboard appear in so many versions that it seems doubtful if the truth can ever be separated from the myths and legends which time has woven about the *Augusta*.

That the ship "ill used by the sea, weakened by the death of half her hands was blown off her course, and forced ashore in a December snowstorm on Block Island" seems clear enough. But the record in the Notarial Protests[2] that it is possible "only one side of the story" was told, adds a touch of mystery that has not been cleared.

Sheffield[3] writes that the vessel is known as the Phantom Ship of Block Island. He says further that the Block Islanders rushed down to the shore when the ship grounded there, and murdered the crew and passengers. The murderers took the most valuable cargo and then burned the ship. She became a phantom ship and appeared every year until all the murderers were killed or died natural deaths. In 1876, when Sheffield wrote, there was a Mr. Benjamin Congdon, then aged 89, who had seen the phantom ship six or seven times. Benjamin S. Knowles of Point Judith, aged 92, had also observed it. According to Sheffield there were at least two survivors of the wreck.

Another version is that the officers took the treasure from the vessel and abandoned her, while the islanders, far from killing the passengers, befriended them. Two of the survivors on the island were women, "Tall" Kattern and "Short" Kattern. Tall Kattern married a negro and had many descendants; Short Kattern lived among families on the island, later dying there. There are still many graves of the shipwrecked victims on the island. Richard Henry Dana's poem about the buccaneers is based on this story. Whittier's poem, the *Palatine*, also concerns the ship.

One of the women passengers, Mary Vanderline, is said to have preferred to keep her cabin on the *Princess Augusta,* as she did not wish to leave her possessions aboard the vessel and go to the homes of the natives ashore. A great storm and a high wind floated the ship off the rocks, and it started out to sea. Block Islanders went aboard to reason with the woman, but she remained adamant, staying on the ship. As the vessel drifted away, one of the men set fire to it, hoping to compel her to leave. Mary Vanderline was stubbornly resolved not to go, however, and soon the flames forced the men to take to their boats. The burning ship with the woman standing dramatically by her possessions amid the flames disappeared over the horizon as the men rowed away.

According to the Reverend Mr. Livermore's account, which quotes the letter of Willey, "the light actually is seen, sometimes one-half mile from shore, where it lights up the walls of a gentleman's rooms through the windows." Strangers suppose it to be a vessel on fire. Willey saw it December 20, 1810. Livermore[4] handles the whole matter rather roughly:

"From this time, it is said, the Palatinate light appeared, and there are many who firmly believe it to be a ship of fire, to which their fantastic and distempered imaginations figure masts, ropes, and flowing sails."

In the year 1778, on the twelfth of December, Newport was swept by a blinding snowstorm still remembered as the "Hessian Gale." The grave Hessian sentries of the British army remained at their posts, faithfully carrying out their orders.[1]

When they failed to come in from their posts, it was believed that some had deserted, but because of the storm no hunt was made; neither could the relieving sentries reach them because of the deep drifts. After the storm went down the changing guard found the missing sentries, still standing at their posts, frozen to death.

An interesting incident of the *Ann Hope* has survived the years. Laden with spice and merchandise, the *Hope* hit around 1806 during a bitter snowstorm on the south end of Block Island. One of the men washed ashore but he appeared more dead than alive. His body was placed above the tide, and after a short time spent in an effort to bring him back to life, one of the rescuers noticed another sailor in the surf.

"Let us try to save that one out there in the water, for this man is as good as dead," said the Block Islander.

"Na! indade, I'm as good as half a dozen dead men!" was the astonishing rejoinder from the apparent corpse on the ground. The *Ann Hope* and her cargo proved a total loss, with the exception of a few bags of coffee, which were salvaged and used by the islanders.[1]

In 1831 Benjamin T. Coe witnessed the unfortunate disaster of the two-masted schooner *Warrior*, which Captain Scudder ran between Boston and New York. The Sound was white with foam in the heavy gale, with the two seas meeting at Sandy Point in great fury. Coe wrote that it was "impossible to describe the awful situation of that vessel when she first came on shore, the seas breaking over her masts, and seven souls hanging to the rigging, not more than 150 yards from us, and completely out of the power of man to render them any assistance."[1]

Bottom up, her masts unstepped, her cargo of cotton and calico coming ashore, the ship was helpless. Sometimes the long bar on which the ship grounded would be nearly naked as the huge billows receded. One giant in the crew, larger and more resolute than the others, realizing that there would be no help from shore, decided to run the gauntlet. Choosing a moment when two large waves were pulling away from the thin strip of stones and sand, he jumped from the *Warrior* and ran for his life. Sprinting along the bar, he had reached a point nearly half way to shore when a towering billow began to form just ahead. Too far from the ship, he could not return. The great wave balanced itself for a moment, then it thundered and crashed on the bar, sweeping with terrific speed at the poor man, until it caught the sailor, knocked him over, and engulfed him. Swept off the bar, the man was not seen again until later when his body was found on the beach.

Although they had lashed themselves to the deck, the others finally were swept into the sea as the vessel broke up and all perished. The seven graves of the victims may still be seen in the northwest corner of the island cemetery. There had probably been twenty-one on board — eighteen men, and three women, all of whom perished.

In 1839 the schooner Jasper bound from Boston to New York hit the east side of the island and was badly damaged. Her cargo of cut stone was thrown over, and the schooner got off. It was not a bad wreck, but the islanders had cause to remember the incident, for many of them took the cut stones to their homes to be made into steps. Spring House, Central House, and the home of Lorenzo Littlefield were among those so adorned.

The first large steamer wrecked at Block Island was the *Palmetto*, which struck Black Rock in 1876. Captain Baker tried to run her into an inlet, but she filled rapidly and went down. The crew and passengers left the ship, rowing to the south end of the island. Sinking to the bottom in seven fathoms of water, the *Palmetto* soon smashed to pieces. For weeks afterwards the merchandise came ashore. One native of Block Island was said to have much more of the leather goods from the cargo than he would ever wear out.

NO MAN'S LAND

During the Revolution a British man-of-war struck on the rocks of East Point and was lost, with many of her crew perishing. A quantity of gold specie in canvas bags went to the bottom. Years later, according to Mrs. Annie M. Wood in her delightful *No Man's Land,* a fisherman was sailing close to shore. On his way to sea, he saw down through the clear water to the bottom, where two bags heavily encrusted with moss and barnacles could be made out. Saying nothing to his companions on board, he planned to return later to the location. Time and time again he passed what he believed to be the spot, but he never again saw the gold bags from the British vessel.

In 1813 the *Amazon,* from Portugal, was wrecked thirty days from Lisbon while carrying a load of salt. A tublike craft was sent out to the vessel by means of a line, and the captain and crew were brought ashore. The second mate, who was carrying the ship's papers and valuables, was lost, but the others all landed safely.

NANTUCKET SHIPWRECKS

ECAUSE of its exposed location in the path of
American coastal traffic as well as almost all shipping to and from the old world, Nantucket has
been the scene of hundreds of marine disasters.[1] The first
wreck, hidden in the mist of Indian folklore, is that of a
French treasure ship which was driven into the gulch west
of Siasconset and entirely destroyed. Survivors of the
catastrophe broke their way through the dense forest to
reach an Indian settlement where they were given shelter
and food. The story is part tradition and part legend, but
within the last fifty years treasure seekers have dug in the
vicinity for the gold which allegedly was never found.

The first recorded disaster of importance was in 1664,
when a vessel bound from the Vineyard to Boston was
lost at Nantucket with all on board drowned or later killed
by the Nantucket Indians. Murdered by his heathen
brothers, a Christian Indian named Joel was the first to
die. No other details of this early shipwreck are known.

Five years later the aunt of Benjamin Franklin,
Bethia Folger Barnard, was drowned with three others as
the canoe[2] in which they were traveling to Nantucket from
the Vineyard overturned. The only survivor was Eleazer
Folger, who clung to the bottom of the canoe, righted it
when the canoe grounded on a shoal, and later reached
Morris Island, Cape Cod.

Tristam Coffin appears prominently in the next few
wrecks, because of his position as military governor at

the island.[3] In the summer of 1673 a Dutch ship, the *Exportation*, commanded by Isaac Mellyne, hit abreast of Siasconset with a cargo of whale oil, tobacco, and cowhide. Coffin was appointed agent[4] for the vessel which proved a total loss.

Five years later the shoals off Nantucket caught a French ship in their grasp. Tristam Coffin became involved in the settlement of the ship's cargo. He was charged with abandoning the ship "to others, with the very best of intentions, but she was soon taken possession of by the people," so Tristam Coffin was fined £343-10s for his negligence in letting the people take over the ship. When he appealed to New York's governor, Sir Edmund Andros, under whose jurisdiction Nantucket operated,[5] the fine was reduced to £150, "Boston money."

A wreck remembered for many years by those who saw it was that of the English sloop *Paoli*, bound for Philadelphia from Halifax. On December 6, 1771, the ship foundered on Great Point in a violent gale and snowstorm. Captain Dewlap and his entire crew reached shore, wet and freezing in the intense cold. The captain and his mate soon perished of exposure, however. Two sailors, attempting to reach a settlement, froze to death at Castine Point. Two other men, together with a boy named Weiderhold, crawled and fought their way to a barn at Squam, where they burrowed in the warm hay. Placing the youth between them, the men covered themselves with several feet of hay and fell asleep. The next day they were discovered by townsmen. Young Weiderhold became a permanent resident of Nantucket, and it is said that his descendants still live there. If those who perished had stayed on the sloop, they would have lived, for the vessel was discovered the next day by the residents of Nantucket, high and dry on the beach.

Three years later the sloop *Rochester*, bound for the African coast, struck on Great Rip, fifteen miles from Sankaty Head.[6] A small boat reached Nantucket from the wreck. The quarter deck washed off the vessel with thirteen of the crew aboard. Not knowing what their fate would be, the shipwrecked sailors had put aboard the quarter deck a barrel of flour and a jug of rum, but before they could try this varied diet, the quarter deck grounded on the southeast part of the island, and all were saved.

The keeper of Great Point Light had an unusual experience in October 1804, when the schooner *Republican* came ashore on the outside of Great Point, close to his lighthouse. After the vessel struck, the captain jumped into the water with his wife in his arms. Swimming ashore with her, he reached land as also did the crew. So grateful was the master of the ship to Keeper George Swain for his hospitality and friendliness that he sold the schooner just as it lay on the shore to the keeper for the bargain price of $50. Swain later broke up the schooner for salvage.[7]

Captain John Barnard of the American privateer *General Armstrong*, successful captor of many English prizes during the War of 1812, saw two of them wrecked around Nantucket Island. On December 21, 1812, the *Sir Sidney Smith* struck on Bass Rip off Siasconset with all on board perishing. A volunteer crew started from Nantucket to help them but turned back because of the weather. Although she had on board a very valuable cargo, nothing was ever recovered from the *Sir Sidney Smith*. The following month another prize to the *General*

Armstrong, the ship *Queen*, went ashore at Nobadeer and broke in two. Soon a very rich cargo began to come up on the beach. Hundreds of people lined the shore, fighting and scrambling for each valuable item as it was sighted in the breakers. Several hundred hogsheads of bottled porter, sauerkraut, cheese, hams, clothing, and various other products smashed their way into the sand. Day after day, night after night, the people paced the beaches, awaiting the offering of the breakers. Estimates as high as $40,000 were made as to the value of the spoils secreted by the residents of Nantucket, but when John Barnard's agents visited the island to recover the cargo, little could be found. Still in existence on the island today are relics of the wreck of the *Queen*. An expert Oyhee swimmer[8] was hired to dive to the bottom and place a sling around the heavier articles from the wreck, after which a capstan on the beach heaved them ashore. Without question John Barnard would have become a rich man had he landed the two prizes, the *Sir Sidney Smith* and the *Queen*, at a New York pier.

Another prize was wrecked at Nantucket during the War of 1812. After the fight between the British frigate *Endymion* and the *Prince of Neufchatel*, American privateer, in which the *Endymion's* efforts to recapture the *Neufchatel's* prize, the *Douglas*, failed completely, the prize floated off Miacomet Shoal and went ashore at Sesachacha. The inhabitants of Nantucket assisted in the handling of the cargo, which consisted of 400 barrels of sugar, 190 puncheons of rum, 400 bags of coffee, 250 bales of cotton, and twenty-two mahogany logs. Many Nantucket people profited from the cargo, as there were no wreck agents in those days, or rather as Gardner says, "everyone appears to have been a self-constituted agent."

From the mariner's point of view, an interesting aftermath developed from a shipwreck on the south side of Nantucket in 1828. The brig *Sarah Ann*, bound to Boston from Savannah under Captain Phillips, struck on the twenty-third of March near Hummock Pond. Her cargo was eventually discharged, and P. H. Folger bought her at public auction for $550. Her owners thought it was a very low sum for such a fine brig. When the *Sarah Ann* was floated off and brought into Nantucket Harbor, the original owners claimed the vessel. In court they lost out, for the chance had been very small that Folger would get the *Sarah Ann* floated free. What had happened after the transaction should not influence conditions at the time of the auction, according to the decision of the court.[9] The case excited considerable attention up and down the coast at the time, the majority of mariners agreeing that the verdict was a fair one.

On December 14, 1828 the brig *Packet* from Saint Petersburg was carrying hemp and iron when she crashed against the south side of the island near Miacomet Pond. The brig began to break up at once. The crew took to the masts, all except the second mate, who left the vessel in a small boat. As he rowed away, the masts went by the board, carrying the other ten members of the crew to their death. Reaching the shore, the mate hunted for shelter from the bitter night, finally noticing a light far in the distance. It was a house in Newton, where a woman who had just passed away was being prepared for burial. As there were no men in the bereaved household, the frightened women would not admit him. When the door shut in his face he started out again, soon finding shelter in another residence a short distance away.

Eight years later a bolt of cloth from the wreck of the *Packet* was found imbedded in the sand, and one of the Nantucket residents folded a fragment of the cloth into a napkin, writing the account of the shipwreck and placing it inside the cloth. The shipwreck expert of Nantucket, Arthur H. Gardner, read the account of the wreck from this paper preserved for many years in the folds of the cloth from the *Packet*.

On March 22, 1829, the schooner *Ranger*, commanded by Captain Wasgate of Salem hit the island near Squam Pond during a snowstorm. The captain and mate made shore, and stumbled in the dense snow into a rail fence which they followed until they came to a barn. The floor was covered with hay, and there they stayed until the storm ended. Back on the schooner three crew members froze to death, unable to reach the forecastle. The same day another schooner, the *Ann*, commanded by Captain Reuben Mossman of Thomaston, Maine, drove ashore near the *Ranger*. Captain Mossman and two men were saved, but three others perished. Two of these were the captain's little sons, whom Mossman carried in his arms for more than a mile, but both died before a house was reached. Six bodies were brought to town from the two vessels and buried from the Methodist Episcopal Church, where all the clergymen on the island assisted in the sad ritual.

The sugar ship *Nathaniel Hooper*, piloted by Captain Bogardus, hit on South Shoal, Nantucket, July 8, 1838. After throwing over her sugar cargo, the crew abandoned the vessel at midnight with all sails set. An hour later a heavy northwest squall freed the *Hooper*, and she drifted

off. Her helm sent the ship toward Boston, and a smack
which sighted her put two sailors aboard. The men sailed
the *Hooper* safely all the way to Boston. A day after the
incident the *Massachusetts* and the sloop *Cony* went out
from Nantucket to look for the *Hooper* but all that could
be found were empty sugar boxes floating on the surface
of the sea. Captain John Bogardus left for Boston, where
he was going to report the loss of his vessel, but on his
arrival was amazed to find her tied up at a pier in the
Massachusetts capital.[10]

On the evening of October 2, 1841, a furious gale
began, which lasted for two days and did not end until
twenty-five vessels were wrecked on or around Nantucket
with considerable loss of life. The storm is still spoken
of as the October Gale. On the morning after the storm
there were nineteen vessels wrecked or stranded around
the island, while within sight of shore the masts of two
others protruded out of water. It was the most unusual
sight ever witnessed by the inhabitants of Nantucket.[11]

The strange trip of the fishing schooner *Minnie* in
this gale is of interest. With foremast cut away, she was
stranded on Brant Point. The crew left the vessel in
safety, and the schooner drove high on the beach, so far
up that later it was decided to launch the vessel inside the
point. The *Minnie* is often spoken of as the only vessel
which ever entered Nantucket Harbor without coming
around Brant Point.

Another curious shipwreck was that of the ship
Joseph Starbuck which left Nantucket for Edgartown,
where she was to be fitted for a whaling voyage. A number
of ladies went aboard to take the trip to Edgartown. On
the morning of November 27, 1842 the steamer *Telegraph*

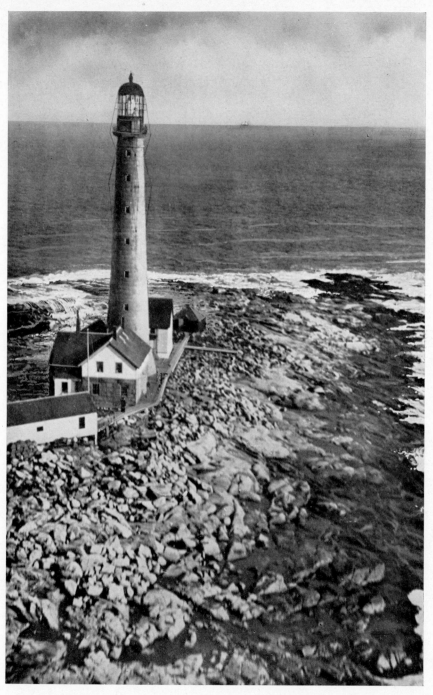

BOON ISLAND, MAINE, WHERE CANNIBALISM WAS NECESSARY
THE NOTTINGHAM GALLEY WAS WRECKED HERE
DECEMBER 11, 1710.

BASED ON FOLGER'S PAINTING

RAMSDELL'S DARING RESCUE
SAVING THE CAPTAIN OF THE SCHOONER TREAT.

THE WYOMING, LOST WITH ALL HANDS NEAR NANTUCKET IN 1924

towed the *Starbuck* out of the harbor and the trip began.
A wind sprang up forcing the ship to lose headway until
finally the *Telegraph* returned to Nantucket after leaving
the *Starbuck* at anchor near Tuckernuck Shoal Lightship.
As the gale increased the chain cables parted, allowing the
ship to drift to the east. The mizzenmast was cut away,
the foresail set, and every effort made to get into Nantucket Harbor, but in vain. The *Starbuck* hit the bar,
going over on her beam ends. It was an awkward and
dangerous situation which the crew faced. The ladies
were placed in as sheltered a position as is possible on a
ship over on her beam ends. The weather began to get
colder, and ice formed whenever the surf hit the vessel.

It was not until morning that the people of Nantucket
noticed the *Starbuck* heeled over. The steamer *Massachusetts* was dispatched at once to the scene, and by careful
maneuvering reached the lee side of the vessel. A long
warp was put in place, and a whaleboat began the perilous
journey from steamer to ship. One by one the ladies were
passed down, until they were all on the whaleboat; then
the difficult trip back began. Ice formed over the crew
and passengers as the whaleboat fought its way through
mountainous waves, but the journey was successful. Four
more trips were made, and an hour later all the shipwrecked victims were safe and sound ashore. The *Starbuck* soon went to pieces. This beautiful ship, built at
Brant Point in 1838, had made only one voyage.

Early in the year 1846 a Scotch ship, the *Earl of
Eglington*, under Captain Niven, left Liverpool for Boston
with a heavy cargo of salt, coal, copper, and dry goods.[12]
On the fourteenth of March the ship struck on the South
Shoal and drifted toward Nantucket, where she grounded

on the Old Man Shoal. Again driving forward, she hit near Nobadeer Pond. Eight of the crew left the ship in two boats, just as the seas made a complete breach over the vessel. One of the boats capsized, drowning two sailors, the others being rescued by men ashore who rushed into the surf for them. The second lifeboat capsized far from shore, and all four aboard were lost. By pantomime the sailors on shore signalled to the men still on the *Egling-ton* to throw over an oar with a line attached. This was done and the oar secured when near shore by a bluefish drail. A larger line was then carefully attached with a paper of instructions tied on. As soon as the signal was given to haul away, the shipwrecked sailors pulled the oar back to the doomed vessel. A sort of sling, capable of holding one man was soon arranged, and by this sling the remainder of the crew was landed. When the captain came ashore the noose gave away, and he dropped into the sea, close enough to the beach to be rescued, however. The ship itself proved a total loss for no appreciable part of the cargo was ever recovered.

In the year 1847 the schooner *Silivae* was wrecked on the west end of Nantucket. After strenuous work, the schooner was got off by one of Nantucket's greatest wreckers, Frederick F. Swain.[13] Swain had lost a leg many years before, but in spite of this handicap floated most of Nantucket's wrecks while he was active.

The winter of 1857 brought severe below-zero weather all over New England, and Nantucket suffered with the rest. Several vessels froze up in the ice. On January 23 the schooner *Conanchet* from Plymouth, in command of Captain Burgess, was caught in the ice and swept against Tuckernuck Shoals. Leaking badly, the *Conanchet* was abandoned. With no boat available, the sailors armed themselves with long planks and oars, crawling and pushing their way across the dangerous ice until Great Point was reached. They arrived in Nantucket when it was eleven degrees below zero, and not one of them was frostbitten. For days afterwards the *Conanchet* drifted about, finally disappearing in the vicinity of the South Shoals Lightship.

The King of Prussia figured in the aftermath of a Great Point Rip shipwreck of 1863. During that year the Prussian bark *Elwine Fredericke,* loaded with coal, struck the rip during a fog. Captain David Patterson and Captain Aaron Coffin reached the scene of the wreck shortly afterwards and saved the fourteen sailors aboard. Almost at once the bark went to pieces. So impressed was the King of Prussia when he heard the story that he sent the one in charge of the rescue boat, Captain David Patterson, a handsome silver chronometer.[14]

One of the most amazing feats of rescue work was performed by Frederick W. Ramsdell of Nantucket on the occasion of the wreck of the schooner *Eveline Treat,* October 21, 1865. For his unusual display of heroism, he was awarded the highest medal of the Massachusetts Humane Society. The *Treat* was on her way from Philadelphia to Gloucester, loaded with coal, when she struck on Miacomet Rip. Discovered at daybreak by the people ashore, she was then 300 feet off the beach. Five of the sailors were lashed in the rigging, the captain, his two sons, and two other men. The schooner's house went by the board shortly afterwards, and the waves swept across her decks. After the mortar and apparatus of the Humane Society were brought to the beach, a small line was shot

M A I N E

Famous New England Shipwrecks

Except Massachusetts Bay

PASSAMAQUODDY BAY

EASTPORT · Campobello I.

Machias

BAY OF FUNDY

GRAND MANAN I.

Machine Seal I.

Englishman Bay

Frenchman Bay

Blue Hill Bay

Millbridge

Petit Manan I.

Grand Manan Bank

① 1

② 2

Mount Desert I.

③ 3

Belfast

PENOBSCOT BAY

Mount Desert Rk

Rockland

④ 4

Matinicus Rk

⑤ 5

AUGUSTA

Kennebec River

Sheepscot R.

Damariscotta R.

⑦ 7

⑥ 6

Monhegan I

⑧ 8

GULF

OF

MAINE

CASCO BAY

Halfway Rk

⑨ 9

PORTLAND

Cape Elizabeth

Saco

Biddeford

⑩ 10

⑪ 11

Cape Porpoise

⑫ 12

Boon I.

Cash's Ledge

Agamenticus Mt.

Cape Neddick

Isles of Shoals

⑬ 13

Fippennies Ledge

Portsmouth

Jeffrey Ledge

NEW HAMPSHIRE

⑭ 14

C. ANN.

Newburyport

⑮ 15

Gloucester

Salem

Lynn

MASSACHUSETTS BAY

Stellwagen Banks

⑯ 16

⑰ 17

BOSTON

MINOTS LT.

CAPE COD

⑱ 18

Plymouth

Cape Cod Bay

Nauset

⑲ 19

MASSACHUSETTS

Buzzards Bay

Cape Cod Canal

⑳ 20

CONN

R. I.

New Bedford

Woods Hole

Monomoy Pt.

Nantucket Sound

Nantucket Shoals

PROVIDENCE

Fall River

NARRAGANSETT BAY

Newport

Martha's Vineyard

MUSKEGET CHAN.

㉒ 22

㉓ 23

㉑ 21

New London

Pt. Judith

SOUND

Gardiners I.

Block I.

㉗ 27

㉖ 26

㉕ 25

㉔ 24

Montauk Pt

Davis. Sh's

Phelps Bk

Asia Rip

N E W   E N G L A N D   W R E C K S

1. SARAH
2. NEW YORK
3. GRAND DESIGN
4. ROYAL TAR
5. ALBANY
6. CATAWAMTEAK
7. ANGEL GABRIEL
8. GEORGE EDMUNDS
9. ANNIE C. MAGUIRE
10. BOHEMIAN
11. WANDBY
12. NOTTINGHAM GALLEY
13. SAGUNTO (?)
14. INDUSTRY
15. WATCH AND WAIT
16. PORTLAND
17. ERFPRINS
18. SOMERSET
19. WHIDAH
20. MONOMOY DISASTER
21. EVELINE TREAT
22. CITY OF COLUMBUS
23. AMAZON
24. METIS
25. LARCHMONT
26. WARRIOR
27. LEXINGTON

across and secured by one of the captain's sons. The boys forced their father to step into a sling, but at the last minute he lost his nerve and climbed back into the shrouds. The mate started ashore, but the rope snarked and stuck when the sling neared the beach. A line was thrown out, which he caught and fastened around his neck, whereupon the mate leaped into the breakers and was pulled up on the beach. One of the captain's sons followed, making the trip successfully.

Three men were left in the rigging of the *Treat* as the afternoon advanced. They agreed that the captain should be sent along next, as he was slowly weakening. A life car which was fastened to the hawser failed to work and was taken down. Finally the young men persuaded the captain to get into the sling, and he started for the beach. When he was midway between ship and shore the line again snarked, and there the poor captain hung bareheaded and in his stocking feet for an hour and a half. As night began to fall, the men in the rigging worked feverishly at the snark, but made little progress.

A young Nantucket man named Frederick Ramsdell volunteered in an effort to save the captain.[15] Fastening a light rope about his waist, Ramsdell started out arm over arm on the hawser until he reached the captain. Cutting the lines on each side of the sling, he retied them and fastened the light rope to the sling. Ramsdell then worked his way back to the beach, and the captain was finally hauled to safety. The other two sailors were soon brought ashore. It was a miraculous feat which Ramsdell had performed.

A notable battle with the treacherous ice floes was fought on February 5, 1871, off the Cliff Shore, when the

five members of the coal schooner *Mary Anna*, were saved
by the men of Nantucket. Captain Lennan had sailed
from South Amboy, anchoring the *Mary Anna* off Chatham. The ice became so thick that she broke from her
moorings and started drifting toward the Nantucket Inner
Bar. So heavily incased in ice, that she was in danger of
sinking, the *Mary Anna* finally stranded on February 4.
The next day her distress flag was sighted from Nantucket,
and the steamer *Island Home* was made ready. After
reaching Brant Point, the rescue steamer was unable to
make further progress as she also became imprisoned in
the ice.

Several attempts made during the day to reach the
schooner failed because the ice was too dangerous to walk
on and boats were soon caught in the enormous floes. At
ten o'clock in the evening a plan was formed to reach the
vessel. Eight men started out over the ice, dragging and
pulling two dories, carrying with them several long planks
and plenty of lines. Whenever the ice would not bear the
weight of the dories, the rescue party would lay the planks
out and slide the boats over them. When the open sea was
encountered, the men rowed the dories across the water.
In this way, two miles of firm ice, rubber ice and water
were traversed by half an hour after midnight. The night
was clear, but the cold stung through the men's heavy garments. They saw the schooner over on her beam ends,
sheathed in ice several inches thick, in ten feet of water.

When they arrived at the *Mary Anna*, the men found
the crew almost frozen to death. The steward, with both
feet frozen, had already bade farewell to his comrades,
who had covered him over with a sail and left him to die.
All the men were soon placed in the two dories, and the

long, dangerous journey back to shore began. The entire party reached Nantucket at three o'clock in the morning, safe and sound. The heroic Nantucket men were each awarded a silver medal by the Massachusetts Humane Society.

An Italian bark, named *Papa Luigi C.*, loaded with wine and brimstone, hit the south side of Nantucket, March 21, 1877. Having a small boat, the crew arrived safely near shore, but the lifeboat went broadside as the breakers caught it. All were saved. The vessel did not go to pieces for over a year, finally breaking up in October 1878.[16]

Captain Roberts of Salem was wrecked aboard the bark *Hazard* with a cargo of hides from Africa on the Old Man Shoal at midnight, February 14, 1881. Leaving the crew to pump, the captain and three men rowed for help. When the vessel began to settle in the water, the second mate and one man went aboard a small raft which was moored astern, but the others decided to stay on the bark. As the float drifted away, the bark settled lower and lower into the water until the others changed their minds and began to swim toward the comparative safety of the raft. It was too late, however, and only one man reached the float, the others drowning.

Later in the afternoon the captain's boat reached Nantucket, but the sailors told such a confusing story that few townspeople believed that a raft was floating off the coast. The next morning the steamer *Island Home* searched the vicinity in vain, so the men were given up for lost. Two months went by when one day the supply ship *Verbena* brought two survivors into Nantucket, the second mate of the *Hazard* and one sailor. When the raft, almost entirely submerged, drifted out to sea the *Island Home* had steamed close by without noticing it.   The shipwrecked men then drifted by the South Shoal Lightship, where the lookout spotted them.   The three men were soon taken aboard, one of them dead from exhaustion.   The two survivors left Nantucket after a brief rest, returning to their homes where they had long been given up for lost.

An unusual story of the sea is the tale of the schooner *French Van Gilder*, the six-master *Alice M. Lawrence*, and the *Unique*.   On March 29, 1885, the three-master *French Van Gilder* struck on Tuckernuck Shoal, and her crew landed safely.   The schooner, loaded with paving blocks, stayed where she struck. Years went by. In 1914, twenty-nine years later, the *Van Gilder* again figured in the news.

On the fifth of December, 1914, the great six-master schooner *Alice M. Lawrence*[17] stranded on Tuckernuck Shoal in the early morning hours, but it was not discovered until later that the *Lawrence* had broken her back by striking the hulk of the *Van Gilder*, wrecked back in 1885. Because of the heavy cargo of paving stones the two schooners could not be separated or taken off the shoal in any way, so after all movable material had been taken off, the 305-foot six-master was abandoned.   On November 27, 1915, the wreck was set afire, burning to the water's edge.   The *Alice M. Lawrence* was one of the largest vessels ever wrecked in the vicinity.

The third part of this strange story took place on July 17, 1917, when the British schooner *Unique* struck squarely on top of the hulk of the *Van Gilder* and the *Lawrence*.   The crew of the Muskeget Coast Guard Station rescued every sailor aboard the *Unique*, which soon became a total loss.

One of the most valiant fights ever put up by a volunteer life saving crew was that enacted on Sunday, January 10, 1886, when the three-master *T. B. Witherspoon* hit on the south side of Nantucket. Captain Alfred H. Anderson, bound from Surinam to Boston, mistook Sankaty Head Light for the flash from Montauk Point, Long Island, in the blinding snowstorm, bringing his schooner up in the breakers near Little Mioxes Pond. News of the disaster reached town, and large groups of people were soon on the shore, watching with that strange fascination which holds crowds at fires, disasters, and shipwrecks. One by one the sailors dropped to their death in the raging sea, which was so rough that a lifeboat could not possibly be launched.

The Surfside Life Saving crew shot several lines over the schooner, but the survivors still on the vessel were powerless to move, having frozen into the rigging. A life raft was launched into the breakers, the men aboard hauling themselves off by a line shot out to the schooner. A huge wave towered over them for a second, then broke with devastating force on the raft, knocking two of the men overboard, but they grabbed the raft and regained its deck. The shock, however, had snapped the hawser, and the life savers were pulled ashore by a second line paid out from the beach. Time after time the mortar sent out its line to the schooner, until at the sixth effort a line struck squarely across the vessel's bow, and was made fast to the forerigging by the two sailors still alive on the *Witherspoon*. A running block with the lines rove through was sent out. By dusk the breeches buoy had been rigged and the men were able to crawl into it.

It was after dark when the two men reached the shore, more dead than alive. One of them, the first mate, had watched his wife and little boy perish when the sea broke into their cabin. It is said that this shipwreck which cost the lives of seven persons was the most sorrowful in Nantucket history. The loss of life in many other cases had been greater, but the victims of the *Witherspoon* wreck lingered for many hours a short distance from safety, only to perish in the waves in full view of hundreds of people on the Nantucket shoreline.[18]

Bound from Manila to Boston with a load of hemp, the ship *Asia* struck on Round Shoal in a severe northeast storm February 20, 1898. Captain Dakin had taken his wife and daughter on the long voyage, and must have suffered terribly with his family before they perished. When the *Asia* began to break up the captain is believed to have given the care of his daughter to the mate. The first news of the disaster was on February 22, when a tug steamed into Wood's Hole with the bodies of the mate and the captain's daughter, the little girl fast in the arms of the mate. It is not known what became of the captain and his wife, but some time later news came that three of the crew had been picked up by the sailors on the *Handkerchief Lightship*. They had been floating in the wintry sea for twenty-four hours. The vessel broke up, her $100,000 cargo coming ashore at Cape Cod, Nantucket, and Martha's Vineyard.

The schooner *Saint Elmo*, built at Rockland, Maine, sailed from that port with a load of lime early in 1898, commanded by Captain Hall. While on the way to New York she struck on the shoals east of Nantucket Island. Two days later Keeper Remsen of Sankaty Light saw the rigging and masts of the sunken vessel, and the Humane Society's boat at Siasconset was sent out to the wreck. As the surfboat approached the wreck a nearby fishing smack signalled to the men, who found the only survivor of the *Saint Elmo* aboard the fishing vessel. The captain, his wife and three seamen had all been washed overboard, the lone sailor clinging to the rigging while the vessel went through a strange series of maneuvers. As the schooner was hove down, the deckload shifted. When she rolled over, the compressed air inside burst out her stern, and she righted and sank until her decks were awash.

In this condition the *Saint Elmo* drifted around the shoals, grounding at low tide and floating at high. Two days and two nights went by before the vessel finally hit the Rose and Crown Shoal, where Keeper Remsen sighted her. The mate later left for home, after a rest from his experience.

The schooner *Stephen Morris* was abandoned early in June 1898, later becoming the object of an unusual chase between the steamer *Petrel* and the underwriter's boat from Nantucket. When the *Morris* was first sighted near Bass Rip off Siasconset on June 5, a tug was sent out after her but failed to find the schooner. The next day off Great Neck Station the steamer *Petrel* spoke a vessel which had fallen in with the schooner a day before. The entire 7th of December was spent cruising around, looking in vain for the derelict. At last it was decided that she had broken up and gone to pieces on the rips.

But the elusive *Morris* had not finished her strange game. A short time later she again appeared, and the *Petrel* started in pursuit immediately. Meanwhile a crew from Nantucket was mustered and soon launched the

underwriter's boat from Surfside. The *Petrel* arrived at
the wreck first and started to tow her to Vineyard Haven
just as the underwriter's boat appeared on the scene. The
lifeboat crew caught up with the slow moving tug and tow,
going aboard the *Morris* to claim her, but it was no use.
The *Petrel* received the $500 salvage money for the
schooner, and the Nantucket lifeboat crew, although pro-
testing vigorously, had done all their work for nothing.

The steam collier *Middlesex* crashed into the five-
master *George P. Hudson* on July 11, 1914. Because of
the crash, the *Hudson's* gasoline tanks exploded, killing
one man. Except for another sailor killed by a falling
mast, the remainder of the crew were rescued by boats
from the *Middlesex*. Captain John Thomas, however, in
keeping with one of the sea's traditions, went down with
his ship. During a severe northeast gale the same fall a
large section of the *Hudson* washed ashore at Quidnet.

The disappearance of the Cross Rip Lightship in
1918 is one of the unexplained mysteries of the sea. Torn
from her moorings February 1 by the heavy ice packs in
the vicinity, the lightship was last seen from Great Point
Light on February 5. At the time it vanished the vessel
was without power, had no sail, and was helpless against
the elements. Tugs and cutters sent out to find her never
located a trace of the ship, and her disappearance became
one of the unsolved mysteries of Nantucket's maritime
history. Not a trace has ever been seen of either the vessel
or her crew of eight men.[19]

The last of that great fleet of Palmer-owned schooners,
the *Dorothy Palmer*, was sailing off Nantucket on March
29, 1923. Perhaps her captain was thinking of the days
when so many of the schooners, all with the last name

Palmer, sailed the seven seas. There had been the *Davis*, wrecked at the entrance to Boston Harbor, the *Prescott* and the *Fuller*, lost off the Georges, and many others, including the *Fanny*, the *Marie*, the *Harwood*, and the *Singleton*. The *Dorothy* alone was still afloat. Suddenly the keel of the *Dorothy Palmer* grounded on the edge of Stone Horse Shoal, and the schooner settled into the sand. The days of the Palmer fleet had ended. Although her crew were all saved, the schooner soon became a total loss.[20]

A terrific blizzard swept the coast on the night of March 11, 1924, sending the great six-masted schooner *Wyoming* to her doom, with all the members of her crew, thirteen in number, going down with the vessel. The *Wyoming* had last been seen at anchor that afternoon near Pollock Rip lightship. The next day her quarterboard came ashore, followed by much wreckage from the 305-foot schooner, and it was feared that she had pounded to pieces during the night. No additional information about the *Wyoming* was ever revealed by the sea.

Closing our remarks on Nantucket, we can conclude by saying that although the shoals around Nantucket have probably caught enough ships and vessels since the beginning of history to make it a greatly feared location, the men of Nantucket have proved themselves of sterling worth in going to the aid of seamen when tossed by the tempest against the shores of "the far-away island."

MARTHA'S VINEYARD

During the same storm of 1778 which wrecked the *General Arnold*, a privateer sloop came ashore at the east end of Martha's Vineyard Island, with seventeen men perishing. Although a fearful gale, it proved a blessing

236 NEW ENGLAND STORMS AND SHIPWRECKS

to the islanders, whose food and supplies had been removed by the British.[1]

Shortly after the gale, one of the residents walking
near the Lagoon Pond found an immense quantity of
striped bass buried in the ice and snow on the beach.
Packed closely together, there were actually thousands of
fish piled up on the beach, evidently washed ashore there
from the wrecked privateer.

The news of the discovery spread rapidly around
Martha's Vineyard and soon the inhabitants were carting
the fish away. As there was little salt on the island the
people packed the bass in the snow. The fish lasted all that
winter, and together with eels, clams, and wild fowl the
fish kept the Vineyard residents from starvation.

At sundown on November 26, 1898, the *Amelia O.
Ireland* anchored near Menemsha Bight in company with
the *Clara Leavitt*. At about ten that night Surfman Manning of the Gay Head Life Saving Station reached Lobster-
ville on his regular patrol along the Martha's Vineyard
shore. In the vicinity of Dogfish Bar he saw the flash of
a torch and realized that a ship must be in trouble. It was
a three-masted schooner, the *Amelia O. Ireland*. Surfman Manning lighted a Coston signal to indicate to those
aboard that the wreck had been sighted, and hurried back
to the station at Gay Head, where Keeper Hayman[1] organized a rescue party. The surfmen rushed down to the
boathouse and decided to transport the surfboat overland
because the stranded schooner lay directly to windward
and the gale was momentarily increasing. The going became so difficult, however, that the keeper sent for the
oxen of Simon Devine, a farmer living a short distance
away, and with the help of these beasts of burden the Gay

Head lifeboat was pulled around to the other side of Menemsha Bight, which they reached at midnight.

The lights of the schooner could now be seen a third of a mile out into the ocean. The shoal broke the heavier seas. So violent was the wind that repeated attempts to launch the boat failed. As the lifesavers struggled on the shore, another schooner loomed up in the night and crashed against the same Dogfish Bar, settling into the water less than a hundred yards from the *Ireland*. At two o'clock, desperate in the face of adversity, the keeper sent for the beach apparatus. Fearing the schooners were too far away, he determined to exhaust every possible effort. As the surfmen went for the ox team, the second schooner started to break up before their eyes. Wreckage soon covered the shore. The surfmen, searching anxiously for bodies of the sailors, found nothing. The second schooner had disappeared completely.

The wind now reached such a pitch that the heavy surfboat was picked up and blown the entire length of the beach, falling into a pool of water almost 300 feet away. As soon as the beach apparatus arrived at daylight, Keeper Hayman made ready to fire the smallest possible line, a number 4, but the wind, now at its peak, upset the faking box. A larger line, number 7, was fired with a six-ounce powder charge, but failed to reach its objective.

Daybreak revealed the figures of men still clinging to the shrouds of the *Ireland*. The other schooner had entirely disintegrated, not even her wreckage remaining where she had struck the night before. The sailors were all believed drowned, but unknown to the surfmen, sailor Philo G. Sparrow had actually made shore in safety, although quite a distance away from the place where the lifesavers had gathered. When the foremast went, he had grabbed a stanchion, and a gigantic wave threw him high on the beach. Crawling on his hands and knees, he reached the bank, laboriously fighting his way up to the road, where he found the home of Charles H. Ryan. Here he aroused the family and told his experience. If he had not been saved, the fate of the three-masted *Clara Leavitt* of Portland, Maine, would have remained in complete oblivion sharing the unknown with the *Addie E. Snow* and the *Pentagoet.*[1]

Back on the shore Keeper Hayman watched with failing hope the growing intensity of the gale. By this time the wind had veered to the north, so that another attempt in the surfboat could be made from a more favorable point. Time and again the picked crew of the station, with three volunteers, charged against the force of the wind, each time thrown back in confusion. Again Keeper Hayman shot the projectile out toward the vessel, but in vain. Sunset was approaching, with a hard night ahead, so Keeper Hayman announced a rest period.

At midnight, when the tide was down again, the wind relented a trifle, and Keeper Hayman made his final effort. One of the best volunteers now decided against going in the surfboat, simply because he felt there was no possible hope of reaching their objective. Successfully, however, the crew launched the boat and slowly but surely shortened the distance to the schooner until the lifeboat reached its goal! Since the port bow of the wreck was found to be encumbered with wreckage, a new attempt was made to get to the schooner at the martingale. As the surfboat hovered underneath, the exhausted sailors dropped one by one into the craft from the schooner. Leaving one man frozen to death in the rigging, the men made for shore.

It was a feat that high praise could not over estimate. For 29 hours the men of Martha's Vineyard had fought for the lives of the sailors on the *Ireland,* and had finally delivered the six then alive to the safety of the shore. The names of the members of this heroic crew follow: N. C. Hayman, Keeper, Francis Manning, Ben Attaquin, Timothy Mayhew, Jesse Smalley, and Samuel Anthony, surfmen, with two volunteers Abram Cooper and Linus Jeffers. The *Amelia G. Ireland* was commanded by Captain Oscar Knapp, and carried a cargo of oil in tanks. Westly Mark, who perished in the rigging was later brought ashore, where his body was buried in the Gay Head graveyard.

The *Port Hunter,* an English steamer sailing for Gravesend Bay, collided with the tug *Covington* on the night of November 2, 1918. Those on board thought that the shock was a torpedo. The *Port Hunter* grounded on the Hedge and Fence Shoal nearby, and a large hole was found in her hull.

A few weeks later material from the steamer showed up in Boston, where it was placed on sale. There had been a $9,000,000 cargo, which eventually was disposed of for $1,000,000. Part of the cargo drifted ashore at Martha's Vineyard, where scores of paper cartons were washed up on the beach.[1]

MASSACHUSETTS BAY

FROM earliest times until the late Eighteenth Century Boston had far more shipping than either New York or Philadelphia, and because of the great number of vessels going to and from the port which was called for over a century "the Mistress of North America" there were many shipping disasters in times of storms and gales. To the more famous storms and wrecks we have devoted individual chapters. Those found here achieved local importance. Literally hundreds had to be omitted in full.

THE 1740 GALE

The December 1740 storm was of outstanding violence around Boston Harbor. Captain Underwood's craft hit the rocks at Rainsford's Island and bilged, Captain Tilden's vessel ran aground at Scituate, while two Newburyport sloops went ashore at Lynn Beach. There were twenty vessels wrecked at Marblehead. Captain McCloud and his entire crew of ten perished when their ship hit the rocks off Scituate. At Nantucket Captain Griffith's ship was wrecked.[1] A sloop belonging to Captain Lowell was wrecked down Massachusetts Bay, but all were saved. Five ships were ashore at Cape Cod, three from the Vineyard, one from North Carolina, and Captain Higgins' vessel bound for Connecticut which came ashore near the Highland.

THE MAGNIFIQUE

On a cool spring morning shortly after the first World War had ended, Captain Charles H. Jennings[1] of the Lovell's Island Range Lights in Boston Harbor was industriously digging in the garden near his house when his spade brought up an object which resembled a coin. Working in the same location, he uncovered several of the round, flat disks, and later brought them into the kitchen of his home, where he and his wife scrubbed one of the objects until the deposit of dirt had been removed. There revealed to them was a gold coin, later found to have a market value of $29. The other coins yielded under the rubbing and scraping to reveal that they were valuable gold and silver pieces of a period between 1650 and 1775.

Although he did not know it at the time, Keeper Jennings had actually uncovered coins from the treasure of the great French man-of-war *Magnifique*, which had been wrecked on Lovell's Island during the Revolutionary War.

In August 1782, the French Fleet was entering Boston Harbor, and David Darling, the pilot of the 74-gun man-of-war *Magnifique*, missed stays in the Narrows. The frigate crashed on the rocks off Lovell's Island, ripped her bottom out, slid over the ledge, and sank in deep water between the ledge and the island. Her career was over.

Pilot Darling lost his position because of the accident, and became the sexton of the Old North Church. His record was known, however, for one day he found written in chalk [2] on the meeting house door:

"Don't you run this ship ashore
As you did the seventy-four."

Attempts were made from time to time to recover the treasure which sank with the ship, but failures were recorded as late as 1869. By this time the entire contour of the island was changing because of the position of the wreck.

The currents of the Narrows created a bar over the skeleton of the *Magnifique,* which in turn connected itself to the island. The bar built up during the storms until even at high water it was visible. When Mayor Shurtleff of Boston visited the island around 1870, he found that the spot where the *Magnifique* sank was dry land, part of the island itself.

Evidently, when the Lighthouse Department erected the keeper's dwelling, they built near the skeleton of the *Magnifique,* and at the time Keeper Jennings dug at the rear of his home, he was actually digging in the soil over the old wreck. Nevertheless Jennings did not become wealthy from the treasure, for later another keeper, in Jennings' opinion, probably obtained coins worth more than $7000 of it. That, however, is another story.

THE ELIZABETH AND ANN

Late in the afternoon of March 6, 1829, Captain William Tewksbury, the famous lifesaver, arrived in Boston from Deer Island with the news that Captain Savage and his entire crew had been lost on the *Elizabeth and Ann* which was then coming ashore a shattered wreck after hitting the rocks off Nahant. Her cargo of oranges and cigars was strewn all along the waterfront from what is now Winthrop Highlands to the end of Deer Island. The captain's watch was found still hanging on a hook in the cabin, when it came up with other wreckage on the Point

Shirley beach. The quarter deck came ashore at Cedar Island at the entrance to Shirley Gut.[1]

The day after the storm the inmates of the poor house in Chelsea, along with several laborers, were gathering kelp and seaweed on the rocks at what is now Fort Heath, Winthrop. One young negro lad, more active than the others, saw a partially submerged plank floating in waist deep water. There seemed to be a white cloth attached to the wood, so the young negro lad waded out into the water to get the plank.

To his astonishment, the boy found the cloth was actually a large canvas bag, torn at one end. He could not easily lift it, but managed to bring it ashore. Pulling it upon the rocks, he opened the sack and found it filled with gold pieces! The others naturally crowded around him, but the overseer was firm, and allowed the boy to keep his discovery, taking him at once to the local Chelsea bank. The money totalled a handsome fortune. Needless to say, the negro's days as a laborer were over, but it would be interesting to know how much money he recovered and his subsequent life history.

Incidentally, the hole in the canvas bag had allowed many of the gold coins to escape into the ocean. Search was made at the time, but nothing was found. Years later, around 1880, the son of the Reverend Mr. Duffield[2] was playing in the sand off Grover's Cliff, Winthrop, when he dug up a coin with his shovel. Taking it to his father, the boy found that he was the happy owner of a gold piece. Word quickly traveled around, as news of that sort does, and soon the entire shoreline was crowded with people searching for gold. Many of them were lucky, as the local papers of the period reported the finding of around

$300. Whether more money is still buried from the wreck of the *Elizabeth and Ann* lost back in 1829 is an interesting question.[3]

THE TEDESCO

The American bark *Tedesco*, hailing from Portland, Maine, homeward bound with a cargo of sherry wine, salt, and raisins, went ashore on Long Rock, about 300 feet east northeast of Galloupe's Point, Swampscott, Sunday night, January 18, 1857. It had been a furious blizzard that swept the coast late in the evening after an unusually calm day. The sea had been so smooth when the fishermen came in that afternoon that they had left their dories just a little above the highwater mark. In the morning nothing but splintered remains could be found.

Captain Peterson of the *Tedesco* had been sailing between Pig Rock and Egg Rock Light[1] in a moderate northwest wind late that afternoon. The wind hauled to the northeast and a furious gale began shortly afterwards. The residents on shore had the impression that the *Tedesco* sailed on up the bay.

The storm was so severe that few people knew of the shipwreck until late in the afternoon when residents discovered the shore strewn with wreckage, including many casks of wine. Every person on the *Tedesco* perished in the surf. Later the bodies of the sailors came ashore on Whale Beach, where townsmen brought them to the Methodist Church. After an impressive funeral, the men were buried in the Swampscott Cemetery.

Two locations in Swampscott are named for the *Tedesco*, whose men perished off the town's shore. The boulder where the bark hit is still called Tedesco Rock, while one of New England's prominent social organizations along the North Shore of Massachusetts is the Tedesco Country Club.[2]

THE VERNON

The British bark *Vernon,* loaded with oranges and lemons, sailed for Boston from Messina, Sicily, during the winter of 1859. Running into heavy seas off the coast, she crashed on Lynn Beach near Little Nahant, February 3. Residents near the shore quickly noticed the shipwreck, and soon hundreds of persons from nearby Lynn and Nahant lined the beach.

A boat which was manned by the mate and two sailors put out for land, but swamped immediately.[1] The craft washed ashore while two of the men were pulled back to the bark by rope. The third sailor, William Bond, drifted to a point near the beach where, just as he was about to sink, he was taken out of the water by Otis Newhall, who had courageously launched a dory into the waves.

The *Vernon* began to break up and the passengers and crew seemed doomed. Zebedee Small manned a lifeboat, but failed after two attempts to get it through the heavy surf. By this time the shore was littered with oranges and lemons which the people quickly gathered as the breakers washed them in.

Captain Miles Blanchard then organized a small group of men and boys who successfully launched their dory and made their way to the doomed *Vernon.*[2] About the same time a group of Swampscott fishermen arrived on the scene with a dory which they had dragged through the snow. The natural rivalry between the two groups of men, representing two sections of the North Shore, stimulated the rescuers to almost superhuman efforts. Soon everyone on the *Vernon* was taken ashore to safety through waves which at times stood the dories on end. For many years afterwards the people of Lynn, Nahant, and Swampscott dated events in relation to the time of the wreck of the British bark *Vernon*.

BOSTON HARBOR'S WORST SHIPWRECK

The *Maritana*, a ship of 991 tons, was built in Quincy, Massachusetts, in 1857, and owned in Providence by Suchet Mauran, 2nd. When the question of a figurehead was discussed, Mauran decided upon a graceful French carving which had been salvaged from the French warship *Berceau* after her capture by the American frigate *Boston* back in the quasi-war with France at the turn of the century. Some years later the figurehead was placed on the ship *Caroline*, which was soon wrecked in a storm. The figurehead was again preserved, this time being placed on the new *Maritana*. The ship's career was fairly uneventful until she sailed from Liverpool, September 25, 1861, with a great cargo of coal, wool, potash, steel, and iron, headed for Boston.[1]

The *Maritana* sighted Highland Light at Cape Cod, November 2 at four-thirty in the afternoon; four hours later she took a bearing on Race Point Light which was, then fifteen miles away to the east southeast. Keeping on her course for Boston Light, the *Maritana* ran into a southeasterly gale while far out in the bay. Shortly after midnight Captain Williams obtained a brief glimpse of Boston Light's welcome flash before snow came down so thick that the light was obscured. Captain Williams ordered the crew to tack ship, but before she could be brought to the wind, breakers were discovered. With a grinding crash, the *Maritana* struck on Egg or Shag Rocks, half a mile to the eastward of Boston Light.

Although the ship was seaworthy, its position on Shag Rocks was almost hopeless. The writer has visited this ugly ledge on several occasions, and believes that there is very little chance for any vessel unfortunate enough to hit here in a storm. Six other disasters to shipping are known to have occurred at Shag Rocks.

Courageous Captain Williams made plans to reach the rocky ledge. A heavy sea was smashing against the hard, unyielding pinnacles which jut out from the water, so that his plans were foredoomed to failure. The ship's longboat was got over, but it was stove in almost at once, while the other ship's boats were crushed to pieces in the davits. At three in the morning the masts were cut away.

A brave seaman named Thomas Haney now swam ashore with a line. Since he could not climb high enough on the ledges to escape the direct force of the mighty billows, he signalled to be hauled back to the boat where he was hoisted over the side, bleeding from scores of jagged cuts. The captain now realized that there was little hope for most of the crew and passengers.

The *Maritana* was new and strong, however, and there was no water below decks at all, hours after the crash. Grinding and chafing on the ledge, the vessel dropped lower and lower as the tide receded. The strain was too great even for a new vessel. Suddenly the captain noticed the ship was beginning to break in two.

"Look out for yourselves!" shouted Captain Williams, and fell to his death in the crevice of the break. The scenes which followed were terrible to witness. With the guiding spirit of the vessel gone the passengers and crew struggled for their lives. Five seamen were able to swim over to Shag Rocks, while seven persons on the ship's poop deck floated against the ledge when the poop came free. All the others, twenty-six in number, were drowned.[2]

Meanwhile, over at Boston Light, Keeper Moses Barrett had noticed the lights of the vessel shortly before midnight. He saw her bearing east northeast when she suddenly changed her course and seemed to be running for the light. At 12:20 she burned her torch lights, enabling him to recognize her as a square-rigger. The snow now came so fast that the ship's lights faded out. Barrett hoped that she had slipped by safely to make her way into the calmer waters of the inner harbor. The gale increased at a fearful rate, with the visibility at daybreak less than one hundred yards. The lighthouse keeper climbed down to the edge of the ocean where he found the standard of a ship, and decided, correctly, that a large vessel had been wrecked nearby.

When the storm lifted a little, the anxious inhabitants of Lighthouse Island were able to see the *Maritana* fast ashore on Shag Rocks. Keeper Barrett knew a lifeboat would not last in the gale. He could do nothing to help. Across Lighthouse Channel lies Hull, and Barrett set the signal for a ship in distress. The wind blew the signal flag to shreds.

By afternoon the wind and the seas had fallen, and Captain Barrett's new signal flag was acknowledged. At two o'clock Pilot Boat *William Sharkey* sent a dory manned by the life savers of Hull ashore at Shag Rocks, where the survivors of the tragedy were rescued. The rescue boat was in charge of Captain Samuel James,[3] a member of the famous life saving family at Hull. The shores of Boston Light received the battered bodies of Captain Williams and five others. Barrett removed the watch and other valuables from Williams' body for safe-keeping.

A more disastrous wreck was never seen. All the outer islands were covered with supplies from the ship.

Captain Hough of the Harbor Police went down to the scene and picked up the ship's papers. The naked body of a woman was recovered from the bar near Bug Light. Across the Narrows at historic Fort Warren this scene was observed by a small group of Confederate prisoners of war. One of them, Lawrence Sangston, had described the storm in his diary[4] the night before, and to give the reader a southerner's views of a New England gale we include it here:

> "Storm increasing, fearful night for ships on the coast; at times the wind would whistle through the casemate windows equal to the shrill whistle of a locomotive engine, and after listening an hour to the howling of the storm, and the waves breaking over the rocks, went to sleep."

The storm was a severe one in Massachusetts Bay. Several other vessels were wrecked, including the bark *Nathaniel Coggswell* at Scituate. All hands were saved from this disaster. The schooner *Emma Wadsworth* went ashore on Spectacle Island in Boston's inner harbor, while the tide swept across Broad Street and Commercial Street in the city itself. Mountainous waves at Revere Beach swept ashore the schooner *Canton* of Newburyport with 20,000 feet of lumber. Hull became an island at the height of the storm. Chimneys, waterspouts, and awnings were blown down everywhere by the gale.

A few days later the figurehead of the ill-fated *Maritana* was brought up to Boston, where it was placed on Lincoln Wharf. The pier later caught fire, and some of the superstitious blamed the figurehead. The graceful wooden figure is now on exhibition at the Marine Room in the Old State House.

The following March part of the body of one of the sailors came up on the beach at Boston Light and was buried on the island. Later in the year the wife of Captain Williams visited Keeper Barrett there, and sat in the shadow of the lighthouse looking out at the merciless ledge which had separated her happy family forever. Keeper Barrett gave the widow the watch and other keepsakes which he had been saving for her. At the time he remarked that it was the worst shipwreck in the history of the harbor, and although over three-quarters of a century have gone by since his remark, it is still true today.

THE 1869 SEPTEMBER GALE

September is, without question, the month of gales. In 1676, 1815, 1821, 1869, 1879, and in 1938 gales hit New England with devastating force, just to mention a few of the many September occasions when the winds have penetrated with telling effect our coastal areas.

On the afternoon of September 8, 1869, a hurricane raged over a narrow fifty-mile-wide strip across Massachusetts and Maine. In Boston the Coliseum Building was wrecked, and with it the great organ and drum located there. Granville M. Clark, standing nearby, was hit when a portion of the wooden sidewalk was torn up and struck him on the skull. He died shortly afterwards.

The Hanover Street Methodist Church lost its steeple, an entire tenement block was levelled in Chelsea, Massachusetts, while the spire of the First Baptist Church in Lynn crashed into the left wing of the edifice. Up and down the coast similar damage was reported.

In Maine the gale was known as the Saxby Gale, as it had been predicted by Saxby.[1] The schooner *Helen Eliza* struck on Peak's Island, Maine, during the gale, and all except one man perished. The survivor, Charles Jordan, floated ashore on a barrel. He drifted near two of his companions, who were clinging to a plank, but they never made the beach.

The well-known steamer *Cambridge* was out in the tempest. Off Monhegan Island at the time, Captain Otis Ingraham brought the two-year-old paddle-wheeler through the gale, but only after her steam pipe and rudder had broken. The *Cambridge*, according to John M. Richardson,[2] drifted almost to the mouth of the Georges River. Captain Ingraham sounded, getting twenty-three fathoms. He ordered both anchors let go when just off the ledges, and the anchors held. Captain Ingraham had saved the *Cambridge* for a career which lasted until 1886, when the steamer broke in two after piling up on the Old Man's Ledge off Port Clyde.

THE GALE OF 1888

The south shore of Massachusetts suffered greatly during the 1888 storm which was a terrible hurricane while it lasted. Minot's Light in particular underwent a terrific battering.

Joseph Frates, Keeper Reamy's assistant at the light, told him that one of the waves which struck the tower on Sunday, November 25, 1888, made his hair actually stand on end. The tower remained firm, however. The wave caused a strong vibration at the time, but Keeper Reamy declared that nothing but an earthquake would ever shake down the lighthouse. We quote from *The Story of Minot's Light:*[1]

> "Keeper Reamy feared that the steamer *Allentown* with eighteen on board had gone down after striking the dangerous reef a mile to the northeast of the lighthouse. He was later asked if he had heard a whistle that fateful night when the *Allentown* was lost.
>
> " 'I did not,' he answered, 'and it would have been impossible to hear a whistle, if it had been within ten feet of the Light, owing to the tremendous roar of the waves as they dashed *over the light.*' "

Fifteen ships were wrecked between Scituate Harbor and Boston in that 1888 hurricane. Life preservers and marked lifeboats soon came ashore in Cohasset to prove that the *Allentown* actually had foundered near Minot's Light, and the *Edward H. Norton*[2] went ashore on the First Cliff, Scituate, with the loss of all fifteen of her crew. The schooner *Sasonoa* drifted by Minot's Light and came ashore on Pleasant Beach, after having snapped her anchor chains in Gloucester Harbor. High and dry, the craft remained a picturesque landmark for many years.

Mr. Fitz-Henry Smith, Jr., of Boston, has written an outstanding account of Boston Bay shipwrecks in which

he includes deeds of valor performed by the lifesavers of
Hull.³ He gives glowing and well-deserved praise to the
heroes who rescued a great many men from death in the
1888 storm, especially signalling out for commendation
Captain Joshua James. One of Captain James' outstanding achievements, according to Mr. Smith, was the rescue
of twenty-nine men in twenty-four hours from five different vessels during the storm.

THE VENETIAN

Heavily loaded with grain, flour, provisions, dressed
beef, 645 live sheep and 845 head of live cattle, the
Furness Liner *Venetian* sailed from the Boston Hoosac
Tunnel Docks shortly before three o'clock on March 2,
1895.

The weather was overcast, but visibility was good as
the *Venetian* drew abeam of the Bird Island Flats and
headed for buoy number 12. Suddenly there was a violent snow squall which blanketed everything around the
423-foot steamer. The pilot was unable to locate a single
identifying marker. A few minutes later the *Venetian* hit
on Governor's Island Flats; her last voyage had lasted less
than an hour. Captain Farthington tried desperately to
back the steamer off, but it was high water, and the tide
slowly receded. Soon afterwards the long Furness liner
snapped her back, and all thoughts of salvage were
abandoned.

Though the thirst-maddened steers which had been
left aboard had to be shot, most of the other cargo was
safely brought ashore. It is said that an enterprising
Brockton shoe manufacturer purchased the rights to ad-
vertise his wares by painting a huge sign extolling the

benefits of his particular brand of shoes on the side of the *Venetian,* and for the whole of the following summer until the *Venetian* was finally broken up, the passengers on the various harbor excursion boats were treated to an unusual advertisement. After various efforts to plan repairs junkmen bought the ship and broke her up.

THE NORSEMAN

During the early morning hours of a very foggy day in March 1899, the freighter *Norseman* drove aground on Tom Moore Rocks off Marblehead. As there was a tremendous sea raging at the time and it was feared that the vessel might go to pieces, lifebelts were quickly passed around. Captain Rees ordered a rocket shot off, while at the same time he blew a distress signal on the *Norseman's* whistle.

At daylight a crew from the Massachusetts Humane Society's station rowed a lifeboat out to the scene, 250 yards from shore. Captain John H. L. Giles, in charge of the surfboat was unable to establish contact with those on the steamer because of the heavy surf. As soon as Captain Giles decided that he could not take off any of the 102 men aboard, he returned to shore.[1] News of the shipwreck spread rapidly; soon the rocks of Marblehead were covered with people.

When the sun came out to disperse the fog, a line was shot across to the stranded *Norseman.* In a short time the breeches buoy was in place, and at eight o'clock that morning, less than five hours after the wreck, the first passenger rode high above the breaking waves to land safely ashore. Another gun was fired across the ship, and another breeches buoy was attached. With the rapid service of

TWO MEN COMING ASHORE ON THE BREECHES BUOY FROM THE
NORSEMAN — WRECKED AT MARBLEHEAD, 1899.

PHOTO FROM THE BOSTON POST

THE ROBERT E. LEE ON MARY ANN ROCKS, MANOMET, 1928
LIFEBOAT SEEN STANDING BY LATER CAPSIZED,
DROWNING THREE OF THE CREW.

THE NANCY ON NANTASKET BEACH, STRANDED FEBRUARY 20, 1927

the two lines, every one of the crew and passengers was ashore within a few hours.

Plans were made to save the *Norseman*. Great crowds gathered daily on the rocks, conjecturing about the possibility of getting her off. Camera tripods were set up in every suitable location, and hundreds of pictures were made. A few days later the combined efforts of the tugs *Juno, Mercury, Pallas,* and *Confidence,* all from Boston, freed the *Norseman*. It was indeed a thrilling spectacle as the victorious tugs started for Boston with the crippled steamer in tow.

THE DAVIS PALMER

Captain Leroy K. McKown anchored the *Davis Palmer* off Finn's Ledge on Christmas Day, 1909. He had hoped to have dinner with his wife that afternoon, but it was not to be, as contrary winds had made him drop anchor three miles off the Winthrop shore. The five-masted schooner swung restlessly as the afternoon waned, while the captain grew more and more worried as the barometer dropped.

By nightfall the first indication of a severe northeast storm was in evidence, and the crew made the ship ready to weather the blow. It was no use, however, for before morning the rising seas had pushed the *Palmer* across from Finn's Ledge, capsizing the great vessel somewhere off Fawn Bar Beacon and drowning the entire crew of twelve men.[1]

On the mainland the snowstorm brought waves and the highest tide since the Minot's Light gale, in fact less than a fraction of an inch below that famous storm and six inches higher than that of the *Portland* Gale. It was the highest tide[2] yet recorded in the twentieth century. The Winthrop seawall was washed out in many sections, houses along the lower part of Fawn Bar Avenue were undermined by the ocean, and Point Shirley was isolated by a gully five feet deep which the tide cut while sweeping across from the ocean to the harbor. One of the two remaining elms on Apple Island went over in the gale.

The people who climbed to the top of Great Head in Winthrop looked down upon a terrible scene from their vantage point atop the 105-foot cliff. The writer was among those who saw the five masts of the *Davis Palmer* as they projected at an angle out of the water a short distance off the Winthrop shore. Captain McKown's wife by this time had been notified of the tragedy, but she still continued to hope that her husband had been rescued. As the days went by she reluctantly became convinced that her husband had perished in the Christmas storm of 1909.

THE MOXIE

The tragedy which befell thirteen young boys from Lynn, Massachusetts, left an impression of unusual degree on all those who were in any way associated with it. On the night of March 29, 1917, the small twenty-three foot motor boat *Moxie* left Stone's Wharf in Lynn at about nine p.m. Shortly before eleven o'clock Winthrop residents walking along the Crest[1] heard shouts for help coming from the ocean. Telephone calls were sent to the Nahant Coast Guard Station. Unfortunately the boat there was out of order, so the Nahant Station telephoned to Hudson Robertson, the owner of the *Moxie*, asking him to go out in search of the persons in trouble. Robertson went down to the wharf, but found his boat missing. This was the first he knew that the boys had taken the boat out.

Meanwhile those on the Winthrop shore had lighted huge bonfires to guide those in trouble to shore, but their cries grew weaker and weaker, finally dying away altogether. Gus Johnson of Winthrop now launched a small dory from the beach, but there was such a heavy ground swell that the dory went over, and Johnson barely reached shore. After vainly staying up until early morning hours, the crowd on the shore dispersed.

Thirteen boys never returned to their Lynn homes, however, and the realization was soon to come that they had all probably drowned in the surf off the Winthrop shore. On the afternoon of April 6, just as this nation was declaring war on Germany, my chum Tom Johnson and I began to walk toward the beach to see if any sign might be found of the missing boat *Moxie*. To our surprise we found that the bodies of the boys were washing in on the beach. In a relatively short time the parents were notified, and pitiful scenes took place as the identifications were made.

THE NANCY

A goodly proportion of the residents now living in Greater Boston have seen the five-masted schooner *Nancy* on the beach at Nantasket. Her story is now one of the sagas of that historic beach which has seen scores of shipwrecks in the past three centuries.

On February 19, 1927, the schooner anchored off Boston Light to ride out an anticipated gale. The next day when a sleet storm hit, the *Nancy* let go three anchors. The wind increased to fifty-five miles an hour. First the anchors dragged and then the chains parted. The schooner began to head for the dreaded Harding's Ledge but Captain E. M. Baird tried the daring maneuver of setting a staysail to clear the dangerous rocks. In this he was successful, and soon the shores of Nantasket Beach loomed ahead in the driving sleet storm. The *Nancy* brought up on the beach about one hundred yards off shore.[1]

Patrolman Ned Gleason of Hull was among the first to sight the *Nancy*, and a volunteer life saving crew was organized. Captains O. C. Olson, Edwin Hatch, Adelbert Nickerson, and eight other volunteers quickly launched the Massachusetts Humane Society's life boat into the breakers and reached the lee of the *Nancy*. The surfmen held the boat fast while the entire crew, one of them holding the ice-covered ship's cat, jumped into the boat. Twenty minutes later all were safe ashore.

The *Nancy* did not break up, and stayed high and dry on the beach for many years. People came from every state in the union to see the five-masted schooner, with those who wished to go aboard paying for the privilege. Every so often, during a run of high tides, efforts were made to launch the schooner, but as the years went by, she became a fixture at Nantasket Beach. One day at high tide she slipped a short distance toward the sea, but grounded again. In another storm she came up ten feet higher than ever.

It was finally arranged that she should be broken up. Her towering masts were acquired by the Hitchcock Quarry in Quincy, and the lumber was taken by residents of Hull.

It was then believed that the people had seen the last of the *Nancy*, but during a northeast storm in the winter of 1940, the keel of the schooner was washed out of the Nantasket sands.

THE ROBERT E. LEE

On the night of March 9, 1928, at the height of a raging snowstorm, the *Robert E. Lee,* considerably off her course, hit the Mary Ann Rocks off Manomet Point, Massachusetts, while running for the Cape Cod Canal. There were 273 men, women, and children aboard.

Captain Harland W. Robinson said that the *Lee* was going at full speed when she struck. Clearing the first of the rocks, the steamer hit four others in rapid succession and then began to ship water on the starboard side. The snow coming in the open wheel house window had affected the compass, Robinson believed.[1]

The discipline of the crew was good, but some of the passengers had to be quieted. A short time after the vessel hit the rocks, the lights failed and the entire ship was blacked out. As the 400-foot steamer rolled back and forth in the darkness, the passengers became uneasy and wandered nervously about the vessel. A short time later the seacocks were opened, allowing the *Robert E. Lee* to settle down on the rocks as in a cradle, and the rolling ceased. It was possible for those on the upper decks to go back to bed, but the water rose higher in the staterooms on the lower decks as the tide came in. All the officers were worried as to what might happen at two o'clock when the tide was high, but the ship held firm. At the turn of the tide the crisis was over.

The next day the Manomet Point Coast Guard Station under Boatswain's Mate Cashman sent its surfboat out to the *Lee,* negotiating with difficulty the giant swells on the way to Mary Ann Rocks. Arriving at the scene of the accident, Cashman went aboard the *Lee,* where he consulted with Captain Robinson about taking the passengers

off the wrecked liner. It was finally agreed that rowing
them all ashore would be not only a long and tedious task,
but one fraught with the danger of capsizing in the
breakers, and so the rescue craft then standing by were
instructed to get ready to receive the passengers from
small boats which could be sent over to them.

The large powerful surfboats at Sagamore and Wood
End were sent for, and Boatswain's Mate Cashman finally
started back for the shore with his men, pleased that satisfactory arrangements had been made. One load of passengers had been ferried across to the patrol boat when
the Manomet lifeboat started back to the beach. It was
then a little past eleven o'clock in the morning, and the
surfboat had reached a position just off Stage Point where
she was making good headway. Suddenly the lifeboat
was lifted clear by an enormous wave and hit by another
before she could settle, sending her straight up into the air.
She came down bottom up. Watchers on the shore saw
several of the men come to the surface as they struggled
in the angry sea. A. A. Proctor, one of the crew, describes[2]
the incident:

> "We were nearly unable to move when we
> landed in the water. All of the seven men in the
> power dory were shocked so badly that we had
> all we could do to grab the boat. . . . First thing
> I knew I began to feel awfully numb. It was a
> tough fight to keep above water."

Three of the crew died as a result of the capsizing,
Boatswain's Mate William H. Cashman, Frank Griswold,
and Edward Stark. The others were rescued and rushed
to the hospital.

Every passenger was taken safely from the *Robert E. Lee* and placed on the patrol boats *Bonham, Active,* and the *C. G. 176.* Seven others returned to Boston on the *Red Wing.* One of them, Gurden S. Worcester of Cambridge, said:

"I was in my stateroom on the saloon deck
when there was a sickening, terrifying crash.
I went on deck and found the other passengers
wandering nervously about trying to find out
what had happened. The snow was whirling
thickly about the ship and I could see nothing.
Suddenly, from someone, came word that a girl
had thrown herself overboard and that we were
stopping to pick her up. . . . The story was false.
But it was typical of the dozens of rumors and
speculative remarks that I heard later."

Worcester and the other six passengers were landed in Boston at 5:15 on Saturday afternoon. Perhaps the most surprised man on board was J. J. Keeley of Winthrop, Massachusetts. Sleeping through the confusion of the shipwreck and subsequent excitement Keeley did not awaken until 7:00 Saturday morning, when he dressed and went down to the ship's barber shop for his morning shave.

The following Sunday thousands of cars jammed the highway around Plymouth to see the wreck of the *Robert E. Lee* off Manomet Point. Later in the month the steamer was pulled from the rocks.

THE NORTHERN SWORD

During a howling February blizzard in 1934, the collier *Northern Sword* came up on the Winthrop beach at a point just below the water tower situated on nearby Great Head. When the storm went down, Captain Sorenson found his craft resting comfortably in three feet of water at low tide, with no apparent danger of disaster.

The local papers soon carried the account of the stranding of the collier, and hundreds came to Winthrop to see the unusual sight. For more than a week the steamer stayed on the shoals near Winthrop. One morning during another storm she was pulled off and floated.[1]

The bar inside of which she grounded has now extended itself to the great seawall on shore, and is called Northern Sword Bar, commemorating the stranding of the collier during the February gale of 1934.[2]

THE ROMANCE

During one of the severe September fogs of 1936, the Provincetown excursion steamer *Romance* and the Boston to New York steamer *New York* collided off Graves Light in outer Boston Harbor. The captain of the New York boat kept his bow wedged against the hole in the side of the *Romance*, allowing the passengers on the smaller craft to climb to safety aboard the *New York*. In this way the quick-wittedness of the *New York's* captain prevented what might have become a tragedy. The *Romance* went down soon afterwards, and the next day her superstructure floated ashore at Winthrop, where souvenir hunters found many a treasure.

THE CITY OF SALISBURY

Entering Boston Harbor on April 22, 1938, in a dense fog, the heavily-laden 419-foot cargo steamer *City of Salisbury* struck an uncharted pinnacle twenty-four feet below the surface, and was unable to move. Loaded with animals, rubber, jute, and many other supplies, the *Salisbury* contained the richest cargo ever wrecked in outer Boston Harbor.[1]

The writer made the first air photograph of the disaster later that afternoon, his plane dropping down in a rift of the fog bank. It was quite a thrill to circle above the huge vessel and to see the animal crates, the Lascars with their life belts on, and the general state of orderly excitement on the steamer as the vessel slowly settled upon the ledge.[2]

Barges began to unload the steamer, but it was too late. Shortly after noon the next day an ominous sound was heard, and the vessel cracked in two. The many animals aboard were hurriedly brought into Boston, with the exception of two snakes and several monkeys which disappeared in the confusion. One of the monkeys appeared later in the week, five miles away on Deer Island where he was seen by Robert Mackey of Point Shirley, while Nelson Maynard of Deer Island found the carcass of a large snake on the same beach.[3]

All the following summer the *City of Salisbury* hung on the pinnacle, with much of the cargo removed by the last of August. Excursion steamers took thousands upon thousands of people out by the wreck, for it was a spectacular sight. The steamer was rechristened the "Zoo Ship" by those who saw it grinding away on the ledge that year. By midsummer the entire forward section had slipped off into deep water, and a crack was developing amidships the remainder of the vessel. When the autumn winds began to blow, the stern alone was above the water. It was a weird sensation to the writer and others who went aboard the after deck two weeks before she sank completely. The grinding and gnashing of the iron rods and broken timbers far down under the water could plainly be heard, and the steamer would shudder and jerk as the ground swell passed alongside. Incidentally, the great September hurricane did not move the wreck at all. A northeasterly storm during October came in out of the Atlantic, and when it had cleared the *City of Salisbury* was no longer visible.[4]

THE MARY E. O'HARA

The last great marine tragedy of Boston Harbor was enacted on January 21, 1941, when nineteen brave men from the fishing schooner *Mary E. O'Hara* fell to their death into the icy seas near Finn's Ledge off the shores of Winthrop.[1] Within a few minutes of the end of her voyage, the *O'Hara* smashed into the barge *Winifred Sheridan* at 3:00 in the morning, sheered off, and settled in forty feet of water.

All but three members of the crew were in their bunks when the collision took place. In an almost unbelievably short time, the schooner went to the bottom. The men were barely able to scramble up into the rigging, to which they clung as the icy waters broke over the schooner. As the hours passed, however, the men grew numbed and weakened, one by one dropping into the sea. It had been impossible to use the dories, as they were buried under tons of ice. Just before the schooner foundered Captain Fred Wilson tried to hack the gripes holding the dories down, but the ice still held them to the deck. The captain hacked away until the water reached his waist before he climbed up to the top lift.

Several boats passed the men. They cried out but

could not be heard above the wind and surf. Then the trawler *North Star* came along. John Sheen cried out, "Hang on, a boat is coming," but when Captain Lars Lunde of the *North Star* arrived, Sheen had already dropped to his death in the freezing sea. By this time the *O'Hara* had listed so that the water was up to the foremast crosstrees. The members of the crew who were rescued were in the rigging about three hours before being taken off. They had watched their friends drop into the ocean, some with the Lord's prayer on their lips, others without even a groan.

Captain Lars Lunde, the master of the rescue vessel *North Star*, estimated that the *O'Hara* sank about 3 a.m. and that he sighted the masts at about 5:40 a.m. The thermometer was 12 above zero at the time. The shouts of the men first attracted his attention; then he saw dimly the masts of the sunken ship. With his engines idling, he slid the *North Star* up alongside and took off the five survivors, Gabriel Welch, Frank Silva, Cecil Crowell, Cecil Larkin, and Stanley Conrad.[2]

Lunde said afterwards that if one of the other three vessels which passed the wreck earlier that bitter morning had heard the cries and stopped, many others and possibly all of those who later perished would have been saved.

CAPE COD SHIPWRECKS

THE great beach at Cape Cod has seen more than three thousand shipwrecks in its long career as guardian of Massachusetts Bay. Beginning in earliest times and extending even to the present day, ships have struck the bending arm of Cape Cod with unfortunate regularity as the years have gone by. The *Sparrowhawk* crashed near Eastham back in 1626, while the last shipwreck to be included in this book is that of the *Teresa Dan*, a two-masted schooner which ran aground during Christmas week, 1942.

THE ALMIRA

On a hillside overlooking Sandwich Harbor on the afternoon of January 16, 1827, stood an old, experienced captain watching a small schooner sail out to sea. So intent in his gaze was the old man that an acquaintance accosted him asking what was the matter.

In response the old sea man raised his hands and said, "Gone out! He will never come in again." His friend reminded him that the wind was southerly, but the old man, totally ignoring this fact, walked away convinced that the ship was doomed.

The master of the schooner in question, the *Almira*, was Captain Josiah Ellis, a large, dignified man, who had concluded that there would be a few days of pleasant weather, and had sailed from Sandwich with a crew of two—his son and another sailor, John Smith, by name.

By early evening the vessel was off Mary Ann Rocks, Manomet, with the northwest sky clear and bright. The temperature dropped so low, however, that the mariners realized that it would be necessary to make the nearest harbor or perish in the bitter cold. They tried to reach Plymouth by tacking, but the wind increased and they failed.

The men realized now that their condition was perilous indeed. The spray soon coated the mainsail with ice and down it came. The vessel was laid to the wind, the foresail braced fore and aft, but the jib which was frozen, could not be hauled down. The wind soon cracked the ice and tore the canvas to shreds. Obeying the helm, the schooner came up to the wind, where it remained.

It was so cold that icicles formed on the bodies of the crew, forcing them all to go below and build a fire in the cabin. When they returned to the deck, they found it covered with ice. The sun rose on the coldest morning of the winter. Captain Ellis and his crew decided to sail back to Sandwich, but when the *Almira* reached a position off the harbor, the men in their frozen condition were unable to maneuver the schooner. The sailors were swept past their homes, where they could see the smoke curling from the chimneys of their houses. The last sail now went to pieces, and the vessel drifted helplessly before the wind. Sandwich, Barnstable, and Yarmouth all were passed, but when the schooner approached Dennis, a ledge of rocks loomed ahead, and the schooner crashed upon them.

From the nearby hill one of the Dennis residents saw the schooner approaching. The vessel was so close to the beach that the watchers ashore could look down on the decks, which were masses of ice. Wondering if anyone might be aboard, they shouted out to the vessel, whereupon the three men slowly emerged from the cabin. Standing like statues in their frozen condition, they indicated that they were in desperate need. A boat was put out to them, making its way with difficulty through the frozen sludge, but a wave swamped it. Those on shore then threw out a warp, which was secured by one of the lifesavers in the swamped dory, and the men were drawn back to the beach.

Out on the *Almira,* the waves still broke over the doomed vessel. One sailor dropped to the deck, and was soon encased in ice. The captain sank down, dying of exposure shortly afterwards. Only the captain's son was still alive. The tide began to rise, freeing the *Almira* from the rocks, and the schooner drifted nearer the shore, where those on the beach boarded her. Young Ellis, the captain's son, eventually recovered, but the prediction of the ancient mariner came true. Captain Josiah Ellis never came in again to Sandwich Harbor.[1]

THE LOSS OF THE FRANKLIN

"Mr. Hopkins of Wellfleet arrived in this city last night and states that the ship Franklin, Capt. Smith from London, of and for Boston, went ashore at Wellfleet, Cape Cod, on Thursday morning, at nine o'clock, and Capt. Smith, with the first mate, and eight others, perished. Twenty of the passengers and crew were saved. The ship went to pieces and her cargo was scattered along the shore."

Thus did the inhabitants of Boston and New England, through the pages of the *Boston Courier* for March

3, 1849, learn of a shipwreck which was destined to attract much attention because of the interest of Henry David Thoreau, and the recovery from the Atlantic of several documents which told the strange story of a planned wreck.

The actual number of persons aboard the *Franklin* was thirty-three, of whom eleven were drowned. The following fall Thoreau visited Cape Cod,[1] walking along the beach where the wreck had taken place. One night he and his friend, William DeCosta, visited the home of Uncle Jack Newcomb, better known as the "Wellfleet Oysterman." Thoreau tells of Newcomb's story of the *Franklin:*

> "He told us the story of the wreck of the Franklin, which took place the previous spring; how a boy came to his house early in the morning to know whose boat that was by the shore, for there was a vessel in distress, and he, being an old man, first ate his breakfast, and then walked over to the top of the hill by the shore, and sat down there, having found a comfortable seat, to see the ship wrecked. She was on the bar, only a quarter of a mile from him, and still nearer to the men on the beach, who had got a boat ready. . . .
>
> " 'I saw the captain get out his boat,' said he; 'he had one little one; and then they jumped into it one after another, down as straight as an arrow. I counted them. There were nine. One was a woman, and she jumped as straight as any of them. Then they shoved off. The sea took

them back, one wave went over them, and when they came up there were six still clinging to the boat; I counted them. The next wave turned the boat bottom upward, and emptied them all out. None of them ever came ashore alive!'"

The lady mentioned as jumping into the lifeboat was Miss Skehan,[2] one of several members of that family aboard the *Franklin*. The little child which the captain held was an eleven-months-old girl, a sister of the Skehan woman.

The *Franklin* began to break up when the lifeboat left the vessel. It was said that the lifeboat was hit by the breakers from twelve to fifteen times as it floated toward the beach. Shortly afterwards the *Franklin* worked its way over the bar and started for the shore. This encouraged the watchers on the beach, who launched a small boat into the tremendous swell then running, and started for the survivors. They let over a line held by the crowd on shore, one of whom was a woman who, it is said, did more than her share.

When the rescue boat arrived at the *Franklin*, they found that one woman had been washed overboard, but all the rest were able to climb into the fishing boat and reach the shore in safety. By this time the *Franklin's* wreckage was strewn up and down the beach. An inhabitant of Cape Cod, writing of the incident two days later, noticed a small boy who had been rescued from the vessel.

"I took the little boy saved up in my lap, yesterday afternoon, and as I looked upon him and the little babe, his sister, also rescued, I could not help exclaiming, in admiration of that providence, without which a sparrow falleth to the ground."

Some time after the wreck Captain Isaiah Hatch of Wellfleet was walking along the beach when he came across a suitcase owned by Captain Charles Smith, the *Franklin's* master. In the valise were incriminating documents indicating that the master was planning to wreck his vessel for the insurance, a deed in which the ship's owners, James W. Wilson and John W. Crafts, were fellow-partners.[3] The captain had become the victim of his own nefarious plan to wreck the *Franklin,* and had not only snuffed out his own life in the attempt, but the lives of ten others. Incidentally, the Boston partners in this crime, Wilson and Crafts, were never properly punished for their share in such a terrible deed.

THE JOSEPHUS

During a heavy April fog in the year 1849 the British ship *Josephus* ran aground on the outer bar off Highland Light.[1] Carrying a cargo of heavy iron rails, the *Josephus* struck during a strong northeasterly gale and soon began to go to pieces. When the fog opened up momentarily, the lighthouse keeper saw the vessel and spread the alarm. A large crowd gathered on the beach within the hour, and efforts were made at once to save the men on the ship.

The masts soon went by the board, scattering the members of the crew to various parts of the *Josephus.* Some could then be seen clinging to the broken ship, their screams echoing even above the roar of the gigantic breakers. Although anxious to help the sailors, the watchers on shore did not dare to risk going out to them in the mountainous seas then pounding the Cape Cod beach.

Suddenly two men were seen running down the side of the Highland Cliff, Jonathan Collins and his friend Daniel Cassidy. Having just returned from a long fishing voyage, the men did not even stop to greet their families, but on hearing of the shipwreck rushed across the town and up to Highland Light. On their arrival at the beach, they found a fisherman's dory which they carried to the water and launched into the high waves. When urged to give up the dangerous attempt, they replied:

"We cannot stand it longer to see these poor fellows being swept into the sea, and we are going to reach them." They had hardly gained a point two hundred feet from shore when a mighty billow loomed over them, poised its tremendous bulk for a moment, and then engulfed the two heroic fishermen. They were not seen again.[2]

Night came, and the cries of the sailors aboard the ship *Josephus* became fainter and fainter, finally stopping completely as the surf continued its ceaseless pounding on the white sands. The powerful beacon in the tower was lighted, and the keeper sat down for a moment, his thoughts on the men who might still be alive off the Highland Cliffs.

About midnight Keeper Hamilton came down from the tower, strangely troubled in his thoughts. He realized that only by a miracle could anyone have reached the shore, but in spite of this he was uneasy. Finally deciding that only a walk along the beach would quiet his nerves, he threw on his overcoat and made his way out to the edge of the cliff. As he descended to the great beach, the Highland lightkeeper noticed that considerable wreckage from the *Josephus* was being buffeted by the waves. In the distance he saw what seemed to be a part of the ship's cabin. As he walked closer, Keeper Hamilton heard a groaning noise coming from the wreckage, and then made out the form of a man clinging desperately to the timbers. Another wave washed the wreckage nearer to the beach. The keeper rushed into the water, grabbed the sailor, threw him over his shoulder, and brought him ashore.

Half an hour later the survivor was carried into the keeper's home, and a doctor sent for. Within a few days the man had completely recovered. Twenty-three of his shipmates and the two heroic fishermen had perished. He alone could tell the story.[3]

A silent watcher of the tragedy was Isaac Morton Small, who later in life spent over half a century reporting shipping for the Boston Chamber of Commerce. Although he witnessed scores of other disasters in his career, Morton Small always carried with him the memory of that April day in 1849 when his mother held him by the hand at the edge of the Highland Cliff, and they watched with dreadful fascination the disaster which befell the *Josephus*.

THE CALEDONIA

A dispatch received at the Merchants Exchange Room in Boston on January 2, 1863, stated that the "British steamer *Caledonia*, Captain Weston, via Portland for N. Y., ran on Peaked Hill during thick weather Wednesday night [December 31, 1862]. She lies about six hundred feet from the beach."

The *Caledonia* had mistaken Race Point Light for Highland Light. It was hoped that she would be got off, but the tide swept out the sand from under her, and when the steam tug *Walpole* reached the scene, the *Caledonia* had broken her back. Most of the cargo, railroad iron and linen, was removed from the ship, which was the same size and model as the famous southern raider *Alabama*. It was also in this storm that the *Monitor*, which fought the *Merrimac*, went down off Cape Hatteras with the loss of thirty-three lives.[1]

THE SHIP PERUVIAN

On the night after Christmas, 1873, a terrific gale swept along Cape Cod, sending mountainous waves high against the cliffs of the Highland there. The ship *Peruvian*, captained by Charles H. Vannah, had sailed from Calcutta several weeks before with a load of tin and sugar. The captain had a special reason for a speedy voyage. His sweetheart, for whom he had been planning a home for several years, was awaiting his return in a New Hampshire town, as this was to be his last voyage.[1]

All had gone well with the *Peruvian* until Christmas Day, when the weather shut in, making any observation impossible. Nevertheless the captain was sure he was off Cape Cod. Keeping the ship sailing northward, he hoped to beat around into calmer waters; but this was not to be. The seas grew more mountainous, the wind increased in violence, and it was impossible to make headway. Just before midnight the vessel struck on the dreaded shoals of Peaked Hill, a mile from shore, and ground its weight into the sands.

All was now chaos in the blackness of the gale. The ship gradually went to pieces, the crew one by one giving up their hopeless fight and dropping off to their death. At daylight the watchers on the beach found the shore littered with wreckage, but only three bodies of the sailors ever reached shore. The disaster had taken place too far out at sea.[2]

Meanwhile Captain Vannah's fiance had made all arrangements to visit Boston just as soon as the ship had been reported as passing the signal station at Cape Cod. Finally, some days after Christmas, word reached Boston of the disaster, and the next day the girl read the overwhelming news that the *Peruvian* had foundered, carrying the man she loved to his death.

THE FRANCIS

Out in the same wild gale which conquered the *Peruvian*, but several miles to the southward, the bark *Francis* was thrown against Cape Cod within five hundred feet of the beach. Settling quickly into the sand, she was observed by watchers along the shore, who located a double ender whaleboat on the bay side of the Cape several miles away. Twenty men dragged the boat to the edge of the pond at North Truro and then slid it across the ice to the Post Office, where a pair of horses and wheels facilitated matters. Great drifts blocked their way to the beach, however, and it was ten o'clock in the morning before the scene of the wreck was reached.[1]

With the double ender launched into the waves, the most difficult part of the journey to the wreck was begun. Out on the *Francis* Captain Kortling, the master, who had been ill for many days in his cabin, was the first to be lowered from the deck into the pitching and tossing whaleboat. The other twenty crewmen were also rescued, but the captain lived only four days after he was brought ashore, as the sickness and exposure proved too much for his weakened body.

Several days later the work of salvage began. The sugar, packed in great straw mats, was hoisted out of the hold day after day, and occasionally one of the packages would break and scatter sugar on the deck. The kind hearted foreman suggested to the twenty-five workmen from nearby Cape towns that it would be all right if they filled their empty dinner pails and baskets with sugar to take home. Gradually the foreman noticed that the size of the dinner containers in which the laborers were transporting their lunches was growing almost daily. At first holding two or three quarts, in a comparatively short time the receptacles which the men were using for their lunches could have accommodated the family laundry. When the shore boat left after work at night, the craft was in danger of swamping, with each of the twenty-five men carrying twenty, thirty, and forty pounds of sugar in what they alleged were lunch baskets. On the day the overseer visited the wreck, the free sugar ended, but not before several of the workmen had obtained enough sugar for nearly a year's supply.

The *Francis*, an iron bark, seemed an attractive proposition for a wrecking company which attempted to raise and float the vessel. The moment came for the floating of the bark, the water was pumped out, and the ship started to rise. The *Francis* came to the surface for a moment, shuddered, and sank at once to the bottom. The waves had worn holes in the bark's iron bottom through which water poured when she lifted off the sand, quickly sending the *Francis* to the bottom again. The wrecking company accepted the inevitable, and left the bark to her fate. Year after year the great storms would expose the iron bark to view, but not since around 1928 has she been seen by watchers from the shore.[2]

THE ITALIAN BARK GIOVANNI

In the winter of the year 1875 the Italian bark *Giovanni* sailed from Palermo with a cargo of sumac, nuts, and brimstone. On March 4, running into a northeast storm off Cape Cod, she drove upon the outer sand bar three miles north of the Highland Life Saving Station. The crew from the Life Saving Station, unable to launch their boat into the mountainous breakers, set up their mortar gun on the beach.

Few thought that the gun could carry to the vessel in the face of that terrific gale, but several attempts were made before the project was abandoned. The bark was seen to be breaking up. Two men jumped from the wheelhouse to wreckage which was beginning to float ashore; one of them soon disappeared from view. The other slowly drifted ashore, where the lifesavers rushed into the sea, joining hands until they formed a living rope. Soon the breakers forced him near the beach, and the foremost man in the chain pulled him from the raging surf. This Italian sailor was the only man rescued from the fifteen on board the *Giovanni*.[1]

All that long night huge bonfires burned on the beach to give hope and encouragement to the survivors on the wreck, but no other person, dead or alive, ever came ashore from the bark. The next day a man was seen to jump from the bow of the vessel and swim to the deckhouse, there to join three of his companions. Soon afterwards the *Giovanni* went to pieces. Although two of the men clung to wreckage until they were halfway ashore, their strength then failed, and they sank beneath the waves.   The drama of the *Giovanni* was over.

THE SLOOP TRUMBULL

On the morning of November 30, 1880, the patrol from the Peaked Hill Bars Station discovered a shipwreck on the outer sand bar a half mile south of the station.   It was the stone sloop *Trumbull,* carrying a deck load of granite from Rockport, Massachusetts, to New York. When she left Rockport the previous afternoon the *Trumbull* carried a crew of five men.

Captain David H. Atkins, in charge at the station, launched the life boat into the surf and six men soon were rowing out to the wreck.   Reaching the scene, Captain Atkins found that he could not approach too near for fear of swamping his craft and so he shouted to the *Trumbull's* crew to jump into the water where they would be picked up.   Three of the sailors leaped into the water, but the captain and mate refused to take the chance, remaining on the sloop.

The life boat returned to the beach with the three sailors, although the captain was troubled by the thought of the two men still out on the sloop.   Finally he announced that he was going to make another attempt to rescue the mariners, and began his second trip.   All went well until the sloop was reached, when the boom and loosened main sheet of the *Trumbull* caught the lifeboat and overturned it.   The surfmen clung desperately to the bottom of the boat, but Captain Atkins, weakened by his efforts earlier in the day, gave up and sank to his death.   Elisha Taylor and Stephen Mayo followed him shortly afterwards.[1]   The other three men began the long swim to shore, where they were hauled out of the water by the man on patrol, John Cole.

With the ocean always performing the unexpected, the incoming tide brought a moderating wind, allowing the stone sloop *Trumbull* to free herself from the dangerous Peaked Hill Bars and continue on her journey down the coast. But the captain and mate of the *Trumbull* must have carried to their dying day the realization that had they obeyed the captain of the life savers and jumped for the life boat, the second trip of the surfmen would not have been necessary.

Later the same afternoon Captain Atkins' own son helped to recover the bodies of the three drowned men. As he carried his father's remains along the beach, it was a proud son who knew that his parent had died carrying out the stern code of the Life Saving Service.[2]

THE MONTE TABOR

An unsolved mystery of the sea was the fate of the Italians aboard the bark *Monte Tabor*, wrecked on the Peaked Hill Bars of Cape Cod, September 14, 1896. Although the loss of life was comparatively small, the shipwreck was never completely explained to the satisfaction of men of the Cape.

The *Monte Tabor*, hailing from Genoa, was loaded with salt from Trapan, Sicily. Struck by a hurricane on September 9, she was trying to make Provincetown Harbor at the time she hit. Patrolman Silvey of the Peaked Hill Station discovered the wreck, but it was impossible to launch the lifeboat. The bark's cabin broke away from the vessel and carried six of the crew ashore to safety. Another young Italian, who reached land by swimming, hid in the beach plum bushes until taken by the life guards. He explained that he expected to be killed if shipwrecked at Cape Cod, which was what the others aboard had told him.[1]

Of those who did not reach land, three committed suicide, according to survivors from the bark, while the remainder of the crew disappeared in the storm. Some say that the captain was so humiliated at the loss of his fine vessel that he killed himself, and two of the other officers followed his example. At the time the survivors claimed it was an Italian custom for the captain of a wrecked craft to take his own life, but this seems to have no basis in fact.[2]

THE COLERAINE

The barge *Coleraine* was one of three which left Bangor, Maine, in April 1915, bound for Philadelphia. Towed out of Bangor Harbor, by the tug *Mars*, the barges encountered heavy weather as the four vessels approached Cape Cod. The following day it began to snow, with the wind setting in from the northeast. At six o'clock that afternoon the captain noticed white water ahead, and realized that he was nearing the Cape. He ordered the cables cut, changed the tug's course, and a few hours later anchored in Provincetown Harbor, where his propeller dropped off.[1]

The three barges, the *Coleraine*, the *Tunnel Ridge*, and the *Manheim* now began to drift against the shores of Cape Cod. One by one they grounded in the sands, but the *Tunnel Ridge* and the *Coleraine* were badly damaged before they hit the beach. The other vessel, in command of Captain George Israel, let go both her anchors, delaying the action of the sea in pushing her up on the beach. By the time she joined the other barges on the shore, the storm had begun to abate, so that the *Manheim* was still in good condition.[2]

The action of the sea soon built up a great breakwater of sand around the *Tunnel Ridge* and the *Coleraine* which were lying stranded one on each side of the *Manheim*. Thus it was impossible to try to float off the uninjured *Manheim* until the two badly wrecked barges were disposed of. It was finally decided to set fire to the wrecked vessels after Captain Israel had allowed the men of Cape Cod to take off the deckhouses from the *Coleraine*. The houses were landed on the beach, cut into smaller sections, and pulled up the steep sides of the Highland cliff by four horses. Made into a three-room building, it soon bore the name of the *Highland House Golf Links*.[3]

On the fourth day of April, 1916, the barge *Manheim* was towed off the beach at Cape Cod. Just a year had elapsed since the wreck of the vessel.

THE 1927 SHIPWRECKS

Two serious shipwrecks occurred on Cape Cod during the year 1927. On February 2, 1927, the three-masted lumber schooner *Montclair* hit the beach at Cape Cod a quarter mile from the Orleans Coast Guard Station. Two men washed ashore on wreckage, but five others were drowned in the great surf. Henry Beston, in his *Outermost House*, gives a fine description of the shipwreck.

Another great storm broke out later in the month. On February 18, the Coast Guard cruiser *238* broke down a mile from the Peaked Hill Bars during the height of the

storm, and radioed for help. Navy craft starting down
from Boston to help the *238* were unable to reach the
doomed cruiser in time. Around midnight the last distress
signals were received on the mainland from the *238*, and
it is believed that she foundered around five o'clock the
next morning. All eight men aboard were lost.

THE TERESA DAN

The last important shipwreck on Cape Cod was that
of the fishing schooner *Teresa Dan,* wrecked one mile north
of Highland Coast Guard Station on December 21, 1942.
Her master was Captain John Hall. After several unsuccessful attempts to free the beam trawler from the sands,
the *Teresa Dan* was sold to Captain Ben Pine, famous
Gloucester fisherman and international racer, who salvaged her on the beach.

THE PORTLAND GALE

WHEN the first chilling winds of a piercing November gale come swirling into the harbors and inlets along the New England Coast, there are gray, aging mariners who recall a night in 1898 when the steamer *Portland* sailed from Boston never to return. The loss of this side-wheeler was the worst marine tragedy of the 19th Century in New England waters.[1] And although the passing years have brought many controversial theories regarding the fate of this handsome steamer, it is probable that the complete story of the *Portland* will never be known.

The gale which caused the loss of the Maine side-wheeler was one of truly cyclonic proportions. It began November 26, 1898, lasting twenty-four hours in violent intensity, and then tapered off to its end. So quickly did it rise that by the time the *Portland* had reached a point off Gloucester, Massachusetts, on her journey from Boston, almost 200 vessels were hurrying for shelter up and down the coast, trying desperately to reach a haven. Gloucester, Vineyard Haven, Provincetown, and Boston were the main objectives of vessels caught in the storm in New England waters. At Martha's Vineyard over twenty ships were damaged or wrecked by the gale, while in Gloucester and Provincetown the shores were strewn with wreckage. Boston Harbor took a severe lashing from the elements, around twenty-five vessels going ashore. In all, 141 different ships were wrecked because of the *Portland* gale in New England.[2]

In such a titanic marine disturbance, we can only cover the outstanding shipwrecks or disasters. The loss of the *Calvin F. Baker*, the *Mertis H. Perry*, the *Albert L. Butler*, and the pilot boat *Columbia* will be considered in detail; the vessels which some claim may have crashed into the *Portland*, the *King Philip*, the *Addie E. Snow*, and the *Pentagoet* will be discussed. The *Portland* itself will be considered at the close of the chapter.

Seven individuals out in the gale have left statements as to the severity of the tempest. Captain Joseph I. Kemp, probably Boston's best known sailing master, who has piloted more than $2,000,000,000.00 worth of shipping from the Fore River yards, was coming into the harbor on that night of 1898. Aboard the tug *Elsie*, Captain Kemp[3] was on the way from Lynn.

"It was the greasiest evening you ever saw, quite similar to the day of the great 1938 hurricane. About seven o'clock it started to spit snow, and a light easterly was blowing. We had towed the barge *Woodside* from Lynn to Quarantine anchorage. Around 7:15 p.m. the *Portland* came down the harbor and passed fairly close to us near Deer Island Light. We landed at Lewis Wharf, and by the next morning they were rowing dories up and down Atlantic Avenue."

Lieutenant Worth G. Ross, assistant inspector of life saving stations in Boston, recorded his impressions[4] of the storm:

"There were at sunset marked indications of approaching bad weather in the vicinity. By midnight it was blowing heavily from the northeast, accompanied by thick snow. Throughout the night the wind and sea increased, and by sunrise of Sunday, November 27, a tremendous gale was raging. Such a violent outburst of the elements had not occurred in this vicinity within the memory of the oldest inhabitant. The wild fury of the wind and driving snow continued without abatement until late in the afternoon. At times the force and roar of the tempest were so appalling as to be indescribable."

Keeper Joshua James, life saver of Hull, Massachusetts, known from Boston to Baltimore for his unsurpassed bravery and rescue work, made some of his most spectacular rescues during that November gale. His comments[5] follow:

"Snow began falling early, and the wind increased until by 10 o'clock it was blowing a gale from the northeast with sleet and snow so thick that we could not see one hundred yards at most. At midnight it was a hurricane."

On the other side of the harbor Keeper Wesley Pingree, well-known around Boston Bay, was marooned at Deer Island Light during the storm. He spent the night in the tower on watch. Some years before his death he signed a statement[6] for the writer about the storm:

"At two o'clock in the afternoon the ocean was as smooth as glass. At five p.m. it had started snowing and the wind was coming up. A little later the Bangor boat went by but returned to the harbor, as the sea was rapidly getting worse. At 7 p.m. the *Portland* came down the channel, and the other boat, anchored in

President Road, whistled a warning to her. At this time the waves were hitting so high that I was lashing my dory fast to the light."

Farther out to sea, on Bug Light at the entrance to Boston Harbor's Narrows, Mrs. Frank Tenney, who kept house for Captain Gershom Freeman, says that she had been digging clams on the bar that afternoon, for there were no signs of the gale then on the way. Later that night the stones thrown up by the waves played strange tunes as they hit the iron supports holding up Bug Light.

Captain William Abbott, who was aboard the steamer *Ohio* when she ran aground at Spectacle Island, said that it had been a terrific experience. "I could hardly see across the ship," were his words.[7]

Keeper Milton H. Reamy of Minot's Light had so often felt the great waves as they crept up the sides of America's most dangerous lighthouse, that he made no particular preparations for the blow when he saw it coming. He took his regular watch in the usual manner, and thought nothing more about it. In the morning, however, when he stepped out on the lower turret of the 114-foot tower, he swept the ocean with his glass, locating many wrecks along the beach. It was only then, said Reamy, that he realized the storm must have been of unusual severity.

The Boston Weather Bureau states definitely that it began snowing at thirty-seven minutes past seven on that Saturday night. At the hour the *Portland* sailed, seven p.m., the barometer in Boston was 29.70, the wind was blowing from the northeast at a rate of thirteen miles an hour, and the weather was cloudy.

A vessel did not have a chance in most cases when

PHOTO THOMAS MARR AND SON

THE ALBERT L. BUTLER ON CAPE COD BEACH, WRECKED
DURING THE PORTLAND GALE.

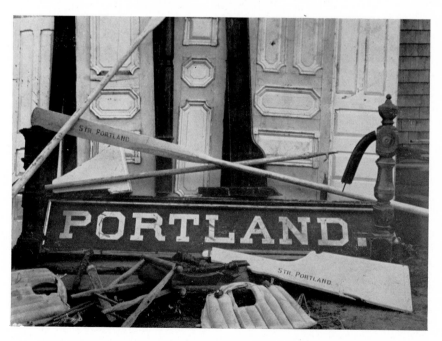

PHOTO THOMAS MARR AND SON

WRECKAGE FROM THE STEAMER PORTLAND
LOST NOVEMBER 27, 1898.

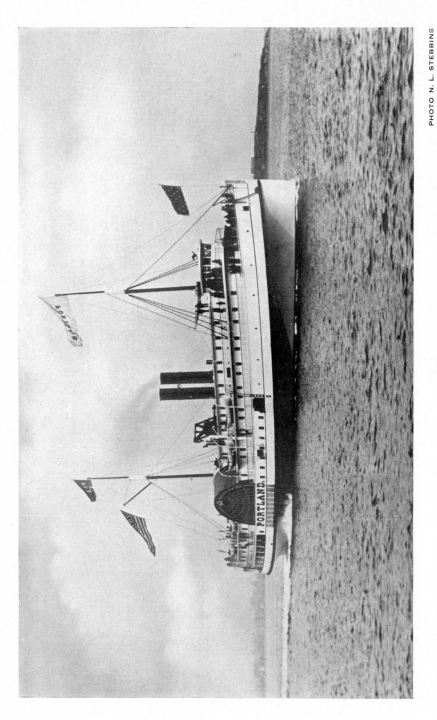

PHOTO N. L. STEBBINS

THE ILL-FATED STEAMER PORTLAND PASSING GOVERNOR'S ISLAND, BOSTON HARBOR
LOST OFF CAPE COD WITH NO SURVIVORS, SUNDAY, NOVEMBER 27, 1898.

caught off a lee shore in such a terrific effort of wind and
storm which developed before sunrise the next morning.
As a result the entire shore from Casco Bay to Cape Cod
was littered with wreckage and disabled ships, with Martha's Vineyard and Nantucket experiencing their share of
the tempest. No one out in the *Portland* Gale ever believed anything else equalled it in intensity. On the 141
vessels wrecked along the New England coast in the hurricane, the loss of life amounted to over 456 persons. The
suddenness and intensity of the storm were probably due
to the rapid increase in energy which took place when two
cyclones, one from the Gulf of Mexico, and one from the
Great Lakes, came together.[8]

THE COLUMBIA

The first of the many wrecks caused by the *Portland*
Gale which we shall discuss was that of the pilot boat
Columbia. The *Columbia's* last known act was to dis-
charge her pilot Captain William Abbott aboard the
steamer *Ohio*, which later pushed ashore on Spectacle
Island. The storm grew worse as the evening wore on,
and it is believed that the *Columbia* was then in the vicinity
of the Boston Lightship. No one escaped the wreck, so
conjecture alone must dictate the story of the loss of the
Columbia.

The following morning Surfman Richard Tobin of
the North Scituate Life Saving Station had the south patrol
along Sand Hills from 8 to 12. His report says:

"I went down the beach to the key post
about three miles from the station. . . . The seas
were coming over with such force that I was
washed into the pond back of the ridge. It was

blowing so hard that that I was obliged to kneel down to get my breath."

At 9:30 Surfman Tobin was on the veranda of the very cottage[1] into which the *Columbia* crashed later in the day. When he returned to the station it was three in the afternoon. The storm was now so intense that no patrol was permitted to leave; in fact not until midnight did the next patrol go out. Surfman John Curran set out on the south patrol this time, and at quarter of two in the morning he sighted a schooner right in the line of his patrol, lying on the beach where she had crashed into a cottage. The wreckage from the shattered building was lying in heaped confusion on the decks of the careened vessel. Since Surfman Tobin had stood on the veranda of that very cottage at 9:30 Sunday morning, the *Columbia* had washed up on the beach between then and 1:45 a.m. on Monday. No one witnessed the disaster and no one ever knew what took place.

By 3:20 that morning Curran had returned to the station and notified the keeper, who visited the scene with three surfmen. On the way they found the body of the *Columbia's* first boatkeeper. The other four men were later found in the vicinity. The wreck of the *Columbia* was complete. The starboard side of the pilot boat had split near the garboard, the planking was torn where she had hung and ground on the rocks, and the sternpost was broken to pieces. The foremast was gone, two anchor chains hung from the hawse pipes, and the anchors were missing. Probably the five men on the pilot boat were dead before the *Columbia* struck the beach, and the fact that both anchors were gone showed that the vessel had attempted unsuccessfully to weather the storm.[2] This opinion was shared by a majority of seafaring men who visited the scene.

The pilot boat *Columbia* was left where she hit on the beach, high above the reach of the normal tides of the years. Made over into a museum, the wreck stayed on the Scituate Beach for about forty years. Thousands visited this vessel during the first quarter of the present century, but about the year 1935 the elements began to make inroads on the wreck, so the Scituate officials ordered the pilot boat burned. Thus ended the career of the Boston pilot boat *Columbia*, the schooner on which five brave men tried unsuccessfully to ride out the *Portland* Gale.

THE CALVIN F. BAKER

The schooner *Calvin F. Baker* encountered heavy weather on the night of November 26, and ran for the safety of Boston Harbor. About three o'clock in the morning of the 27th when the storm had reached terrific proportions, the captain saw Boston Light loom up on the port bow, and the schooner crashed almost instantly against a submerged ledge in back of Lighthouse Island. Everyone aboard made for the rigging as the breakers swept over the ship, and the schooner careened to and fro in her rocky cradle on the ledge.

Keeper Henry L. Pingree of Boston Light[1] saw the schooner but the waves at that time were sweeping the entire island, preventing him from helping the unfortunate sailors. All that Sunday the *Baker* rocked in her cradle, the helpless men calling for aid from their precarious positions in the rigging of the ship. The mother of one of the assistant keepers was so affected by the shock of hearing the frozen men calling for aid throughout that day and the following night that she died shortly afterwards.[2]

At dusk during the evening of the *Portland* gale there was a momentary lull in the storm, which gave Keeper Joshua James of the Point Allerton Coast Guard Station an opportunity to look out on the ocean with his telescope. James sighted the spars and masts of the *Baker* showing behind Lighthouse Island, but, since he and his men were nearly exhausted, having already that day saved the crew of the *Henry R. Tilton* and coal *Barge No. 1*,[3] they reluctantly decided against attempting any more rescues so late in the day.

When the first glimmer of dawn appeared the next morning, Keeper James anxiously focused his glass on Lighthouse Island. He saw that the wreck was still there and that the distress signal flag at Boston Light was flying. Engaging the services of the tug *Ariel* to tow him across the harbor in his surfboat, he let go the tow line when reaching the lee of Boston Light. Keeper James now steered his craft across the bar between the lighthouse and Great Brewster Island, finally reaching the *Calvin F. Baker.*

With the arrival of the surfboat, the men who were still alive took heart. First mate Burgess S. Howland had fallen to his death the day before, while second mate Isaacs disappeared during the night. Just before the surfboat arrived, the master of the *Calvin F. Baker* noticed Willis Studley, the steward, standing with his hand against the taffrail. When a shout failed to arouse him, the captain hit the man heavily on the shoulder to wake him up, but Studley fell over to the deck. He had frozen to death while leaning against the rail, and the captain's blow had

keeled his body over. When Keeper James boarded the
Baker he found the five sailors huddled on a remnant of
the forward deck of the schooner. They were all taken
into the surfboat, the four living and the one dead man.
A short time later they were inside the life saving station,
their experiences in the *Portland* gale at an end.

THE MERTIS H. PERRY

With 15,000 pounds of fish in her holds, the fishing
schooner *Mertis H. Perry* was coming into Boston Bay
when the gale hit. Snow and sleet shut in around 9:30
that Saturday evening, and at eleven the captain wore ship
to edge offshore. At midnight the jib split, the main gaff
snapped, and the vessel could make no further headway,
so the crew lowered the foresail and let go the port anchor.
The snow descended in such quantities that visibility was
entirely blocked out. When the port anchor failed to
hold, the starboard anchor was let go. The *Perry* now
fetched up, but with the storm increasing the crew of
fourteen knew the vessel would soon start to drag anchor
again.[1]

Sometime early that Sunday morning the dreaded
event happened—all on board felt the anchors begin to
drag. Gradually the *Perry* worked her way into shallow
water. The captain ordered the masts cut away. Soon
afterwards the port anchor cable parted, and the starboard chain separated around seven in the morning. Their
only chance was to run before the wind toward shore,
trusting that they would strike a sandy beach.

Now in the heavy breakers, the *Perry* hit bottom.
The tide was coming in, carrying the *Perry* along with it.
The sailors had no idea where they might be. When about

200 yards off the beach sailor William Bagnell of Cape Breton Island died of exposure. Captain Joshua Pike decided to try to reach shore, so jumped over the side with a part of a broken dory. He was never seen again.

A few minutes later a gigantic breaker seized the schooner and pushed her high up on the beach so that the jib boom actually hung over the banking above the shore. They had hit at Brant Rock, Massachusetts. Four of the sailors dropped from the schooner's jib boom down on the bank, but then another wave pulled the *Perry* around broadside. The remaining fishermen threw a line to the men on shore, but before it could be used the schooner again swung around into her former position, with the jib boom over the bank. Six men jumped to safety. Joseph Veader, however, leaped just as another billow swept around the bow, and fell into the surf. He lost his life.

The survivors were now all ashore. George Bagnall soon died from exposure as he lay on the sandbank, and when the others started to look for shelter Charles Forbes could not keep up with them. Near death from exhaustion, Forbes begged the others to go on without him. After walking some distance, they found a farmhouse. Knocking at the door, they met the owner, Mr. Ames, who took them in and also sent two of his men back to the wreck to bring back Forbes. But the unfortunate fisherman had died there on the bank. Nine of the sailors were saved aboard the *Perry*, while five perished because of the wreck.[2]

At nearby Brant Rock Life Saving Station the surfmen were energetically attempting to save their wave-battered building which was filled with many residents who had sought safety from the high tides there. As wave after wave smashed against the edifice and the tide rose even higher, the women and children were ordered up-stairs. A few minutes later the surf crashed open the boatroom doors and swept through the dining room windows. Fearing that the entire structure would be carried away, the men threw open the rear doors, allowing the tide to sweep through the lower floor of the station while the second floor remained intact. The tide finally began to go down, and as soon as the area around the station was bare, all the women and children were taken over to the Union Chapel, a stone church nearby, which was considered safe. That night the surfmen joined the townspeople in the church, and the night went by without further trouble.

THE ALBERT L. BUTLER

When the *Portland* gale hit the *Albert L. Butler*, the schooner was forty miles east southeast of Highland Light. By midnight the wind was blowing from the northeast, and at seven the next morning the captain wore ship under bare poles. No sooner had the schooner got around than a tremendous sea boarded her, drove portions of her deck load of logwood through the rigging, carried away booms and gaffs, and smashed into hatches, leaving the *Butler* a helpless wreck. Oil bags proved of no value when put over. At about ten that morning shore breakers were under her forefoot. The sea was frightful by this time — greater than the captain had ever seen before. A short time later the *Butler* swung broadside high on the Cape Cod sands.

Surfman B. F. Henderson from the Peaked Hill Life Saving Station and Surfman Benjamin Kelly from the

High Head Station had just met and parted near the half-way house, over which the surf was breaking, when the *Albert L. Butler* loomed up before them out of the storm within the limits of the Peaked Hill Bar Station. Within a half hour Henderson had returned to the station. Soon the beach wagon was manned and on the way down the beach toward the wreck. As they made their way through the swirling snow, a flash of lightning came, followed by a clap of thunder. Captain Michael F. Hogan, of the *Ruth M. Martin,* out in the same wild storm, believed the flash to be from the *Portland,* which he thought might have blown up at the time. As scores of residents in the vicinity of Cape Cod heard the thunder during the *Portland* gale, the captain must have mistaken the lightning for an explosion.[1]

Reaching the scene of the wreck, the rescuers found a man on the bank. Since he was not seriously injured, they left him there to save those still on the *Butler*. Four sailors were seen in the rigging, only fifty yards away. The life savers fired a Lyle gun, dropping a number seven line between the mainmast and the mizzenmast, but the sailors ignored the life line completely. Another shot was fired, this time right across the deck. One of the sailors, instead of reading the tally board of instructions sent out with the whip line, merely made the tail block fast to the mizzen rigging, and without waiting for the hawser or breeches buoy, tried to reach shore by the whip block. Of course the slender line sagged until it was in the surf, but the men on shore hauled him as rapidly as possible through the breakers. He was lucky to reach shore alive, but he did make it. Shortly afterwards the mizzenmast gave way and crashed forward. If the sailors had only waited a few minutes, another line would have been sent out, but evidently they became panic stricken by the crashing mast and tried to get ashore by the whip line, as the other sailor had done. The falling mast fouled the line, and though the surfmen pulled hard, the snarked rope would not run freely through the tail block. Just as a gigantic wave formed on the other side of the vessel, the line jammed. As the wave struck, it buried the ship under tons of water. The tragedy is mentioned[2] in the official report of Captain Cook: "I had hold of the whip line, and could feel when the sailors lost their grasp. They were washed off, and that is the last we know of them." A moment later a surfman heard a moan coming from under the bank and rushed over to find a man crying for help. He had been cast up on the shore some time before.

There was now no sign of life on the *Butler*. After the surfman had taken the survivors back to the station an unexpected incident took place. As the tide went out, more and more of the beach was exposed until the vessel was at the water's edge. Just as the surfmen were about to climb aboard the wreck, they heard a scramble, and two men, who had been in the cabin all the time without the knowledge of their shipmates, jumped to the beach. They were taken to the life saving station, where the five members of the crew were brought together again.

After the storm the *Albert L. Butler* remained on the beach for many weeks a picturesque wreck, its masts and fittings gradually stripped by the wreckers of the Cape. It was here on the beach near the *Butler* that much of the material from the *Portland* later washed up.

THE PORTLAND

Regardless of the number of other vessels sunk or wrecked during the terrific hurricane of November 1898, mention of this gale usually brings back one outstanding event in the minds of New England inhabitants — the loss of the steamer *Portland*.[1] Although nearly half a century has elapsed since the momentous night when she steamed out to meet the gale which proved her doom, there are many who still vividly recall the famous vessel which gave her name to that devastating cyclone.

The 291-foot steamer *Portland*, designed by William P. Pattee, was built at the Bath, Maine, shipyards in 1890.[2] She was one of the outstanding paddle-wheelers of the time. Seaworthy and of great strength, the *Portland* was unusually spacious and comfortable. When photographed on her trial run by N. L. Stebbins,[3] the greatest marine cameraman of his day, the white and gold trimmed steamer appeared as a vessel of beautiful lines on her way down Boston Harbor. Drawing eleven feet of water, the *Portland* could navigate Broad Sound Channel in Boston's outer harbor, and with her beam of forty-two feet she was considered an ideal craft for the trip to Portland.

Since November 26, 1898, was the Saturday after Thanksgiving, there were more passengers than usual who wished to make the journey to Portland that night. Many were returning to Maine from Philadelphia, New York, or farther south, where they had been with their folks on the holiday. That morning the weather was pleasantly fair, with a light breeze. As the day wore on, however, the clouds above Boston grew heavier, giving first evidences of an advancing condition of grave danger.[4] A tremendous cyclone from the Gulf of Mexico was about to join forces with a storm of only slightly lesser proportions roaring across from the Great Lakes.[5]

Meanwhile, the loading of the steamer's freight continued at India Wharf in Boston. The passengers who had made reservations for the journey began to come aboard. Some of them later cancelled their accommodations, but the majority, more than one hundred people, sailed with the ship. Together with the crew, there were 176 persons aboard the *Portland* by sailing time.[6]

The general manager of the Portland Steam Packet Company, John F. Liscomb, on receiving warning of the approaching storm from New York, tried to communicate by phone from Portland with the steamer's captain, Hollis H. Blanchard.[7] Failing in this, he left word that the *Portland's* companion ship, the newer *Bay State*, would not leave Portland until nine o'clock, when the size of the storm could be better gauged. When he returned at 5:30, Blanchard talked over the phone to the *Bay State's* captain, Alexander Dennison, called because of his comparative youthfulness the "Kid Pilot."[8]

Captain Dennison told Blanchard of manager Liscomb's suggestion to hold the *Portland* until nine o'clock. Captain Blanchard replied that the *Portland* would sail on schedule at seven, giving as his reason the direction of the storm, which he predicted would not reach the city of Portland until after the steamer had safely docked. Dennison, said Blanchard, would be proceeding southward, and would run into the storm before he reached Boston.

The fact that the two captains talked over the phone that day has given rise to the popular legend that Captain Blanchard sailed contrary to the advice of the general manager because he was anxious to prove his sailing abilities superior to those of Captain Dennison by steaming into Portland Harbor where the *Bay State* would still be at the wharf. There seems to be no foundation in fact for this tale, to which many still cling.

Captains of passenger vessels invariably feel the responsibility for so many lives which depend upon their skill and judgment. Those who really knew Captain Blanchard were convinced that he was no exception. His decision was based upon his best judgment and at least twelve other sea captains[9] have admitted that under similar conditions they would have reasoned and acted as he did.

Throughout the day special bulletins from the weather bureau arrived. At 10:33 a.m. the bureau informed C. F. Williams, the line's Boston agent, that a storm of considerable intensity was on the way. At 3:15 p.m. a special report from New York stated that a northeast snowstorm had already begun there. At 6:07, fifty-three minutes before sailing time, the final notice arrived with the information that it was still snowing in New York, but that the wind had backed around to northwest. This news gave Captain Blanchard confidence that he could reach Portland ahead of the storm as he had done many times before. Agent Williams then left India Wharf for his home.[10] At precisely seven o'clock that November evening the final departing whistle from the *Portland* split the chill night air of Boston's Atlantic Avenue, and Captain Hollis Blanchard sailed into the unknown.

Many claim that it was snowing when the *Portland* left her pier at seven o'clock. Wesley Pingree, down at Deer Island Light, later mistakenly remembered that it had begun to snow around five that afternoon.[11] The official report of the Boston Weather Bureau, which can hardly be wrong, stated that the snow began to fall at 7:37, two and one-half hours later than Pingree's recollection claims. While the fact that the lighthouse is five miles down the harbor from the city would account for some discrepancy in time, the difference could hardly be so great. Besides, Captain Kemp, who was near Deer Island Light, stated positively that the snow did not start there until about seven o'clock.

It is commonly believed that the *Portland* was never seen again after leaving Boston. Nothing could be further from the facts. The records tell a remarkable story.

The Bangor boat *Kennebec* dropped anchor in President Road just before the *Portland* proceeded down the harbor. Although Captain Collins had started for Bangor, the threatening storm caused him to return to safety. As the *Portland* steamed by, he whistled what seemed by others to be a warning to Captain Blanchard, but the latter, unheeding, continued out to sea.[12]

A short time later the incoming *Mount Desert,* piloted by Captain William A. Roix, passed the *Portland* just as both vessels drew abeam of Graves Ledge in Boston's outer bay. According to Thomas Harrison Eames,[13] those in the wheel house of the *Mount Desert* expected to see the *Portland* come about and return to port, but she followed her regular course until the lights faded in the distance.

Captain William Thomas of Bailey's Island, Maine, master of the fisherman *Maud S.,* saw the lights of the *Portland* when he was 3¾ miles southwest of Thacher's Island. Believing that his wife was on the steamer, Thomas naturally was watching for the *Portland* with unusual attention. Less than two miles away from the side-wheeler at the time, Thomas thought that the steamer was closer to shore than usual. He said[14] to his crew, "There goes the *Portland*. She will probably run close to Thacher's." It was then two and a half hours after Blanchard had sailed from Boston. Nothing at that time led Thomas to believe that the captain of the *Portland* was foolhardy in continuing her journey. Incidentally, Thomas' wife was not on the *Portland*, having made fortunate use of the privilege of changing her mind.

Captain A. A. Tarr[15] of Thacher's Island twin lights off Gloucester agreed with Thomas about weather conditions at the time the *Portland* passed that point. He said that it seemed so nearly normal weather at the time the ship was scheduled to pass the island that he did not even bother to look for the sparkle of the lights of the sidewheeler. There seemed to him to be no reason why the *Portland* should not have reached that point at the usual time as the wind and sea were not boisterous. Moreover, we have the evidence of another man stationed at Thacher's Island. Captain Lynes B. Hathaway of Brockton, master workman of the Lighthouse Department, at about 9:30 or shortly afterwards was in the smoking room which the workmen used on the island when he saw the *Portland's* lights as the steamer passed within 500 feet of the shore, between Thacher's and the Londoner Ledge. The *Portland*, then on schedule, continued up the coast.[16]

Around eleven o'clock, less than ninety minutes after Captain Hathaway saw the steamer, Captain Reuben Cameron of the schooner *Grayling* sighted the *Portland* twelve miles south by east of Thacher's Island.[17] Thus, without question, the vessel had changed her course. The *Portland* came so near to the *Grayling* that Captain Cameron burned a Coston flare to warn the steamer away. The paddle-wheeler at this time seemed rolling and pitching badly, although her superstructure appeared intact.

Also in the vicinity was the schooner *Florence E. Stearns.* At approximately 11:15 p.m. her master Frank Stearns passed a paddle-wheel steamer, doubtless the *Portland,* as there was no other vessel of her type in the area. Half an hour later Captain D. J. Pellier of the schooner *Edgar Randall,*[18] then fourteen miles southeast by east of Eastern Point, Gloucester, noticed a large vessel bearing down upon him out of the night. Pellier swung the *Randall* away and escaped a collision, but had time to see that the ship was a paddle-wheel steamer. At the time, he believed that the steamer's superstructure had been damaged, but how accurately he could see from the lurching deck of a small schooner is a matter of conjecture.

Meanwhile the storm had increased in intensity. In Portland at noon there had been a north wind blowing at 19 miles per hour, which increased at 2 p.m. to 26, changing to northeast at 3 o'clock, then increasing to 36 miles per hour at 7 that evening. Having swung around to north at 6 p.m., the wind shifted to northeast an hour later. There were spells of wind which blew during this period at almost a mile a minute. The official weather bureau records at Boston indicate that the wind velocity increased from 14 miles per hour at seven o'clock to 31 miles per hour at midnight. Occasionally the wind reached almost unbelievable intensity; many gusts of at least 72 miles per hour were experienced. The barometer at Boston dropped from 29:70 at seven to 29:44 at twelve.[19]

Shipping all along the coast scurried for shelter. Vessel after vessel, failing to reach a safe harbor, was tossed ashore along Nantasket Beach and the North Shore of Massachusetts, while every coastal town and city in the path of the storm was fearfully battered. Giant breakers swept through many main thoroughfares, and the tide, as measured at Cohasset, rose even higher than it had during the record Minot's Light gale which toppled over the lighthouse.[20]

When we left the *Portland,* she had changed her course off Thacher's Island and, probably damaged, seemed not to be making progress toward her destination but rather, to be engaged in tactics designed to enable her to weather the storm.

Just how far on her scheduled journey did the *Portland* go? There were those, including the late yachting enthusiast and newsman, William U. Swan, who believed that the *Portland* reached a point north of Boon Island[21] off Portsmouth on her voyage up the coast. This belief is hard to reconcile with the known facts. If the side-wheeler passed the Londoner Ledge off Thacher's Island around or shortly after 9:30, she could not have attained a position near Boon Island, many miles to the north, at the same time have changed her course, and still be twelve miles southeast of Thacher's Island ninety minutes later at eleven p.m. Logically it would seem that the *Portland* never attained a position more than five miles north of Thacher's Island.

Captain Albert Bragg, master of the steamer *Horatio Hall,*[22] sailed out of Portland Harbor approximately an hour after Captain Blanchard steamed from Boston that Saturday night. The wind and sea were light when the *Hall* left her dock. Bragg's course took him sixteen miles east of Boon Island and forty miles east of Thacher's

Island, but the storm hit with such unprecedented fury that he hove to about one in the morning, staying in that position until eight a.m. "I never saw such a storm in my life," was his statement.[23]

Captain Frank Scripture of Rockport, Massachusetts, described how the gale seemed to travel in veins, as indicated on shore by the track it made through forests. Not within his memory had there been such a hurricane as that which hit Cape Ann shortly before midnight. Nevertheless, said Scripture, when the *Portland* sailed there was no reason why a prudent captain should not leave Boston. The storm came on more rapidly than any other he ever experienced on Cape Ann. Probably when the cyclone surprised Captain Blanchard somewhere north of Thacher's Island Lights, the *Portland's* master headed her out to sea to ride out the gale, as he had done before.[24]

Exactly six hours after the *Portland* was sighted by Captain Pellier of the *Edgar Randall,* off Eastern Point, Gloucester, Captain Samuel O. Fisher of the Race Point Life Saving Station on Cape Cod, standing at the foot of his bed[25] at the station, heard, he says, four sharp blasts from a steamer's whistle. It was 5:45 a.m. Sunday, November 27.

"I went out," said Fisher, "and glanced at the clock and rang the gong for the boat." He then telephoned to the Peaked Hill Bars Station and afterwards sent a man down the beach to look for the wreck. The sea and tide were then combining to make conditions the worst Fisher had ever seen.

The storm continued in violence until about nine o'clock that Sunday morning when a surprising event took place.   Cape Cod's Life Saving District Superintendent, Benjamin C. Sparrow, tells[26] us about it:

> "Between 9 and 10:30 o'clock a.m. on Sunday Nov. 27 there was a partial breaking up of the gale, the wind became moderate, the sun shone for a short time, and the atmosphere cleared to an extent which disclosed two coast-wise steamers passing southward, also a fishing schooner lying to under short sail. . . . About eleven o'clock a.m. the gale again increased and vision was obscure from the offing until after day-light on Monday morning."

As the *Portland* and the *Pentagoet* were the only two steamers of their type in the vicinity, it is reasonable to assume that they were the vessels sighted during the partial breakup in the storm.

Miss Lillian Small, daughter of the Boston Chamber of Commerce ship observer, Isaac Morton Small, also saw the *Portland* during the lull in the gale from her home near the Highland Light.

The fishing schooner mentioned in Superintendent Sparrow's report was the *Ruth M. Martin*.   Aboard the schooner was Captain Michael Francis Hogan,[27] with a crew of twenty-six men.   Making Chatham Light at ten that Saturday night, he tried to anchor but failed.   The next morning he had reached a point off Highland Light, where around the middle of the morning, during the lull in the storm, Hogan noticed a large white steamer which appeared to be underway.   The superstructure did not seem to be damaged noticeably.   Captain Hogan, anxious to save his schooner, put a distress flag in his rigging to attract the attention of the vessel, which he later believed to be the *Portland* as it was the only steamer of its type anywhere in the vicinity.[28] Patrick Droohan, the man in the crew who placed the distress flag in the rigging, said that the *Portland* was visible for two hours that morning, until the storm set in again. As it turned out, the *Ruth M. Martin* escaped while the *Portland* foundered. Hogan worked the *Martin* around Cape Cod's Race Point and into Provincetown Harbor safely.

On the basis of the evidence of Hogan and Droohan, if the *Portland* was first seen in midmorning, about half past nine, and was visible for two hours, it must have been at least eleven thirty when she faded from sight. This point should be remembered in order to estimate the approximate time of the *Portland's* sinking.

The people on the *Portland* must have seen Hogan's schooner and the cliffs of the Highlands. They probably were congratulating themselves on escaping from the terrific gale, when the weather began to shut in again. First the cliffs faded from view in the gathering snowstorm, then the fishing boat was lost to sight. Whether the *Portland* and the *Pentagoet* ever sighted each other will probably never be known, although they were both seen from the Cape. Sometime during the evening the *Portland* came to her end. Imagination must describe her last hours. We cannot do better than quote from the pen[29] of Thomas Harrison Eames:

"It seems probable that the intense smashing she received through the night had weakened her, and finally the pounding of the sea under her guards opened her up and allowed tons of water to rush into the hull, flooding engine and boiler rooms, drowning the men working there, and depriving the ship of her power. The passengers above must have experienced a sense of horrified dismay as the vibration of the engines stopped and the ship swung around broadside to the oncoming seas, lurching sickeningly and settling deeper each moment. The water crashing into the helpless vessel would smash any lifeboats which may have remained, tear off doors, and burst through windows and ports, ripping away the sheathing of the superstructure and washing helpless occupants of staterooms to death in a churning sea.

"As she took her final plunge, the superstructure was probably torn away at the main deck and was smashed to kindling wood. Those inside were thrown into the icy water as the wooden deckhouse disintegrated, some being killed outright by falling beams and other debris, others being caught in the wreckage and carried under the surface to drown, while many who had equipped themselves with lifebelts or who succeeded in grasping floating wreckage were benumbed by the frigid water and hammered so unmercifully by the gigantic waves that they soon died."

On the Cape Cod shore, the afternoon came to an end. The bitter wind continued to fill the air with snow and sand, making it nearly unbearable for Surfman Johnson of the Peaked Hill Bars Station, who was plodding his lonely way through the gale along the beach. He knew that another life saver was pushing toward him from the

Race Point Coast Guard Station several miles away, and that ahead was the Half Way House where the two were to meet. The gale increased and the waves, swept in by the tides, rose higher and higher.

Finally arriving at the Half Way House, Johnson met his fellow watchman, Surfman Bickers, exchanged a story or two, spoke of the gale, and started back along the windswept beach. The darkness increased. At 7:20, Johnson thought he saw something thrown up by the incoming tide. Keeping his eye on the object, he fought his way down to the shore, ran the last few steps to avoid an oncoming breaker, reached down, picked up his find, and hastily retreated to the bank above the surf. In the dim light of his lantern he examined the object. It was a life-belt, and on it he read the words *Steamer Portland of Portland.*[30] Even then he had no reason to suppose anything but that the boat had lost a life preserver.

Here is his statement:[31]

"I was bound west toward the station, when I found the first thing that landed from the steamer. It was a lifebelt and it was one-half mile east of the station. At 7:45 o'clock that evening I found the next seen wreckage, a creamery can, 40-quart, I guess. It was right below our station, and nine or ten more of them, all empty and stoppered tightly came on there closely together.

"Jim Kelly succeeded me on the eastern beat, leaving the station at 8:20 p.m. and at 9:30 he found doors and other light woodwork from the *Portland* on the shore. When I found the lifebelt the wind was north northeast."

Only two months ago,[32] Surfman George Henry Bickers, who after his service at the Race Point Station became Keeper of the Wood End Life Saving Station, told the writer of his meeting with Johnson that night.

"I had the dog watch with Johnnie; he started walking eastward toward me from Race Point and I began the long hike westward from Peaked Hill. We met as usual at the Half Way House. Neither of us had noticed anything on the beach at that time. After he left me around seven he picked up a life belt, and later a large, empty milk can."

It was not until dead high tide, around eleven o'clock Sunday night, that the real flood of wreckage started to come ashore. Edwin B. Tyler of the Race Point crew found doors, electric light bulbs, wash stand tops, and other wreckage, but his most important discovery was the upper part of a steamer's cabin, about ten feet square, painted yellow and red. The colors were not those of the *Portland,* but of another steamer, the *Pentagoet,* thus piling mystery upon mystery.

When the midnight watch returned the beach was buried with wreckage and debris from the *Portland.* Mattresses, chairs, upholstery, windows, doors, and paneling all came ashore in a great mass shortly before midnight. Jot Small, former Provincetown lifesaver comments[33] as follows:

"In my opinion, the *Portland* hit on Peaked Hill Bars and went all to pieces. That is the only way one can explain the mass of wreckage in one place. To prove my statement, no bodies could have come ashore as fast as they did unless the

Portland was fairly near shore. The bodies do not float as woodwork does, but the tide and waves push and roll them along the bottom until they reached shallow water, when they get into the undertow and are tossed up on the beach."

There are other theories of the *Portland's* last hours besides those of Thomas Harrison Eames and Jonathan Small, already quoted. The finding of the *Pentagoet's* cabin with the wreckage of the *Portland* has given rise to the theory that the two steamers were in collision. The *Pentagoet* was on a voyage from New York to Rockland, Maine, with a Rockland master, Captain Orris R. Ingraham,[34] and fifteen men, and she carried a great load of Christmas toys and holiday gifts for Rockland stores. She was sighted off Highland Light the night the storm began. It is improbable to assume that a collision occurred as no bodies from the *Pentagoet* were ever found. Had the two steamers met their doom together, bodies from both vessels instead of from the *Portland* alone would have washed ashore.

Very few mariners at the time considered the possibility of a collision between the *Portland* and the 162-ton schooner *Addie E. Snow*,[35] but later the brother of the schooner's captain examined some of the *Portland's* wreckage on the beach. To his surprise, Captain Brown's brother found the *Addie E. Snow's* medicine chest in the *Portland* litter, and afterwards found several other articles which had been on the schooner. The crew all perished with their captain, and none of their bodies was ever found.

Others believe that the schooner *King Philip*, heavily loaded with coal, collided with the *Portland* during the storm. The *King Philip* was last seen by the schooner *Alicia B. Crosby*. Her master, George W. Bunker,[36] said later that she was a mile and a half on his lee near the Hue and Cry Ledge off Cape Elizabeth at eight p.m. Saturday night. The two vessels had been following a similar course since Friday, November 25, and were together when they made Cape Elizabeth Light. Entering Portland Harbor, where she dropped anchor at 1:45 a.m., the *Crosby* rode out the storm safely. The *King Philip* was never seen afloat again.

Wreckage from the *King Philip* as it came up on the beach at Brewster, Cape Cod, was first identified by William U. Swan, covering the story for the Associated Press:[37]

"On the Wednesday after the *Portland* went down I helped pull the bodies of two poor negro waiters from the surf. It was blowing like the very devil at the time, for another northeaster had set in. I later drove across to the beach at Brewster where I heard that some wreckage had come ashore on the inside of the Cape. I stopped at the home of a fisherman who was having a quarrel with his wife, and he directed me down to the beach where the wreckage had come in. There were some pieces of a schooner's deck timbers, with a steam pump three feet high attached, painted green. I found a metal tag with a serial number on the pump, which had been sold by a Boston firm.

"Anxious to find the name of the schooner, I returned to Orleans, where all lines to Boston were down. I cabled a message to Boston by way of France, Ireland, Newfoundland, New

York City, and Albany. The message finally
reached Boston and was delivered. I received
my reply the next day. The steam pump was
from the schooner *King Phillip*. If the *Portland* had collided with the *King Phillip* wreckage
from both vessels would have come in together."

Wreckage from the *Portland* came ashore Sunday
night, while no wreckage from the *King Philip* washed up
until the following Wednesday, far inside the arm of the
Cape. Thus we must assume that the two vessels foundered
many miles from each other, and any belief in a collision
between them can have no foundation considering what
we know to be true.

Recalling Keeper A. C. Fisher's belief that he heard
four blasts from a steamer's whistle at 5:45 a.m. Sunday,
we offer a statement made by one of the surfmen then at
the Race Point Life Saving Station. This Cape Cod man,
who later became captain at the Wood End Station, told[38]
the writer a few months ago that in his opinion Keeper
Fisher never heard any whistles:

"We told him what he really heard was the
wind whistling through the steel guy rods holding the chimney on the roof, but he did not like
us to say that. All of the rest of us knew that
was what he really heard. On the day he was to
take the train for Portland to testify about the
shipwreck, I was standing by the door as he
started out.

" 'I would have taken you with me,' Captain Fisher said, 'but you had an opinion of your
own.' "

These were the words spoken to my Provincetown friend, who prefers not to have his name mentioned in connection with this particular story.

Another veteran life saver of the Cape whose opinion must be considered was Captain W. W. Cook of the Peaked Hill Bars Station. His statement[39] follows:

> "The steamer never got as far as the Peaked Hill Bars, but foundered. I do not think that the captain was trying to reach the lee of the Cape for shelter. If a vessel can be kept head to in a storm, she can, perhaps, ride it out. If she cannot be controlled, and falls into the trough of the sea, she is gone. The *Portland's* whole upper works were swept off by the sea, and she went down like a sounding lead. And there she is now. She will never come ashore, she is in too deep water."

If we accept Cook's theory that the *Portland* went down soon after the superstructure was swept away, then she foundered around nine that night, as the watches were stopped at an average time of 9:15.

Souvenirs from the *Portland* are many. There are four different wheels of the *Portland* said to be in existence. That owned by Charles Ayling, of Centerville, is one of the authentic ones.[40] The *Portland's* speaking trumpet, plainly marked *Portland,* was brought up to Boston in the summer of 1899 and sold for $10, to be crated and shipped out west. A local oil dealer bought one of the life raft cylinders and painted it red, filling the hollow metal container with fuel and selling kerosene from it on the streets of Boston.[41]

Cy Young, well-known antique dealer of Province-town, was over on Cape Cod Beach early the day after the wreck, collecting a large amount of material from the steamer's superstructure and cabins. Loading an odd as-sortment of bunks, cabin posts, empty coffins, bottles of rum, life belts, doors, and cabin posts on his huge cart, he drove his team across the dunes to his home in Province-town. He later sold twelve of the large cabin posts for $100. The writer acquired two doors of the *Portland* from Mr. Young in 1941.[42]

In the spring of 1899 Captain Thomas of the *Maud S.*, who had seen the *Portland* near Thacher's Island the night of the storm, caught articles in his fishing trawl which were later identified as coming from the *Portland*. The location where the discovery was made was said to be $22\frac{3}{4}$ miles east of Boston Light, 24 miles north, $\frac{3}{4}$ west from Highland Light, and $14\frac{1}{2}$ miles southeast from Thacher's Island. When the material was brought into Boston, Steward Harris, formerly on the *Portland*, and electrician Burnett, also on the same craft, identified the material. A number of small brackets actually recut by the steward to fit the *Portland's* bunks were recognized by Harris, while Burnett was able to identify several light sockets and brackets as part of his own electrical work.[43]

Lieutenant Nicholas J. Halpine, formerly in charge of the U. S. Hydrographic office in Boston, contested the authenticity of the articles. None of them came from the *Portland*, in Halpine's opinion, as the ship had not gone down where the find was made.

"I am still of the opinion," he said in March 1899, "that the wreck of the *Portland* lies outside of the Peaked Hill Bars somewhere, and I am equally confident that I can locate her and bring her into harbor, and I intend to do it, too." Many summers have come and gone since this confident statement was made, but the hull of the *Portland* still eludes all efforts of those who wish to find her.[44]

During another gale Captain Hollis H. Blanchard had headed the *Portland* for the open sea and kept her there until the blow went down. Is it not reasonable to assume that he did the same in this storm? Would he not keep her headed into the northeast gale, carrying the rudder a point or two into the east, gradually working off the coast?

In this way he was slowly taken down toward Cape Cod, until in the morning he found himself off the fatal beach, the storm having carried him at a faster rate than he could steam against it. When he saw his position, the battle was almost won, for if the storm had then ended, he might have rounded Cape Cod's Race Point and entered Provincetown Harbor. But such a happy ending was not in store for Hollis H. Blanchard.

We do not question, as did Lieutenant Halpine, the authenticity of the material picked up by the *Maud S.* Without a doubt, during her terrible trip across the bay she lost some of her superstructure in the gale's buffeting, including stateroom panels, lifeboats, and even perhaps her pilot house. But she continued afloat, in the writer's opinion, for about twenty-four hours after being sighted by the *Maud S.*

There are many reasons why the *Portland* did not go down on the northern edge of the Stellwagen or Middle Bank, as indicated by the find of Captain Thomas. If the *Portland* sank at any time before ten p.m. Sunday night, when the wind shifted to a more northerly direction, the wreckage must by necessity have drifted to leeward. A glance at the map should convince the reader that the flotsam would have gone in a southwesterly direction, not south, and landed along the inner shores of Massachusetts Bay.

Surface tides on the night of the hurricane were dominated by the wind, and the wind was northeast. When the first object, a life belt, was driven ashore at 7:20 Sunday night, the wind as stated by the man who found the preserver was north northeast, whereas the Stellwagen Bank's northern edge is in a northwesterly direction.

There is a much more conclusive point. The fragments of paddleboxes, life cars, door blinds, staterooms, and the like were heaped almost entirely in a half mile area between Race Point Station and the Peaked Hill Bar Station. How could this great mass of debris drift contrary to a northeast gale for twenty-four miles across as rough a stretch of water as there is? If such a heaping pile of wreckage travelled even ten miles, it would have been scattered up and down the shore.

The heavier freight came up on the beach farther east than the lighter windswept superstructure. The barrels, trunks, firkens, tubs, and boxes filled with all types of eatables and merchandise, could not under any imaginative prompting have bumped, thudded, and pushed their way twenty-four miles along the bottom of the sea. All of this material actually came ashore at a point more distant from Thomas' location than the lighter, floating woodwork. Who can claim that the heavier freight would travel farther on the bottom of the sea than the woodwork floated on top? It is much more sensible to assume that the *Port-*

land went down at a point from three to five miles off the shore, with the wreckage masses soon washing up on the lee beach of Cape Cod.

The Provincetown lifesaver, Jot Small, is still hale and hearty, living down in Provincetown. When the writer met the well-known surfman of former days he asked Jot why there were so many different opinions on the Cape about the loss of the *Portland*.

"Take my advice," said Jonathan Small.[45] "Don't try to understand it, for that would be impossible. It is just a mystery, and it always will be. There is so much that can't be explained, so many things happened that just couldn't happen, that we are all mystified by the whole affair. What happened to the *Portland* will always stay a mystery from start to finish. Mark me well!"

We have tried to present as reasonable an account of the *Portland's* last hours as could be pieced together from the evidence. The *Portland*, seen by persons at Cape Cod and on the schooner *Ruth M. Martin* was definitely afloat after eleven o'clock that Sunday morning. Watches found on the bodies of victims were practically all stopped around 9:15,[46] indicating the sinking of the steamer at about that time. As the steamer was seen afloat after that hour on Sunday morning, then the *Portland* must have foundered shortly after nine that night, as evidenced by the terrific amount of wreckage which hit the beach within the next three hours. Combining all the known facts, this seems the only conclusion which can be made.

Somewhere in the swirling depths of the great beach at Cape Cod lies the answer to all our queries. Almost two generations have gone by since the *Portland* sank beneath the waves off the North Truro Beach, and relatively little has been discovered during the intervening period. It is improbable that we shall ever learn much more than is now known about New England's greatest sea mystery, but if she is located, the chances are that the *Portland* will be found off the changing sands of the Peaked Hill Bars.

NOTES

THE SOMERSET

1. Major Pitcairn, whose alleged tomb I saw in Westminster Abbey in 1942, actually is buried at the Old North Church in Boston, for the remains of the wrong man were sent to England.
2. Samuel Adams Drake, *Old Landmarks of Boston*, [1872] p. 214.
3. The battle at Chelsea Creek has been inexcusably neglected by historians.
4. Captain McNeill's journal is published by the Massachusetts Historical Society in the *Proceedings*, vol. 55, p. 91.
5. Ourry is only one of several recorded spellings of the *Somerset* captain's name.
6. Edward Rowe Snow, *Sailing Down Boston Bay*, [1941] p. 65.
7. Massachusetts Archives, vol. 200, fol. 187.
8. *Ibid.*, fol. 192.
9. Eastham's food cost ran to 392 pounds; Harwich 78 pounds; Yarmouth 19 pounds; Sandwich 40 pounds.
10. The guard ship *Rising Empire* was first chosen, but as the *Penet* was older and less sea worthy it was made the prison ship.
11. Massachusetts Archives, vol. 169, fol. 353.
12. *Ibid.*, vol 175, fol. 125.
13. E. Ward Wilder acquired the sampson post of the *Somerset*.
14. From an interview with Coastguardsman Henrique November 2, 1941.

THE 1635 TEMPEST

1. Point Allerton, Hull, is named for Isaac Allerton.
2. Thacher is also spelled Thatcher.
3. Samuel Adams Drake, *New England Legends and Folk-lore*, [1901] p. 245 ff.
4. Thacher is believed to have reached land near what is now the fog signal.
5. Samuel Adams Drake, *New England Legends and Folk-lore*, p. 252.
6. *Bradford's History of Plimoth Plantation*, [1928] p. 401 f.
7. J. Henry Cartland, *Twenty Years at Pemaquid*, [1914] p. 69 f.
8. John Johnston, *A History of Bristol and Bremen*, [1873] p. 80. At the Essex Institute in Salem there are preserved two Jacobean chairs which came ashore from the wreck of the *Angel Gabriel*.
8. Sidney Perley, *Historic Storms of New England*, [1891] p. 4 f.
9. Cape Sable is at the southern extremity of Nova Scotia.

CANNIBALISM IN MAINE

1. John Dean, *A narrative of the Shipwreck of the Nottingham Galley, & c.* [1730] p. 1.
2. *Ibid.*, p. 17 ff.
3. Christopher Langman, *A true account of the voyage of the Nottingham Galley*, [1711].
4. William R. Dean of Boston, around 1870, questioned the authenticity of the Langman account.

THE WHIDAH

1. Two sources of further research are *A Relation . . . in the Shipwreck of . . . Pirates*, published at Boston in 1717, and *The Trial of Eight Persons Indited for Piracy*, a Boston publication of 1718.
2. The work was published in London in 1726.
3. G. F. Dow and J. H. Edmonds, *Pirates of the New England Coast*, [1923] p. 122.
4. Only two other Cape Cod wrecks have had greater loss of life, the *Portland* and the *Erfprins*.
5. Both Nix's Mate Island and Bird Island were used for this purpose.

THE GALE OF 1723

1. No accurate record was made of the 1723 storm, but J. H. Edmonds estimated it a 16 feet.
2. Fitz-Henry Smith, Jr., has an interesting discussion of the storms and high tides in Bostonian Society *Publications*, vol. II, Second Series, "Storms and Shipwrecks in Boston Bay," page 16.
3. John Hayes was keeper at historic Boston Light from 1718 until 1733.
4. This location was known for many years as Hunt's Corner.

THE GRAND DESIGN

1. Greenleaf and Jonathan P. Cilley, *The Mount Desert Widow*, p. 1.
2. Descendants have in many cases perpetuated the name Asbell, as in Robert Asbell Snow of Rockland, Maine.
3. The boy was afterwards lost at sea.
4. Rev. Henry White, *History of New England*, [1841] p. 203 ff.

NOTES *323*

THE GENERAL ARNOLD

1. Forty-six Pilgrims died during the first winter.
2. During the storm at Boston a driver and his oxen froze to death standing up, caught in the great drifts at Boston Neck.
3. *Hyannis Patriot*, October 21, 1937.
4. Downs later became prominent in his community, and years later Amos Otis penned the story of Downs' terrible adventure aboard the *Arnold*.
5. The term "moon-curser" as used up to 100 years ago has now become "moon-cusser," as evidenced by Henry C. Kittredge's *Mooncussers of Cape Cod*.

THE ERFPRINS

1. Located about due east of Newcastle, England, and about half way to Denmark.
2. J. C. De Jonge, *Geschiedenis van het Nederlandsche Zeewezen*, [1845] p. 360.
3. *Ibid.*, p. 361.
4. Evidently this was the last observation which the captain obtained.

THE 1786 STORM

1. Sidney Perley, *Historic Storms of New England*, p. 126.
2. *Ibid.*, p. 127.
3. *Ibid.*, p. 128.
4. Edward Rowe Snow, *The Islands of Boston Harbor*, [1935] p. 229.
5. From letter of David H. Cowell to E. R. Snow, August 15, 1943.
6. Frederick W. A. S. Brown, an interesting character down Boston Bay, was the signal man at Deer Island, and later the telegraph representative on State Street.
7. This edifice was located across from Kilby Street.
8. There is no record in New England history of any other storm with as great a fall of snow.

THE TRIPLE SHIPWRECKS

1. A fine painting of the *Volusia* is in the Marine Room of the Peabody Museum in Salem
2. Thomas Knox was keeper at Boston Light from 1783 until 1811.
3. Sidney Perley, *Historic Storms of New England*, p. 166.
4. Shebnah Rich, *Truro, Cape Cod, or Land Marks and Sea Marks*, [1883] p. 492.

THE STORM OF OCTOBER 1804

1. *Boston Gazette*, October 11, 1804, carries a good account of the gale.
2. *The Diary of William Bentley, D. D.*, [1905] vol. III, p. 117.

THE SEPTEMBER GALE OF 1815

1. *Boston Gazette*, September 25, 1815.
2. *Columbian Centinel*, October 4, 1815.
3. The prose is from Holmes' *Pages from an Old Volume of Life*, page 163 of the 1892 edition, while the poetry is copied from Walter Channing's *New England Hurricanes*, page 9.

THE ROYAL TAR

1. William IV of England reigned from 1830 to 1837.
2. Roy Coombs of Vinalhaven is said to have part of the elephant's skeleton.
3. The passenger's name was Hinson Patten. Another passenger, Captain Waite of Portland, clung to the rudder chain with two others holding on to him.
4. The location of the Isle of Haut is west of Vinalhaven, south of Deer Island, and southwest of Swan's Island.

THE TRIPLE HURRICANES

1. Fitz-Henry Smith, Jr., in Bostonian Society, *Publication*, vol. II, Second Series "Storms and Shipwrecks in Boston Bay," p. 22.
2. A complete story of the three hurricanes is contained in a pamphlet published in 1840, entitled *Awful Calamities or the Shipwrecks of December 1839 . . . on the Coast of Massachusetts.*
3. John J. Currier, *History of Newburyport, Mass.*, vol. II, p. 18.
4. Fitz-Henry Smith, Jr., "Storms and Shipwrecks," p. 23 f.
5. Sidney Perley, *Historic Storms of New England*, p. 278.

THE LEXINGTON

1. In some of the accounts, the family is referred to as Hutchinson.
2. Follen Street, in Cambridge, is named for Mr. Follen.
3. All quotations are from the volume by S. A. Howland, entitled *Steamboat Disasters and Railroad Accidents in the United States*, published in 1840.

THE SAINT JOHN

1. *Boston Daily Bee,* October 8, 1849.
2. *The Boston Daily Mail,* October 9, 1849.
3. Henry David Thoreau, *Cape Cod,* [1896] p. 4.
4. *Ibid.,* p. 9 ff.
5. The inscription reads: This cross was erected and dedicated May 30, 1914 by the A. O. H. and L. A. A. O. H. of Massachusetts to mark the final resting place of about forty five Irish emigrants from a total company of ninety nine who lost their lives on Grampus Ledge off Cohasset October 7, 1849 in the wreck of the Brig St. John from Galway Ireland R. I. P.

THE MINOT'S LIGHT STORM

1. The entire height of the tower was seventy-five feet.
2. Edward Rowe Snow, *The Islands of Boston Harbor,* p. 229.
3. *Boston Journal,* April 18, 1851.
4. Perley, *Storms,* p. 305.
5. Edward Rowe Snow, *The Story of Minot's Light,* [1940] p. 56.
6. The tower was first lighted by Keeper Joshua Wilder.

THE CITY OF COLUMBUS

1. Nickerson's Wharf was across Northern Avenue Bridge in South Boston.
2. The hull was found inside the buoy.
3. In 1887 the Gate City hit the same ledge, but stayed on, and no one was lost.
4. *The Boston Post,* February 9, 1884.
5. Estimates run from 99 to 107 on the number drowned.
6. *Frank Leslie's Illustrated Newspaper,* January 26, 1884, p. 358.

A NANTUCKET RESCUE

1. *Boston Daily Globe,* January 14, 1912.
2. Arthur H. Gardner, *Shipwrecks around Nantucket,* [1915] p. 145.
3. *Ibid.,* p. 113.

THE JASON

1. Captain Harold Foss of Boston told the writer once of the sailor who was the sole survivor in three different wrecks. He then gave up the sea.
2. William U. Swan is the authority for this part of the story.
3. Jot Small says that the boy told him he had floated ashore and then grasped the jute bale to prevent the undertow from pulling him back.

THE MONOMOY DISASTER

1. Dr. William Flynn of Dorchester did much research for this chapter.
2. J. W. Dalton, *The Life Savers of Cape Cod,* [1902] p. 133 ff.
3. Henry C. Kittredge, *Cape Cod, Its People and Their History.* [1930] p. 230.
4. The actual sum amounted to $36,583.52.

THE LARCHMONT

1. *Boston Globe,* February 13, 1907.
2. *Boston Post,* February 14, 1907.
3. *Boston Herald,* February 17, 1907.
4. *Boston Post,* February 17, 1907.

THE FAIRFAX-PINTHIS

1. *Boston Post,* June 12, 1930.
2. *Boston Herald,* June 17, 1930.
3. *Boston Globe,* June 15, 1930.

THE NEW ENGLAND HURRICANE

1. 682 is the estimate of those who wrote the *New England Hurricane.*
2. *The Boston Post,* September 24, 1938.
3. Providence Journal Company, *The Great Hurricane and Tidal Wave—Rhode Island.*
4. A geologist has suggested that the 1815 hurricane may have been equally as high as the 1938 blast, the difference being caused by the settling of the land around the building.
5. Providence Journal Company, *Hurricane and Tidal Wave.*
6. The September Gale of 1869 severely damaged this lighthouse.
7. *New England Hurricane,* [1938] p. 121.
8. Massachusetts lost over 100 persons.
9. Reynolds Printing, *1938 Hurricane Pictures, New Bedford and Vicinity.*
10. *The Boston Post,* September 22, 1938.
11. *New England Hurricane,* p. 211.
12. *Ibid.,* p. 195 ff.
13. *Boston Herald,* September 23, 1938.

MAINE AND NEW HAMPSHIRE
THE PLYMOUTH PINNACE
1. Bradford's History "Of Plimoth Plantation." [1928] p. 187.
2. *Ibid.*, p. 187, f.

THE ALBANY
1. From an interview with my cousin, Willis Snow.
2. Charles A. E. Long, *Matinicus Isle*, p. 87.
3. Joshua Thorndyke's home on Metinic Island had been raided three times by the British, once from the *Albany*.

THE ADAMS
1. George L. Hosmer, *An Historical Sketch of the Town of Deer Isle, Maine*, [1886] p. 233 f

THE NEW YORK
1. This same vessel had blown up several years before with the loss of many passengers.

THE SARAH
1. From interview with Captain Ernest Delesdernier Sproul.

THE BOHEMIAN
1. Alden's Rock is located about half way between the Hue and Cry Ledge and Cape Elizabeth Light.
2. In his *Lighthouses of the Maine Coast*, Robert Thayer Sterling writes a fine account of the wreck of the *Bohemian*.
3. From an interview with former Mayor Fitzgerald.

THE GALE OF 1888
1. The *Rockland Courier-Gazette* carries a good account of the storm in Maine.
2. *Rockland Courier-Gazette*, November 27, 1888.

THE PORTLAND GALE
1. Interview with Will Snow in 1940.
2. From a letter now in the possession of the writer.

THE PEMAQUID SHIPWRECKS
1. *The Boston Post*, September 18, 1903.
2. *Ibid.*

THE CATAWAMTEAK
1. Captain Joshua Rowe also was aboard the clipper ship *Crystal Palace* when she made her record run to Melbourne from Boston in 1854.
2. From a letter in the writer's possession.

THE GOAT ISLAND SHIPWRECKS
1. Interview with Captain John I. Snow, 1940.

THE WANDBY
1. Interview with Captain John I. Snow, 1940.
2. Cash's Ledge is about 100 miles to the eastward of Newburyport, Massachusetts.

THE CITY OF ROCKLAND
1. *Boston Post*, "The Observant Citizen," September 2, 1943.
2. Thomas Harrison Eames of Belmont, Massachusetts, recently presented the writer with a section of the *Rockland* timber.

ADDITIONAL ITEMS
The *Carolyn* went ashore on Metinic Island in 1912.
The *W. G. Butman* was coming up from Matinicus when she suddenly filled and went down, but no one was lost. This occurred May 27, 1915.
The *Governor Bodwell* was wrecked on Spindle Ledge near the entrance of Swan's Island Harbor in January 1924. John I. Snow got her off, and she was rebuilt, but later entirely destroyed by fire.
The *Wawenock*, a three-master, struck on McGlathery Island in 1929, where she could not be got off.
The *Lucy R.* was an unlucky ship, a Nova Scotia three-master which was wrecked on Matinicus Island. John I. Snow bought her, but she never caused "anyone anything but trouble" was the way John I. expressed himself. At one time outfitted for an expedition which was given up, she was last seen in Portuguese trade, and foundered off that coast some time later.

THE ISLES OF SHOALS
1. The *Sagunto* was later said to have reached Boston Harbor.
2. The verses are from her brother Oscar's book, *Ninety Years at the Isles of Shoals*.
3. Captain Bill Wincapaw inaugurated this practice back in 1926.

THE KATAHDIN

1. Making her first trip in 1863, the vessel was active until 1894.
2. In John M. Richardson's outstanding contribution, *Steamboat Lore of the Penobscot*, the *Katahdin* is pictured after her experiences in the gale.

THE OLIVER DYER

1. *Annual Report of the . . . Life Saving Service*, 1889, p. 27.
2. *Ibid.*, p. 28 f.

SOUTHERN NEW ENGLAND

1. The *Metis* was of 1359 tons.
2. *Boston Daily Globe*, August 31, 1872.

THE NARRAGANSETT

1. *Boston Daily Advertiser*, July 14, 1880.
2. *Ibid.*
3. Captain Nye afterwards admitted he had not learned the correct fog signal.

BLOCK ISLAND

1. Palatinate lands were located in Germany on the Rhine and in Bavaria.
2. Notarial Protests, vol. IV, 392 f.
3. William P. Sheffield, *Historical Sketch of Block Island*, p. 39.
4. Rev. S. T. Livermore, *A History of Block Island*, p. 124.

THE HESSIAN GALE

1. Wilfred G. Munroe, *Picturesque Rhode Island*, [1881] p. 205.

THE ANN HOPE

1. Livermore, *Block Island*, 126.

THE WARRIOR

1. *Ibid.*, 127.

NANTUCKET AND MARTHA'S VINEYARD

1. Arthur H. Gardner's fine volume lists over 700 wrecks around Nantucket.
2. A canoe in earlier times was a substantial lapstreak dory.
3. Arthur H. Gardner, *Wrecks around Nantucket*, [1915] p. 12.
4. Cyprian Southack was the first mariner to chart this shoal accurately.
5. Tristam Coffin was placed under court martial.
6. Sir Edmund Andros was later to be captured in 1689 and imprisoned at Castle Island in Boston Harbor.
7. Arthur H. Gardner, *Wrecks around Nantucket*, p. 18.
8. This man is believed to have come from Oahu, one of the Hawaiian Islands.
9. Arthur H. Gardner, *Wrecks around Nantucket*, p. 32.
10. *Boston Courier*, July 11, 1838.
11. This October gale brought great devastation to Cape Cod. Truro lost fifty-seven men; Yarmouth ten; twenty from Dennis. Captain Knowles' fight against this storm is described in Henry C. Kittredge's *Cape Cod*.
12. *Boston Courier*, March 16, 1846.
13. The *Silivae* was his last wreck, however, for he died shortly afterwards.
14. Arthur H. Gardner, *Wrecks around Nantucket*, p. 72.
15. For this feat of bravery Ramsdell was presented with the silver medal of the Massachusetts Humane Society.
16. Arthur H. Gardner, *Wrecks around Nantucket*, p. 90.
17. Built at Bath, Maine, in 1906, her gross tonnage was 3,132.
18. Arthur H. Gardner, *Wrecks around Nantucket*, p. 107.
19. Harry B. Turner's additional collection of Nantucket Shipwrecks, added to Arthur H. Gardner's volume in 1930, contains the information.
20. Others in the Palmer fleet include *Baker*, *Elizabeth*, the second *Fanny*, *Maud*, and *Paul*. With the exception of *Fanny*, they were all lost in 1915.

MARTHA'S VINEYARD

1. The British sailors and marines had systematically taken all food from the island.

AMELIA O. IRELAND

1. *Annual Report of the . . . Life Saving Service*, 1899, p. 41, ff.

ADDITIONAL ITEMS

On January 5, 1856, a great gale swept the Vineyard bringing a tide six feet higher than ordinary gales from the northeast. More than six vessels were wrecked at Holmes Hole.

The schooner *Christiana* was sunk on Hawes Shoal outside of Cape Poge with only one survivor; forty bodies were picked up from this storm in Nantucket.

The Gale of 1869 blew off Fairhaven's church steeple.

The storm of 1878 caused the capsizing of the bark *Sarah*, with twenty-two drowned.

The Hurricane of 1938 was considered to be worse than that of 1815, which caused tides twenty-three feet above normal.

MASSACHUSETTS BAY
THE 1740 GALE

1. In this period the vessels were listed by the names of the captains.

THE MAGNIFIQUE

1. Jennings was Keeper of Boston Light from 1916 until 1919.
2. Nathaniel Bradstreet Shurtleff, *Boston*, [1871] p. 552.

THE ELIZABETH AND ANN

1. The Minot's Light Storm destroyed all vestiges of this island.
2. Edward Rowe Snow, *Historical Facts about Winthrop*, [1939] Episode 21.
3. Only rocks remain today where the sandy area was.

THE TEDESCO

1. Egg Rock Light was first lighted September 15, 1856, discontinued 1922. The brig *Judge Hathaway* and the schooner *Geneva* both came ashore in the same gale.
3. A painting of the *Tedesco* accompanies Fitz-Henry Smith's article on "Some Old Fashioned Winters in Boston," Massachusetts Historical Society, *Proceedings*, vol. 65 p. 294.

THE VERNON

1. *Salem Gazette*, February 5, 1859.
2. *Boston Globe*, April 24, 1925.

BOSTON HARBOR'S WORST SHIPWRECK

1. Fitz-Henry Smith, Jr., in Bostonian Society, *Publications*, vol. II, Second Series, "Storms and Shipwrecks in Boston Bay," p. 35 ff.
2. This is the largest number lost in Boston Harbor. The Thompson's Island disaster of 1842 cost the lives of twenty-five, while the *Mary E. O'Hara* tragedy of 1941 totalled twenty deaths.
3. Samuel James was a son of the William James who helped save the crew of the *Tremont* in 1844, and brother of Joshua James.
4. Edward Rowe Snow, *Historic Fort Warren* [1941] p. 22.

THE 1869 GALE

1. According to information furnished by Capt. Sproul.
2. John M. Richardson, *Steamboat Lore of the Penobscot*.

THE 1888 GALE

1. Edward Rowe Snow, *Minot's Light*, p. 94.
2. This schooner had previously left Canada under spectacular conditions.
3. Fitz-Henry Smith, Jr., in Bostonian Society, *Publications*, vol. II, Second Series, "Storms and Shipwrecks in Boston Bay," p. 9 ff.

THE NORSEMAN

1. *Boston Post*, March 30, 1899.

THE DAVIS PALMER

1. *Boston Globe*, December 27, 1909.
2. The Minot's Light tide averaged 15.62 feet in Boston, while the Portland tide was 14.94 in Boston. The 1909 storm was 15.60 feet. Two residents of Everett drowned when the tides flooded the area.

THE MOXIE

1. The Crest is Winthrop's Shore Drive.

THE NANCY

1. *Boston Post*, February 21, 1927.
   In the same storm the *C G 238* was lost with eight men off Highland Light.

THE ROBERT E. LEE

1. *Boston Herald*, March 9, 1928.
2. *Ibid.*

THE NORTHERN SWORD

1. The writer performed an unusual duty when he delivered mail to the stranded collier, as the postman was unable to reach the ship.
2. This new bar runs parallel to and about an eighth of a mile to the northward of Winthrop Bar, erroneously called Fawn Bar.

THE CITY OF SALISBURY

1. The cargo was valued at approximately $1,500,000.
2. Captain Owen Morris was the master of the City of Salisbury.
3. Interview with Robert Mackey, October 1943.
4. Material was still being removed from the hold as late as 1942.

THE MARY E. O'HARA

1. Finn's Ledge is approximately half the distance from Winthrop's water tower to Graves Light.
2. The writer interviewed Crowell one week after the incident.

ADDITIONAL ITEMS

A sloop from the West Indies hit at what is now Winthrop in 1682, and her treasure went down a short distance off the shore.
The ship *Mary* was wrecked on Connyhasset Rocks, January 22, 1683. The ship *Elizabeth* was wrecked on the same rocks March 23, 1686, with a load of rum. The *Hazard* also hit there in 1715.
In March 1823 the *Rebecca Ann* hit on the reef of Norman's Woe, with everyone on board except one sailor perishing within a few minutes.
The brig *Joachim*, Captain Drew, struck on Middle Brewster Island in February 1829, with two of the crew lost. Boston Light Keeper Bruce rescued the survivors.
In 1885 the *A. G. Brooks* was wrecked on the outside of Deer Island, Boston Harbor. Forty-four lives in all were lost in the Gale of 1888 in Massachusetts.
Nahant shipwrecks of importance include the *Peggy* at Little Nahant in 1795; the *Exile* in 1851 at Long Beach; the *Prairie Flower* off Nahant in 1858 with several prominent Bostonians lost; the *Lion* in 1864; the *Alsatian* in 1896 near the Spouting Horn; and the *Charles S. Briggs* near Little Nahant in 1899.
Cape Ann wrecks include the *Abigail* in 1790 on the Londoner; the *Howard* in 1907; the brig *Persia* near Brace's Rock, with everyone on board lost, including the son of the eminent L. A. Lauriat, early in the 19th century.
In November 1883 six schooners went down off George's Banks with seventy-six men lost.
Salem Wrecks include the *Martha* of Portland in 1803 and the *Favorite* in 1805.
The *Mryra B. Weaver* was brought into Boston Harbor about 50 years ago with the body of a woman frozen to death in the rigging. Refitted, it was later named *Pendleton's Satisaction* and is mentioned in the list of Maine shipwrecks.

CAPE COD

THE ALMIRA

1. Sidney Perley, *Storms of New England*, p. 242 ff.

THE FRANKLIN

1. Henry David Thoreau, *Cape Cod*, p. 123 ff.
2. *Boston Courier*, March 3, 1849.
3. Henry C. Kittredge, *Mooncussers of Cape Cod*, [1937] p. 136 ff.

THE JOSEPHUS

1. Henry C. Kittredge, *Cape Cod*, [1930] p. 222.
2. Isaac Morton Small, *Shipwrecks on Cape Cod*, p. 9.
3. *Ibid.*, p. 9.

THE CALEDONIA

1. Henry C. Kittredge has a fine lithograph of the *Caledonia* in his *Cape Cod*, p. 220.

THE PERUVIAN

1. Isaac M. Small, *Cape Cod Shipwrecks*, p. 14.
2. 28 perished in the disaster.

THE FRANCIS

1. Capt. E. P. Worthen of Highland Station was in charge of the rescue.
2. Isaac M. Small, *Cape Cod Shipwrecks*, p. 18.

THE GIOVANNI

1. J. W. Dalton, in his *Life Savers of Cape Cod*, says that no one was saved.

THE TRUMBULL

1. Elisha Taylor, just before he sank, said to Isaiah Young, father of Cy Young, "Isaiah, have you got a chew?" Isaiah, struggling in the water, finally got his tobacco out. Elisha took a big bite, smiled in satisfaction, and slipped beneath the waves to his death.
2. J. W. Dalton, *The Life Savers of Cape Cod*, p. 21.

THE MONTE TABOR

1. Interview with G. H. Bickers.
2. An investigation later proved that the captain had taken his own life.

THE COLERAINE

1. The *Mars* was owned by the Reading Railroad Company.
2. Isaac M. Small, *Cape Cod Shipwrecks*, p. 69.
3. The building was later used as a summer cottage.

THE PORTLAND GALE

1. The *Saint John*, with 143 was second in the number drowned.
2. *Blue Hill Meteorological Observatory*, Bulletin No. 2, 1899, A. E. Sweetland, "Two Remarkable Snow-Storms."
3. From an interview with the writer.
4. *Annual Report of the Operations of the United States Life-Saving Service*, [1839] p. 26.
5. *Ibid.*, p. 26.
6. From the statement of Wesley Pingree.
7. The *Ohio* was later got off the Spectacle Island beach.
8. "Two Remarkable Snow-Storms."

THE COLUMBIA

1. *Annual Report of the* . . .*Life-Saving Service*, 1899, p. 28.
2. *Ibid.*, p. 29.

THE CALVIN F. BAKER

1. Keeper at Boston Light from 1894 until 1909.
2. Interview with Wesley Pingree.
3. Fitz-Henry Smith, Jr., in Bostonian Society, *Publications*, vol. II, Second Series, "Storms and Shipwrecks in Boston Bay," p. 57 ff.

THE MERTIS H. PERRY

1. *Annual Report of the* . . . *Life-Saving Service*, 1899, p. 33, f.
2. *Ibid.*, p. 36.

THE ALBERT L. BUTLER

1. From interview with the relatives of Michael Hogan.
2. *Annual Report of the* . . . *Life-Saving Service*, 1899, p. 41.

THE PORTLAND

1. Amos E. Haggett, of N. E. Shipbuilding Co., was in charge of building the *Portland* which took fifteen months and ended May, 1890.
2. Perhaps the only pictures still in existence of her interiors were made by F. L. King of the *Boston Post.*
3. Stebbins published his *Coast Pilot*, from scores of pictures which he took up and down the New England coast in 1890.
4. From talks with waterfront residents of Boston, Provincetown, and Portland.
5. "Two Remarkable Snow-Storms."
6. There were 108 passengers and 68 crew members.
7. From testimony at the examination into the loss of the *Portland.*
8. *The Boston Herald*, November 27, 1938.
9. Seven of them were under oath at the time of their statements.
10. The exact time was 6:15 p. m.
11. From his signed statement in the writer's possession.
12. Keeper Pingree believed a warning was definitely given.
13. From an interview with Thomas Harrison Eames in 1940.
14. From testimony at the examination into the loss of the *Portland.*
15. From a letter in the possession of the writer.
16. From his testimony at the examination.
17. Thomas Harrison Eames, in the *New England Quarterly*, vol. XIII, no. 2 p. 194 "The Wreck of the Steamer 'Portland!' "
18. The writer talked with Captain Pellier at Ten Pound Island in 1936, and Captain Pellier believed the superstructure of the *Portland* badly damaged when he saw it that night.
19. From copies of Weather Bureau charts in the possession of the writer.
20. The high tide marks are still visible from the two storms of 1851 and 1898 on the rocks near the keeper's residence on Government Island, Cohasset.
21. Boon Island is about sixty-five miles in a northeasterly direction from Boston.
22. The capstan cover from the *Horatio Hallis* at the Boston Old State House.
23. From Captain Bragg's testimony at the examination.
24. From Captain Scripture's testimony.
25. From Captain Fisher's testimony.
26. From a letter in the possession of the writer.
27. Captain Hogan's descendants live in Billerica.
28. There was no other paddle-wheel steamer within one hundred miles.
29. Thomas Harrison Eames, "*The Wreck of the Steamer 'Portland.'* " p. 197 f.
30. All the lift belts were not marked alike.
31. From statement in the possession of the writer.
32. From interview with George Henry Bickers.
33. From interview with Jot Small.
34. Orris R. Ingraham was the twin brother of Otis Ingraham, both sea captains of Rockland, Maine.
35. Named for Addie E. Snow, granddaughter of Israel Snow who founded the Snow shipyards in Rockland, Maine.
36. From his testimony at the examination.
37. William U. Swan did much independent research in an effort to solve the mystery of what happened to the *Portland.*
38. The man in question will gladly answer any letters addressed to him through the medium of the writer.
39. From a statement in the possession of the writer.
40. Mr. Ayling has a sworn affidavit that the crew of the High Head Station picked up the wheel with other wreckage from the *Portland.*
41. *Boston Transcript*, August 31, 1899.
42. The doors in question had lain undisturbed in Mr. Young's back yard for almost 43 years.
43. *The Boston Post*, April 25, 1899.
44. On June 29, 1934 Captain Charles Carver recovered several articles believed to be from the Portland. In 1936 Captain Ault brought up bathroom fixtures.
45. Interview with Jot Small.
46. According to statement of George Henry Bickers and others.

MAINE SHIPWRECKS

Adams, 1814.
Addie E. Snow, 1898, Capt. Brown, Peaked
 Hill Bars.
Addie Ryarson, 1880, White Head.
Africa, 1902, Capt. Masters, Libby Island.
Alice Clark.
Alida, 1898, Spruce Island.
America, 1803, Capt. Morse.
Amos Cutler, 1912 (?), Capt. Morris.
Anna Barker, 1898, Capt. Blake, Southern
 Island.
Angel Gabriel, 1635, Pemaquid Point.
Annie C. Maguire, 1886, Portland Head.
Annie Freeman, 1878.
Ara, 1927, Little Dick Island.
Argo, 1782, Capt. Trevett.
Asa, 1818, Coombs.
Astral, 1902, Mount Desert.
Atlantic, 1839.
Aurora, 1809, Capt. Isley.
Australia, 1885.

Barge 767, 1918 (?), Vinalhaven.
Barge 791, 1933, Rockland.
Bay State, 1915, McKinney's Point.
Bertha E. Glover, 1898, Vinalhaven.
Black Swan, 1879, Chatham Bar.
Blasson.
Bodwell, 1924, Capt. Kent, Swan's Ledge;
 1931, Capt. Kent, Swan's Island.
Bohemian, 1864, Capt. Bolan, Portland.
Break of Day, 1893, Rockland.
Brig (a), 1890, Wooden Ball.
Brooklyn, 1883.

Caledonia, 1878, Capt. Davidson, Libby
 Island.
California, 1900, Capt. France, Portland.
Cambridge, 1886, Old Man's Ledge.
Cameo, 1875, Metinic.
Carlotta, 1873.
Carolyn, 1912, Metinic.
Carrie C. Miles, 1898, Portland.
Carrie Pickering, 1895.
Casco, Capt. Laselle.
Castine, 1935, Bay Ledges.
Catawamteak, Monhegan.
Charles, 1907.
Charles H. Tuckey, 1920.
Chase, 1873.
Chewink II, 1902, Metinic.
City of Portland, Crescent Beach.
City of Rockland, 1904, Crescent Beach;
 1923, Kennebec River.
Clara Bella, 1900, Capt. Pulk, Two Bush.
Columbia, 1800, Capt. Dunning.
Columbus, 1851.
Columbus, 1912, North Triangles.
Commodore Perry, 1845.
Cora Etta, 1887, Capt. Fales.
Cornelia, 1918, Little Fawn Bar.
Cullen, No. 18, 1938, Searsport.
Cumberland, 1918.
Cyrus McKown, 1885.

D. W. Hammond, 1887, Capt. Flanders,
 Portland.
Daniel McLeod.
Derrick Scow (a), 1938, Deer Isle.
David Faust, 1910, The Brothers.
Don, 1747, Mount Desert.
Dorothy L. Brinkman.
Dove, 1850, Capt. Crockett.
Duncan, 1855, Capt. Porter.
Durego, 1873.

E. Arcaularius, Capt. Stevens, Cuttyhunk.
E. G. Willard, 1898, Capt. Aylward.
E. S. Pendleton, 1859.
Edmunds, 1903, Poole.
Edwardo, 1870, Cutler.
Edward W. Murdock, 1907?, Machias Bay.
Elizabeth Howard, 1915.
Eliza Crowell, 1866.
Ella F. Crowell, 1898, Vineyard Haven.
Ella U. Dora.
Empire, 1885, Portland.
Etna, 1884, Portland.
Exact, 1888.
Excelsior, 1856.

F. C. Lockhart, 1923, Libby Islands.
Fame, Capt McDonald, Libby Islands.
Fannie May, 1898.
Fenimore, 1918, York River.
Flora, 1888, Capt. Lee, Boot Head, Quoddy.
Flora Condon, 1907, Vinalhaven.
Florida, 1838, Damariscotta.
Foaming Billow, 1860.
Forrest Belle, 1869.
Forrester, 1851.
Fortune, 1851, Capt. Stearns.
Freisdale, Wooden Ledges.

G. & B. Morse, 1884, Portland.
George and James, 1845.
Georgietta, 1898, Spruce Head.
Gladys M. Taylor, 1920, Matinicus.
Grace E. Stevens, 1926, Rockland.
Grampus, 1851.
Grand Design, 1741, Mount Desert.
Gussie Blaisdell, 1912.
Guy Mannering, 1867, Matinicus Island.

H. C. Higginson, 1888, Capt. Fales.
Hanover.
Harriet B, 1925, Lubec.
Hay schooner, (a), 1888, Webster's Head.
Helena, 1910, Old Woman.
Helen Eliza, 1869.
Hercules.
Hockamoac, 1866.
Huntress, 1930, Greenlaw.
Hurricane, 1898.

I. K. Stetson, 1909, Boyce.
Ida Grover, 1890, Matinicus.
Idella Small, Bay View, Massachusetts.
Industry, 1770, Patterson.
Irvington.
Isidore, 1842, Capt. Foss.
Island Bell, 1877.
Island City, 1898, Vineyard Haven.

J. T. Morse, 1915, Capt. Shute, Moose
 Head; 1924, Stonington.
James Boyce, Pleasant Island.
James A. Brown, 1898, Vineyard Haven.
John B., 1857, Rockland.
John Douglass, White Head.
John H. Myers, 1925, Capt. Myers, Libby
 Island.
John G. Dennis, 1864.

Katahdin, 1886, Capt. Homer.
Kearsage, 1903, Seal Island.
Kendrick Fish, 1899, Capt. Gilbert, Port-
 land.
King Phillip, 1898, Capt. Cod.
Knowlton, 1907, Capt. Healey, Block Island
 Sound.

L. A. Johnson, 1877, Mahlman.
Lake Huron, 1886.
Laura Jane, 1866, Portland Head.
Lena White, 1898, Capt. Gray.
Lincoln, 1846.
Lingan, 1822, Capt. Haskell.
Lion, 1851, Capt. Pressey.
Little Fanny, 1875, Capt. Doughty.
Lobster smack, (a), 1910, Outer Penobscot.
Lochinnvar, 1832, Capt. Doughty.
Loihocla, 1919.
Lotus, 1910.
Lucy R.

Mabel Hall, 1940, Block Island.
Mary E. Olys, 1920.
Mattie E. Eaton, 1888, Capt. Gamage.
Maud C., 1888, Green's Landing.
Maud S., 1888, Owl's Head.
Maud Snare, 1908 (?), Hart's Island.
Menemon Sanford, 1856, Capt. Sanford, Thatcher's Island.
Middlesex, 1922, Trundy's Reef.
Milo. 1825, Robinson.
Montreal, 1873.
Minerva, 1855.
Morris and Cliff, 1922, Union River.
Myra J. Wooster, 1934, Friendship.

Nellie Short, 1869.
New York, 1826, Capt. Harrod.
Niagara, 1850.
Nile, Ash Island.
Northern Light, 1925.
Norumbega, Clark's Island.

Palm, 1916, Robinson's Rock.
Pagonia, 1886.
Pearl, 1849.
Pendleton's Satisfaction, Islesboro.
Penobscot, 1903, Two Bush.
Pentagoet, 1898, Capt. Ingraham, Cape Cod.
Persian Monarch, 1886.
Polias, 1920, Port Clyde.
Portland, 1898, Capt. Blanchard, Cape Cod.
Post Boy, Otter Island Ledge.
Princeport, 1892, Capt. Brown, Libby Island.

Rawley, 1888.
Rebecca Ann, 1823, Capt. Walker.
Rebecca Douglass, 1907, Vinalhaven.
Rising States, 1833.
Robert W., 1923.

Robert Peel, 1845, Metinic.
Robert Ripley, 1888, Capt. Cooper.
Rockland, Capt. Greene, Lower Gangway.
Romeo, 1878, Metinic.
Royal Tar, 1836, Capt. Reed, Fox Island.

S. F. Maher, 1898.
Samuel Rankin, 1857.
Sankaty, 1924, New Bedford.
Sarah, 1851, Chaleur Bay.
Sardinian, 1907, Wreck Point, Metinic.
Schooners, 1883, George's Bank.
Seguin, 1940, Kennebec River.
Sinbad, Channel Rock.
Sophronia, 1869.
Susan P. Thurlow, 1897.

Tamerlane, 1849, Capt. Green.
Thomas H. Lawrence, 1939, Bay Ledges.
Thorndyke, 1835.
Tilden, 1867, Capt. Sylvester.
Tizar, 1866.
Tom Thumb, 1836, Boon Island.
Torrey, 1879, Capt. Bray.
Treaty, 1880, White Islands.

Ulysses, 1877.

Vinalhaven, 1893, Capt. Webster, Rockland.
Vinalhaven, 1938, Rockland.
Voice of God.
Violet, 1850.

W. C. Wellington, 1872, Capt. Thompson.
W. K. Butman, 1915, Outer Rockland Harbor.
Wandby, 1921.
Wanderer, 1924, Cuttyhunk.
Warren, 1875, Pickering.
Washington B. Thomas, 1903.
Waterwitch, 1878.
Wawenock, 1929, McGlatheny, Land Harbor.
Will W. Chase, 1877, Capt. Desmond.
William Booth, 1930 Roberts Harbor.
William McLoon, 1888, Capt. Smith.
William L. Elkins, Cape Elizabeth.
William L. Elkins, 1915.
Willie Martin, 1888, Capt. Perry.
Woodruff, 1898, Northport.

Yankee Maid, 1890.

Zealand.
Zeaman, 1922, Metinic.

INDEX

INDEX

333

57, 60, 65, 70, 71, 73, 75, 87,
89, 90, 94, 97, 122, 124, 139,
156, 158, 163, 196, 214, 232,
246, 268–284, 291, 297, 298,
307, 308, 309, 310, 314, 315,
316, 317, 318, 320
Cape Cod Canal, 261
Cape Cod Light, 94
Cape Elizabeth, Me., 191, 314
Cape Elizabeth Light, 314
Cape Hatteras, 276
Cape of Good Hope, 154
Cape Porpoise, 197, 198, 201
Cape Sable, 46, 50
Captain Magee Storm, 64–72
Caroline, 246
Carrie C. Miles, 194
Casco Bay, 291
Cashman, William H., 261, 262
Cash's Ledge, 198
Cassidy, Daniel, 274
Castine, 184, 189
Castine, 199
Castine Point, Nantucket, 215
Castle Island, 31
Catawamteack, 196
Cathcart, Charles B., 153
Catholic Church, Pawtucket,
131
Cedar Island, 243
Centerville, 316
Central House, 212
Central Street, Boston, 133
C. G. 176, 263
Charles, Capt., 156
Charles H. Tuckey, 197
Charles River, 22, 98, 131
Charlestown, 22, 23
Charlestown Beach, R. I., 174
Charlestown Bridge, 107, 133
Charlestown Ferry, 56
Chase, Keeper Walter N., 146,
147, 148, 153
Chase, Surfman, 160
Chatham, 25, 57, 156, 159, 162,
228
Chatham, England, 21
Chatham Light, 308
Chelsea, 23
Chelsea, 31, 97, 122, 243, 251
Chelsea Bridge, 133
Chelsea Creek, 23, 31
Chestnut St., Chelsea, 122
Childs, Capt. George, 108, 109,
118
Christian, 214
City Hall, Fall River, 178
City of Columbus, 139–145
City of New York, 207
City of Rockland, 198
City of Salisbury, 264, 265, 266
City Point, Boston, 179
Clara Leavitt, 236, 238
Clark, Granville M., 250
Cliff Shore, 227
Clinton, 23
Coast Guard, 171
Coast Guard Cruiser *238*, 283,
284
Coen, Benjamin T., 211
Coffin, Capt. Aaron, 225
Coffin, Tristam, 214, 215
Cohasset, 94, 104, 122, 123, 124,
125, 127, 128, 130, 135, 138,
252, 306
Cohasset Rocks, 127
Cole, Capt. Daniel, 157
Cole, John, 281
Cole, Pilot, 88
Coleraine, 282, 283
Coliseum Building, 250
Collins, Capt., 303

Collin's Cove, Salem, 132
Collins, Jonathan, 274
Columbia, 286, 291, 292, 293
Columbia Road Breakwater, 179
Columbia Yacht Club, 179
Columbiana, 107
Commercial Street, Boston, 249
Conanchet, 224, 225
Conanicut Island, 176
Concord, 22, 23
Concord, N. H., 93
Confederate, 249
Confidence, 257
Congdon, Mr. Benjamin, 209
Connecticut, 177, 204, 240
Connecticut, 177
Conimcut Point, 176
Conrad, Stanley, 267
Constitution Hill, Providence,
96
Cony, 220
Conyngham, 197
Cook, Capt., 107, 299
Cook, George M., 196
Cook, Capt. James, 88
Cook, Samuel, 88
Cook, Capt. W. W., 316
Coombs, Captain Leighton, 199
Cooper, Abram, 239
Coskata Beach, 146
Coskata Life Saving Station, 146
Coston signal flare, 203, 236, 305
Courier-Gazette, 193
Covington, 239
Cowell, David H., 84
Cowell, John, 84
Cowell, Joseph, 84
Cox, Benjamin, 117
Crafts, John W., 273
Cranberry Islands, 61
Crest, 258
Crosby, 314
Cross Rip Lightship, 234
Crowell, Cecil, 267
Crowley, David, 109, 119, 120
Crumpstey, Capt. Andrew, 53,
54
Cuba, 51
Cumberland, 30, 197
Curran, Surfman John, 292
Curtis, Weston, 195
Cushing, Maine, 183
Custom House, 130, 133
Cuttyhunk Island, 141
Cyron, Edward, 30

Dacia, 171
Dakin, Capt., 232
Damariscotta, Maine, 83
Damariscove, 182
Dana, Richard Henry, 209
Danvers, 94, 97, 131
Darling, Pilot David, 241
Dartmouth, Earl of, 21
Davenport, 105, 106
Davis, Thomas, 51, 54, 55, 56
Davis Palmer, 235, 257, 258
Dead Man's Hollow, 32
Dead Man's Point, 61
Deane, Capt. John, 47, 48, 50
Decatur Street, East Boston,
131
December 1740, Gale, 240
DeCosta, William, 56, 271
Deer Isle, Maine, 189
Deer Island, Mass.. 131, 242,
265
Deer Island Light, 286, 287,
302, 303
Dennis, 269
Dennison, Capt. Alexander, 301,
302

Dept. of Commerce, 175
Deposit, 105
Derby Wharf, Salem, 132
Devil's Back, 140
Devil's Bridge, 140, 142, 145
Devine, Simon, 236
Dewlap, Capt., 215
Dexter, 143
Dexter's Locomotive Museum,
99
Dix's Island, 198
Doane, Col., 29
Doane, Justice, 54
Doane, Capt. Hezekiah, 156
Dobbins, Rev., 71
Dogfish Bar, 236, 237
Dogger Bank, 73, 74
Dolliver's Neck, 194
Dorchester, Mass., 58
Dorchester, Mass., 131
Dorothy Palmer, 234, 235
Douglas, 217
Dove, 94
Downs, Barnabas, Sr., 71
Downs, Barnabas, 70, 71, 72
Droohan, Patrick, 309
Duffield, Rev., 243
Duley, Michael, 132
Dunn, Capt. Lawrence H., 180
Dutch, 73, 74, 215
Dyer, Capt. 100

Eames, Thomas H., 309, 312,
313
Earl of Dartmouth, 21
Earl of Eglington, 223, 224
East Boston, 104, 131
East Indiamen, 87–92
East River, 108
East Point, 213
Eastern Point, 305, 307
Eastham, 29, 55, 268
Eastham Tavern, 54
Eastport, 103
Eastport Harbor, 99
Eastport, Maine, 190
Eaton, Ebenezer, 94
Eckstrom, Fannie, 190
Edgar Randall, 305, 307
Edgartown, 194, 220
Edward H. Norton, 252
E. G. Willard, 195
Egg Rock, Boston Harbor, 247
Egg Rock Light, 244
Eldridge, Capt., 159, 160, 161
Eldridge, Jessie H., 153
Eliot, William, 35
Elizabeth and Ann, 242, 244
Ella F. Crowell, 195
Ellis, Capt. Josiah, 268, 269, 270
Ellis, Surfman, 159, 160, 162,
163
Ellsworth, 171, 194
Elsie, 286
Elwell, Mr., 184
Elwell, Samuel, 81, 82, 83
Elwine Fredericke, 225
Emerson Rocks, 132
Emma Wadsworth, 249
Endicott, Gov., 97
Endymion, 217
England, 21, 23, 32, 35, 40, 45,
51, 52, 59, 99, 154, 155, 158,
182
English, 73, 215, 216, 239
English Channel, 74
Episcopal Church, East Boston
131
Erfprins, 73
Esterhill, Eddie, 180
Esterhill, Capt. Fred, 180
Eubank, John V., 171

1944, A YEAR OF GALES AND DISASTER

THE 1944 HURRICANE

Strangely similar in sequence to the September 1823 storm which followed the disastrous hurricane of September 1815, the September gale of 1944 followed uncomfortably close to the great New England hurricane of September 1938. Communities and counties which the 1938 blast had dealt with either kindly or not too severely were devastated by the 1944 blow, while other locations completely escaped the overwhelming disaster which befell them six years earlier.

Although the loss of life ashore was relatively small in 1944, with thirty-one deaths in northeastern United States, there was a different story to tell at sea. A destroyer, a lightship, and two other government craft were sunk with heavy loss of life, in great contrast to the 1938 gale.

Cape Cod and Martha's Vineyard were hit heavily in 1944. Warning after warning had gone out over the radio all day September 14, and mass evacuations had been completed in many sections of New England by evening. Between nine and ten at night the wind increased rapidly, with 100 miles an hour a common reading before midnight.

Fortunately the hurricane held off until the tide had been going out for three hours, preventing such terrific damage as occurred in 1938 when the tremendous tidal

waves swept over various sections of New England. But
the wind again proved its strength by destroying thousands of trees and hundreds upon hundreds of houses.
Cape Cod suffered severely from Falmouth all the way
to Provincetown, which was the scene of outstanding damage. The town hall roof, the Methodist Church steeple,
and the town pier roof in Provincetown were all carried
away. Shortly before 1:30 a.m. Chatham experienced a
wind of 105 miles an hour. The Wareham railroad bridge
collapsed at the height of the gale. The Methodist church
steeple at West Dennis was blown over and speared its
way into the roof of the edifice. Camp Edwards and
nearby Otis Field were raked by the gale, while at South
Sea Village in South Yarmouth a near tidal wave piled
houses and cottages upon each other in hopeless confusion. There were many freak accidents. Electric light
service was either curtailed or non-existant on Cape Cod
after the storm.

Southern Massachusetts again suffered heavily.
Beach cottages in the area were severely damaged. The
entire New Bedford section reported a disaster as great
or greater than 1938, with Mayor Arthur N. Harriman
estimating that losses would reach nearly $5,000,000.
Station WMBH radio tower collapsed, Dan's Pavilion was
totally destroyed, and Fort Rodman was badly battered.
The Fairhaven Bridge was five feet under water. Three
yachts and several small boats were found high and dry
on the bridge when the tide went down.

At the height of the storm, Martha's Vineyard suffered overwhelming damage, with the Edgartown waterfront torn asunder, resembling a shambles in many sections. The steamship pier at Oak Bluffs was wrecked.

The southwestern section of Nantucket was severely dealt with by the hurricane as it swept along but the losses there were not to be compared with what Martha's Vineyard suffered.

Telephone damage was severe with 70,000 telephones out of order in New England because of the gale. The service was restored with alacrity and dispatch whenever possible, and the telephone linemen deserve much credit for the rapidity with which lines were replaced and communication again made possible.

An early visitor to the Cape after the hurricane, Alton Hall Blackington took many remarkable pictures of the 1944 disaster. Riding along through roads made almost impassable by storm debris, he was able to photograph and record many of the unusual incidents of the hurricane.

Rhode Island escaped with minor losses, chiefly confined to Portsmouth, Newport, and Warwick, amounting to less than $500,000.

In the first gasp of relief that the storm was not as devastating as the 1938 gale, people in northern New England were inclined to minimize in their minds the terrific and overwhelming effects of the gale which hit the Cape, New Bedford, and Martha's Vineyard with greater intensity than its predecessor. One should not forget that many beautiful locations in these sections of Massachusetts were irreparably damaged. The hurricane on Cape Cod alone is said to have cost $50,000,000.

Located near the Sow and Pigs Ledge to the south of Cuttyhunk, the Vineyard Sound Lightship has been a well-known sea marker to the sailor and voyager. Forced to stay at its post when other ships fled to safety before the great hurricane, the Vineyard Lightship went down with all eleven of the ship's company, probably at the height of the gale. The captain of the doomed vessel, Warrant Officer J. Edgar Sevigny, had planned to reach home on leave the day after the hurricane hit, but the skipper of the lightship went down with his vessel.

Built in Baltimore in 1901, the 129-foot lightship weathered the 1938 hurricane and scores of other storms without damage, only to disappear completely in the 1944 gale. Several of the bodies of the men were found, and it is said that the hull of the vessel was located.

The loss of life because of the 1944 hurricane aboard the Destroyer *Warrington*, the Coast Guard Cutters *Jackson* and *Bedloe*, the Minesweeper *XMS-409*, and the Vineyard Lightship reached the unprecedented total of 344 killed or missing. While the survivor list was not made known, without question the percentage of loss was extremely heavy.

THE STORM AT CLEVELAND LEDGE LIGHT

Just as the famous Minot's Ledge Light underwent its baptism of storm in 1851 after its erection in 1850, so did the Cleveland Ledge Light experience its initial test during the hurricane of 1944. The light is located six miles west of the Cape Cod Canal. While Minot's Light fell over into the sea, the Cleveland Ledge Light built in 1941, successfully "rode out" the gale which threatened its safety.

Lieutenant Olie P. Swenson of Bourne was commanding officer aboard the lighthouse when the hurricane hit from the southeast around eight o'clock September 14.

Four hours later the wind changed to southwest, and within half an hour a glass block skylight on the southwest side of the tower gave away, allowing tons of water to pour into the lighthouse. The entire personnel of nine men rushed to the engine room, where they bailed the water from the floor. As they worked other waves came crashing down upon them, and only the presence of a porcelain laundry tub into which they emptied their pails saved the day. The tub drained quickly every pail of water thrown into it.

Some of the coastguardsmen tried to stop up the break in the skylight, but were thrown back by the force of the waves which swept in.

The men were only able to stop the water rising in the battery room when it had reached a point less than two inches from the top of the batteries. One by one various pieces of electrical equipment flared out a flaming warning as it was short circuited. Finally Seaman LaMar Steed and Chiefboatswain's Mate Thomas E. Norris managed to reach the broken glass block and erect a barrier of oil drums, planking, and mattresses against the sea. The two men saved the lighthouse from being extinguished at a time when both the telephone and the radio were out of order.

During the gale, the launch secured to the davits thirty feet above high water mark was badly damaged by the force of the waves. The little wire-haired terrier, the only other occupant of the tower besides the nine men, showed great fright during the ordeal. But the nine men of Cleveland Ledge Light had successfully "ridden out" the first real test of the lighthouse.

THE TRIPLE STORMS OF NOVEMBER 1944

Three gales which struck the New England coast late in November caused great damage and spectacular surf in many localities. A storm which reached its height on November 17 sent breakers entirely over the top of 114-foot Minot's Light, while it pushed tons of sand and boulders up on the great Shore Drive in Winthrop, Massachusetts. Aided by a scheduled run of high tides the surf leaped the high sea wall and came down many of the Winthrop streets, filling cellars and stalling autos everywhere along the areas near the beach.

Down at Sandwich, Massachusetts, however, a tug and the coal barge it was towing were in serious trouble. Late Thursday night the barge began to suffer from the huge billows which were breaking entirely over her. The two men aboard, Captain Kidd of New Bedford and donkey-man Ules Hines, worked all night long on the pumps, but when Friday morning came it was seen that the barge was going down. Captain Oliver Givens of the tug then started toward the sinking barge, but the craft foundered before Givens could reach the location.

Thrown into the icy waters, the two barge men stayed afloat until a rescue craft from the Sandwich Coast Guard Station reached them. Exhausted, the sailors were pulled into the Coast Guard craft and later taken ashore. Meanwhile, however, the tug became fouled from the hawser from the barge, and was even then washing ashore, her wheel hopelessly tangled by the hawser. The alert watchers from the Sandwich Coast Guard Station soon had a breeches buoy set up and fired a line out to the tug. One sailor, a powerful swimmer, did not wait for the ride ashore, but jumped into the raging surf and swam to the beach. He was William Craig, of Decatur, Texas.

One by one the other crew members were brought ashore in the breeches buoy. Even the dog Jock arrived safely, in the arms of Chief Engineer Robert Marnell. Only Captain Givens was left on the tug. As he started ashore the tug shifted, putting a great strain on the lines which snapped and dropped him into the raging sea. But the coastguardsmen were ready. Seaman Donald H. Ward of Portland, Maine, unhesitatingly plunged into the roaring surf and swam out to Captain Givens. After releasing him from the lines, Ward swam ashore with Captain Givens. It was a perilous undertaking, but Seaman Ward did not falter in the face of what he believed to be his duty. Another great rescue had been accomplished by members of the United States Coast Guard, able successors to the old Life Saving Service.

The following Saturday and Sunday the waves continued to hit the New England shores with terrific force. Some as high as 115 feet were reported on Sunday from Great Brewster Island in outer Boston Harbor. The waves diminished somewhat by Monday, but that afternoon the first signs of another storm were noticed.

The second November gale of 1944 hit with tremendous force the next day. Again Winthrop, Massachusetts, received the worst damage along the coast. All Tuesday afternoon and Wednesday morning the waves made up higher and higher, until a great section of the Winthrop seawall in the vicinity of Myrtle Avenue collapsed and fell into the sea. The waves then proceeded to eat away the boulevard, and by 4 o'clock that Wednesday afternoon were reaching buildings across the forty-foot driveway. Water again poured down the streets, inundating the entire section, with two to three feet of water showing in several locations.

At high tide, which occurred shortly before 5 p.m., crowds had gathered to watch the fury of the storm at its spectacular height. Fortunate enough to climb up to the roof of a nearby house, I had my camera set hopefully waiting. A great cry from the hundreds watching the surf warned that a billow of spectacular size was even then advancing toward the beach, with a huge crest about to break. Then with a crash which could be heard for miles, jarring everyone in the vicinity, the wave struck the battered seawall. Shooting up, up, and up, until we were all spellbound by its grandeur and magnificence, the mighty ocean surge reached its peak. It was then that the picture which forms the frontispiece of this edition was taken.

The third of the November 1944 storms was the worst. Late in the night of November 29th the roar of the sea up and down the coast could be heard as it ushered in another gale, and before dawn the next morning New England knew it was in for another siege of ocean battering.

The tide at Boston came in with such fury that the reading of 13.8 feet was as high as it had been in the history of the Coast and Geodetic Survey records. Office buildings as far from the waterfront as the corner of Broad and Custom House Street were flooded. Tea Wharf, Long Wharf, and Central Wharf were among those inundated, while Atlantic Avenue was submerged in many places.

Winthrop, Massachusetts, for the third time that month, felt the tremendous force of the sea with the ocean pouring down its streets and filling hundreds of cellars. It was truly a discouraging experience for the inhabitants. The tide was the highest for many years, allowing canoeists to paddle along Shirley Street in that town.

Vast areas were under water in Salem. Historic Derby Wharf was completely covered, while the railroad tunnel at Washington and Bridge Street was flooded and filled with floating debris.

The storm was one of the worst ever to hit the Maine coast. Portland's waterfront experienced record tides and many disasters, one of the worst being the collapse of a grain elevator. Camden damage was high. A 10,000 gallon fuel tank there drained into the harbor when the high tide smashed a feed pipe. Rockland, famous maritime center, suffered considerably at the height of the storm. The tide, high at 11:30 a.m., caused damage which amounted to $40,000, at the Lafayette Packing Company, while a chimney in the city toppled into the street. Narrowly missing two small girls, the chimney wrecked an auto owned by Manager Tryon of the Western Union. Disaster befell the fishing vessel *Nancy*, moored off Rockland's public landing. The 42-foot craft, owned by Raymond Dow, dragged anchor to end her career smashing against the nearby retaining wall. The *Nancy* later sank, a total loss.

Nor was Cape Cod, already crippled by the hurricane, spared from this new storm. All along the great arm of land leading up to Provincetown the gale took its toll. In South Dartmouth twelve motorists were rescued by New Bedford firemen after they had been trapped in the swirling current at Padanavan Bridge.

Regardless of what other claim it may have to posterity, the year 1944, with four great storms, several disastrous shipwrecks, and one mighty hurricane, must go down in history as a year to be remembered in the storm and shipwreck annals of New England.

SOUTHERN NEW ENGLAND SHIPWRECKS

Based on Records of United States Engineers at Newport, R. I., furnished by Miss E. E. Freeman of Wellfleet, Mass.

*   *   *   *

Name, Date, and Location or nearest point are given when known.
All vessels are Schooners, unless otherwise indicated.
Abbreviations, when used, are explained below:

Br	= British	Sm	= Fishing Smack
Bk	= Bark	Sl	= Sloop
Bkt	= Barkentine	Sp	= Ship
Bg	= Brig	St	= Steamer
Sc	= Schooner	Yt	= Yacht

1. "Ayr," 1890, Napatree Point
2. Alice M. Ridgeway, 1891, Branch Hill Light
3. A. H. Hurlburt, 1890, Narragansett Pier
4. Alice C. Jordan, 1898, Vineyard Sound
5. Addison Center, 1900, Race Point
6. Addie P. Avery, Pamet River
7. Anna E. Kischum, Peaked Hill
8. American Chief, Orleans or Nauset
9. Anna D. Price, Peaked Hill
10. American Lloyds, Highland Light
11. Albert W. Smirk, Orleans
12. Annie F. Contan, Chatham
13. Alfred Keen, Race Point
14. Abbie H. Hodgman, Shovelful
15. A. H. Glover, Race Point
16. Abel W. Parker, Orleans
17. A. F. Ames, High Head
18. Alice Raymond, Race Point
19. Albert H. Cross
20. Abden Keene, Peaked Hill
21. Annis, 1883, Nausett
22. Bk, Altamaha
23. Amazon, Race Point
25. Sp, Asia, 1898, Great Round Shoal
26. Annie Laurie
27. Sp, Antoinette, 1889, Tuckernuck
28. Argo, 1896
29. Artemus Tirrel, 1889, Shovelful
30. Albert Woodbury, Monomoy
31. Annie E. Moore, 1890, Handkerchief
32. Ada H. Pevere, Chatham
33. Anna Elizabeth, 1890, Chatham
34. Anna Eliza, 1880, Wood End
35. Amelia G. Weyland, 1890, Chatham
36. Augustus Hunt, 1891, Bearses Shoal
37. Alice J. Crabtree, 1891, Handkerchief
38. Augustus W. Yates, Provincetown
39. Annie W. Akers, 1893, Shovelful
40. Andrew Peters, 1894, Common Flats
41. Abbie S. Walker, 1894, Provincetown
42. A. M. Burham, 1895, Handkerchief
43. Br Sc, Arthur M. Gibson, 1896, Handkerchief
44. Alfaretta S. Suare, 1897, Stone Horse
45. Anna L. Sanborn, 1896, Monomoy
46. Aetna, 1894, Handkerchief
47. Alneida, 1896, Race Point
48. Ann, 1896, Orleans
49. Br Sc, A. G. Heisler, 1897, Cahoons Hollow
50. Br Sc, Arona, 1898, Handkerchief
51. Albert L. Butler, 1898, Peaked Hill
52. Agnes, 1898, Provincetown
53. Allen H. Jones, 1898, Provincetown
54. Alice B. Phillips, 1899, Race Point
55. Sl, Active, 1899, Wood End
56. Ada J. Campbell, 1899, Wood End
57. Sl, Avalon, 1900, Nauset
58. Annie E. Lane, 1901, Nantucket Shoal
59. Yt, Adventure, 1901, Wood End
60. Alfred W. Fiske, 1901, Monomoy
61. Br Sc, Atrato, 1901, Handkerchief
62. Amanda E., 1901, Chathams Roads
63. Alice T. Boardman, 1902, Harding's Beach
64. Br Sc, Annie Laura, 1902, Shovelful
65. Ada F. Brown, 1903, Stone Horse
66. Albert T. Stearns, 1903, Shovelfull
67. Agnes E. Manson, 1903, Rose & Crown
68. Br Bk, Abertina, 1903, Muskegat Shoals
69. Alaska, 1900, Nantucket Bar
70. Annie E. Randolph, 1897, Orleans
71. Adelaide, Pt. Judith
72. A. H. Bowman, Pt. Judith
73. Alida, W. of Pt. Judith
74. Amelia, 1864, Pt. Judith
75. American Eagle, 1870, S. Pt. Judith
76. St, Acusionet, 1870, S. Pt. Judith
77. Anna R. Eaton, 1875, Block Island
78. A. E. Sterris, 1876, Block Island
79. Armistice, 1878, Whale Rock
80. Alexander, 1879, Block Island
81. St, Ashland, 1879, Point Judith
82. Arctic, 1879, Stephens Cove
83. Annie Whiting, 1883, Block Island
84. Adrianna, 1884, Block Island
85. Annie Godfrey, 1884, Block Island
86. Annie Steel, 1884, Block Island
87. Augusta, 1884, Lewis Pt., B. I.
88. Ada Herbert, 1884, E. Block Island
89. Anna B. Jacobs, 1885, Block Island
90. Anthony Benton, 1885, Watch Hill
91. Argo, 1885, Fishers Island
92. Almon Bacon, 1885, Pt. Judith
93. Allen Green, 1886, Pt. Judith
94. Annie Steel, 1886, Block Island
95. Achilles, 1887, Lewis Pt.
96. Artist, 1888, Napatree Pt.
97. Anita, 1888, Pt. Judith
98. Annie G., 1888, Block Island
99. Bk, Alexander Campbell, 1888, Block Island
100. Avenger, 1890, Watch Hill
101. A. H. Hurlburt, 1890, Narragansett Pier
102. A. J. Boardman, 1891, N. Block Island
103. Alice M. Ridgeway, 1891, Watch Hill Beach
104. Arvesta, 1893, Dickens Reef
105. Agricola, 1894, Napatree Pt.
106. Allen, 1894, Fishers Island
107. Active, 1895, Old Break, B. I.
108. Angie, 1896, Dick Spring, B. I.
109. Arabella, 1897, Block Island
110. Sl, Anna M., 1897, Block Island

111. Ann Elizabeth, 1902, New Shoreham
112. Amanda E., 1902, Pt. Judith
113. Ava, 1898, Dandy Point
114. Actress, 1898, Brentons Point
115. Agnes, 1898, Pt. Judith
116. Addie M. Anderson, 1899, N. Whale Rock
117. Sm, Annie, 1899, Quonochoutaug
118. Alma, 1899, New Shoreham
119. Annie E. Fowler, 1900, New Shoreham
120. Sl, Ariel, 1902, Quonochoutaug
121. Sl, Allison, 1902, Watch Hill
122. Alfred Huddel, 1876, Lion's Head
123. Acorn, 1891, Beaver Tail
124. Addie, 1903, W. Port Hyannis Harbor
125. Belle R. Hill, 1896, Watch Hill
126. Blue Jay, 1896, Point Judith
127. B. D. Haskins, 1885, Nauset
128. Belle A. Nauss, Pamet River
129. Bkt, Belmont, Peaked Hill
130. Bg, Black Swan
131. Belle R. Hull, 1896, Watch Hill
132. Benjamin Cole, 1898, Watch Hill
133. Br Sc, Bessie Parker, 1895, Shovelful
134. Benjamin Oliver, 1895, Bearses Shoal
135. Boyd & Leeds, 1897, Race Point
136. Sl, Braganza, 1902, Wood End
137. Sl, Blackbird, 1900, Cahoons Hollow
138. Braganza, 1902, Race Point
139. Belle Hundy, 1896, Long Shoal
140. B. L. Shuman, 1896, Hawes Shoal
141. Br Bg, ..., 1862, Point Judith
142. Bg, ..., 1862, Point Judith
143. Bayuduci, 1877, Block Island
144. Bobb, 1883, Block Island
145. Belle O'Neil, 1883, Beaver Tail
146. Berbie Vierce, 1886, Block Island
147. Barge, Bonanza, 1886, Watch Hill
148. Black Swan, 1887, New Shoreham
149. Bill Stowe, 1890, Narragansett Pier Beach
150. Bradford & French, 1894, Dickens Point
151. Brunhild, 1895, Sugar Reef, Watch Hill
152. Blue Jay, 1896, Point Judith
153. Bessie M. Dewitt, 1896, Block Island
154. Sl, Bess, 1897, Point Judith
155. Sl, Bannent, 1897, Narragansett Pier
156. Benjamin D. Price, 1899, Short Beaver Tail
157. Bucco, 1886, Lion's Head
158. Bg, ..., 1867, Brenton's Reef
159. Bg, ..., 1865, Beaver Tail
160. Bg, ..., 1865, Beaver Tail
161. Bk, ..., 1870, Jones Ledge
162. Charles S. Rogers, 1879, Cape Cod
163. City of Gloucester, 1879, Whaleman's Shoal
164. Carrie E. Sayward, 1898, Provincetown
165. Sl, Carrie Lida, 1898, Provincetown
166. Carl D. Lothrop, Race Point
167. Cyrus Chamberlain, Peaked Hill
168. Sl, C. E. Trumbull, Peaked Hill
169. Clina, 1887, Orleans
170. City of Augusta, Peaked Hill
171. C. E. Schmidt, Chatham
172. Bg, Clara J. Adams, 1881, Highland
173. Chatanooga, 1890, Orleans
174. Clara Jane, Peaked Hill
175. Br Sc, Cricket, 1893, High Head
176. Commander, Race Point
177. C. A. Campbell, 1895, Pamet River
178. Calvin P. Harris, Race Point
179. Bg, Circassian, 1896, Chatham
180. Carrie M. Richardson, Race Point
181. Calvin B. Orcutt, 1894, Pollock Rip
182. Carrie W., 1887, Highland
183. St, Cottage City, 1893, Chatham Bar
184. Bg, Clement, Whale Rock
185. Chalmet, 1893, Pollock Rip
186. Clarice Walker, 1895, Stone Horse
187. Br Sc, Clifton, 1896, Shovelful
188. Centennial, 1896, Peaked Hill
189. Cora C. Meadow, 1896, Bearses Shoal
190. Caviare, 1896, Provincetown
191. Br Sc, Clifford, 1897, Wood End
192. Cora E. Smith, 1897, Shovelful
193. C. W. Morse, 1897, Race Point
194. Carrie E. Philips, 1897, Wood End
195. Carrie E. Payson, 1898, Chatham
196. Champion, 1898, Provincetown
197. Cathie C. Berrig, 1899, Peaked Hill
198. Clarence H. Venner, 1899, Shovelfull
199. Carrie C., 1899, Wood End
200. Barge, Calabria, 1899, Monomoy
201. Barge, CRR of N. J., 1900, Monomoy
202. Clara Jane, 1901, Orleans
203. Br Sc, Colonia, 1901, Wood End
204. Cavaire, 1902, Wood End
205. Cape Cod, 1902, Provincetown
206. Clara Goodwin, 1903, Pollock Rip
207. Carlotta, 1895, Tuckernuck Shoal
208. Canary, 1899, Muskeget
209. Clara Goodwin, 1903, Monomoy
210. Bk, C. B. Hamilton, 1866, Pt. Judith
211. Catherine W. May, 1876, Pt. Judith
212. Caroline Kuneshe, 1877, Block Island
213. Cat, ..., 1879, Harbor Neck Pt, Block Isl.
214. Cat, ..., 1880, Napatru Pt.
215. Cuckoo, 1882, Pt. Judith
216. Convenient, 1883, Block Island
217. St, George W. Danielson, 1883, Block Island
218. Charles L. Mitchell, 1883, Fishers Island
219. C. B. Payne, 1883, Block Island
220. Connecticut, 1883, East, Block Island
221. Clarissa Allen, 1884, Stonington Pt.
222. Cleo Chileot, 1886, East, Watch Hill
223. C. W. Lock, 1886, Napatree Pt.
224. Commodore, 1888, New Shoreham
225. Clifton, 1888, Meeting House Shoal
226. Clifton, 1888, Pt. Judith
227. St, Crown Prince, 1889, Scarborough Beach
228. Carrie A. Lane, 1890, Napatree Pt.
229. Cat, Bessie Fiske, 1894, New Shoreham
230. Cassia, 1894, New Shoreham
231. Sl, Cora, 1895, Brentons Pt.
232. Clarissa Allen, 1896, Pt. Judith
233. Chehegan, 1897, Block Island
234. Coguette, 1892, New Shoreham
235. Sl, Crocodile, 1898, Quonockontaug
236. Caroline Ann Cornelia, 1876, Beaver Tail
237. Concord, 1843, Shoemakers Place
238. Chas. E. Raymond, 1868, Long Gully
239. Daniel M. French, 1889, Watch Hill Light
240. D. B. Haskins, 1885, Nauset
241. Druid, Pamet River
242. David S. Siner, 1889, Pollock Rip
243. Daniel B. Fearing, 1896, Cahoons Hollow
244. Dora Mathews, 1902, Monomoy
245. Danom, 1890, Chatham
246. Dora M. French, 1893, Shovelful
247. Delaware, 1899, Shovelful
248. Damietta & Joanna, 1901, Shovelful
249. Douglas Haynes, 1901, Little Round Shoal
250. Damozella, 1899, Eel Point
251. David J. Lee, 1836, Nauset
252. Dawson City, 1903, Peaked Hill
253. Dove, 1887, Bordens Reef
254. Douglas Haynes, 1890, Brentons Reef
255. Sl, Douglas Haynes, 1899, Watch Hill
256. Sl, Due, 1903, Block Island
257. David A. Barry, 1875, North Beaver Tail
258. E. W. Merchant, 1887, Shovelful Shoal
259. Ethel Ward, 1892, Cape Cod
260. Emma M. Dyer, 1899, Cape Cod
261. Eliza, 1899, Rose & Crown Shoal
262. Elsie M. Smith, 1902, Chatham Bar
263. Sl, Eagle, 1902, Off Gay Head
264. Edna Harwood, N. E. Nauset
265. Edith B. Coombs, Off High Head
266. Effie Sweet, 1880, Off High Head
267. E. H. Weaver, 1888, Pleasant Bay
268. Edmund, Off Chatham
269. Ethel Swift, Peaked Hill
270. Effort, Chatham
271. Ethel Maud, 1897, Race Point
272. Eddie Pierce, High Head
273. Emma K. Smalley, 1891, Chatham
274. Emma, Nauset
275. Esther Ward, 1892, Chatham
276. Bg, Emily T. Sheldon, Highland
277. Everett Webster, 1890, Stone Horse Shoal
278. Emma G. Edwards, 1879, N. E. Tuckernuck
279. Ellen Perkins, 1896, Great Point
280. E. L. Dow, 1899, Coskata

281. Emma C. Middleton, 1900, Great Point
282. E. A. Williams, 1891, Monomoy
283. Edith T. Gandy, 1891, Monomoy
284. Elizabeth M. Cook, 1892, Monomoy
285. Eva May, 1892, Handkerchief
286. Eliza B. Emory, 1893, Common Flats
287. Ella B. Kimball, 1894, Common Flats
288. Errola C., 1894, Common Flats
289. Edith and May, 1894, Common Flats
290. Ellen Morrison, 1894, Shovelful
291. Sl, Elgin, 1894, Monomoy
292. Eliza Levansaler, 1895, Race Point
293. Ellen Lincoln, 1895, Nauset
294. Edith L. Conley, 1896, Handkerchief
295. Edgar Randall, 1896, Race Point
296. St, Elihu Thompson, 1897, Pollock
297. Empress, 1897, Monomoy Pt.
298. Excelsior, 1898, Handkerchief
299. Eva Lender, 1898, Chatham
300. Sl, Ella Frances, 1898, Provincetown
301. Eliza, 1899, Rose & Crown Reef
302. Empire State, 1899, Cahoons Hollow
303. Electa Baily, 1901, Chatham Roads
304. Bk, Ethel, 1901, Monomoy
305. Emma D. Endicott, 1902, Chatham
306. Elsie M. Smith, 1902, Orleans
307. Edward Burton, 1902, Handkerchief
308. Emeline G. Sawyer, 1903–, Common Flats
309. Edwarda, 1895, Great Point Rip
310. E. L. Dow, 1899, Nantucket
311. Enterprise, 1896, Long Shoal
312. Emma Bacon, Point Judith
313. Ella, Point Judith
314. Eastern Star, Point Judith
315. Sl, Elizabeth, Point Judith
316. Eve, Noyes Beach
317. Express Tilton, 1874, Beaver Tail
318. E. A. Hooper, 1878, Block Island
319. Edward H. Norton, 1881, Narragansett Pier
320. Emma K. Small, 1883, Block Island
321. Eva Maud, 1884, Wicopesset Island
322. Ellen Maria, 1883, Catumb
323. Earl P. Mason, 1888, Point Judith
324. Ellen B., 1888, Block Island
325. Eddie H. Weeks, 1891, Block Island
326. East Wind, 1892, Pt. Judith
327. Sl, Ethel Swift, 1893, Bonnet Pt.
328. E. F. Gammage, 1893, New Shoreham
329. Earl & Nettie, 1894, Block Island
330. Eddie H. Weeks, 1894, Block Island
331. Sl, Edna, 1894, Sandy Pt.
332. Eva Leonard, 1895, Rugged Pt.
333. Evelyn, 1895, Block Island
334. Emerald, 1896, New Shoreham
335. Edith Bacon, 1897, New Shoreham
336. Edward M. Laughlin, 1897, Pt. Judith
337. Edward H. Smead, 1898, Block Island
338. Emily, 1899, Watch Hill
339. Estrella Day, 1870, Beaver Tail
340. Ezra H. Day, 1869, Whale Rock
341. Fortuna, 1894, Off Race Point
342. Fortuna, 1896, Highland Light
343. Farmer R. Walker, 1899, Race Point
344. Florence Pearl, 1899, Shovelful Shoal
345. Francis Hatch, Off Chatham
346. Fred & Elmer, 1894, Provincetown
347. Bk, Fram (Norwegian), 1878, High Head
348. Geo. S. Tarbell, 1891, Bearses Shoal
349. Bkt, F. A. Willey, Off Cahoons Hollow
350. Fred Walton, 1890, Pollock Rip
351. Fawn, Off Orleans
352. Florida, 1891, Handkerchief
353. Bk, Fredericka, 1883, Pleasant Bay
354. Francis S. Orne, 1891, Shovelful
355. Bk, Francisco, Chatham
356. Fleetwing, 1893, Coskata
357. F. H. Odiorne, 1888, Handkerchief
358. Franklin, 1888, Provincetown
359. Franklin, 1893, Bearses Shoal
360. Barge, Fidelia, 1894, Pollock Rip
361. Br St, Forest Holms, 1896, Cahoon's Hollow
362. Frank Foster, 1898, Provincetown
363. F. H. Smith, 1898, Provincetown
364. Florence Pearl, 1899, Handkerchief
365. Francis Whalen, 1901, Provincetown

366. Florida, 1898, Cahoon's Hollow
367. Fly Away, 1902, Stone Horse
368. Frances R. Rand, 1900, Tuckernuck
369. Franklin Pierce, 1883, Block Island
370. Favorite, 1884, E. Block Island
371. Fred A. Carl, 1825, Watch Hill
372. Sl, Flesun, 1887, Watson Pier
373. Sl, Favorite, 1887, New Shoreham
374. Frank Herbert, 1889, Narraganset Pier
375. F. W. Fredson, 1890, Old Schooner Pt.
376. F. A. Pike, 1890, Catumb Reef
377. Sl, Fashion, 1892, Ft. Adams
378. Fannie Whitmore, 1894, Noyes Beach
379. F. M. Allen, 1895, Napatru Pt.
380. Four Brothers, 1896, Common Pt. Cove, B.I.
381. Fellowship, 1852, Hulls Cove
382. Florida, 1871, Lion's Head
383. George A. Pierce, 1901, Catumb Rocks
384. Gertie Smith, 1902, Newport
385. Giovanni, Highland & High Head
386. George H. Squires, Off Nauset
387. Gov. J. Y. Smith, Race Point
388. Granite State, Off Pleasant Bay
389. George M. Adams, Nauset
390. General Scott, Off Highland Light
391. George F. Edmunds, 1890, Handkerchief
392. Grecian, Off Pleasant Bay
393. George Nevinger, Great Pt. Light
394. George S. Tarbell, 1888, Pollock Rip
395. Grampus, 1890, Shovelfull
396. George B. Marble, 1892, Chatham Roads
397. Grey Eagle, 1890, Wellfleet
398. Gertie S. Winsor, 1896, Race Point
399. Grace C. Hadley, 1895, Shovelful
400. Bkt, Golden Sheaf, 1896, Pollock Rip
401. Sl, Gracie, 1898, Provincetown
402. Sl, Golden Eagle, 1899, Wood End
403. St, Angelia B. Nickerson, Provincetown
404. Gladstone, 1901, Wood End
405. Gen. Sheridan, 1900, Highland
406. Br Sp, George Walker, Pt. Judith
407. George R. Smith, 1902, Monomoy Point
408. Bg, Guard, 1884, Watch Hill Race
409. George Walker, 1882, Wicopessit Island
410. Barge, Gerogette, 1887, Block Island
411. Gardiner Colby, 1887, Block Island
412. Sl, Guenn, 1888, Napatree
413. Glimpse, 1887, Lower Pier Dock
414. George A. Upton, 1896, Newport
415. George E. Bentley, 1895, N. Block Island
416. Sl, Genevieve, 1902, New Shoreham
417. Bg, Highlander, 1893, Fishers Island
418. Harry Friend, 1893, Shovelful Shoal
419. Henry A. Paull, Race Point
420. Henry Lippet, Pamet River
421. Hannah E. Shubert, Off Highland
422. Hattie I. Philips, 1890, Handkerchief
423. H. A. Dewitt, 1888, Common Flats
424. Hyena, 1890, Wood End
425. Henry A. Little, Pollock Rip
426. Henry L. Philips, 1891, Long Point
427. Helen R. Low, 1892, Provincetown
428. Harry L. Whelan, 1892, Billingsgate
429. Harmona, 1892, Handkerchief
430. Bkt, Harry Nowell, Pollock Rip
431. Henry Washington, 1895, Pollock Rip
432. Harriet C. Kalin, 1895, Pollock Rip
433. Hattie & Lottie, Bearses Shoal
434. Haroldine, 1895, Nauset
435. Barge, H. C. Libby, 1897, Nantucket
436. Helen G. Moseley, 1898, Bearses Shoal
437. Bkt, Harriet S. Jackson, 1898, Monomoy
438. Harrie M. Young, 1898, Provincetown
439. Helena, 1899, Peaked Hill
440. Sl, Helen, 1899, High Head
441. Humboldt, 1899, Monomoy
442. Helen, 1900, Orleans
443. Horace W. Macomber, 1902, Nauset
444. Henry, 1902, Peaked Hill
445. Br Sc, Helen Maud, 1903, Shovelful
446. Henry B. Fiske, 1903, Monomoy Pt.
447. Helen L. Smith, Point Judith
448. Harriet Lewis, 1874, Beaver Tail
449. Henry W., 1875, Point Judith
450. Henry H. Scavy, 1875, Point Judith

451. Henry J. May, 1876, Block Island
452. Sl, Hadley, 1884, Fishers Island
453. Hope Haines, 1885, Catumb Reef
454. Harry A. Barry, 1887, S. Pt. Judith
455. Hornet, 1887, New Shoreham
456. Henry H. Olds, 1888, N. W. Whale Rock
457. Henry White, 1892, Quonochoutaug
458. H. A. Dening, 1894, Watch Hill
459. St, Harry E., 1895, Brentons Reef
460. Henry L. Wyman, 1896, E. Block Island
461. Helen F. Whitten, 1896, Newport
462. H. M. Rowley, 1897, Block Island
463. Israel H. Day, 1867, Whale Rock
464. Ira Laffrinier, 1897, Nauset
465. Ida May, 1889, Handkerchief
466. Isiah K. Stetson, 1898, Shoveful
467. Isiah Hart, 1897, Pollock Rip
468. Sc Yt, Ivanhoe, Monomoy
469. Isaac Collins, 1898, Provincetown
470. Independence, 1862, N. Pt. Judith
471. Isaac Webb, Noyes Beach
472. Imogene Diverty, 1873, Pt. Judith
473. St, Commodore, 1863, Pt. Judith
474. Island Belle, 1884, Block Island
475. Illinoise, 1880, Pt. Judith
476. Isabella Jewett, 1886, W. Quaug Beach
477. Idlewild, 1884, Sand Hill Cove, Pt. Judith
478. Isaac H. Borden, 1888, Pt. Judith
479. Ida & Jane, 1887, New Shoreham
480. Irene, 1898, Mussel Bar
481. Sl, Inez, 1896, New Shoreham
482. Ira & Abbey, 1898, Pt. Judith
483. Juno, 1880, Provincetown
484. J. W. Campbell, 1896, Off Long Island
485. John Rommel, Jr., Race Point
486. J. H. Ells, 1887, Off Nauset
487. J. G. Babcock, Off Orleans
488. Joseph G. Stover, 1887, Pleasant Bay
489. John L. Merrill, Off Peaked Hill
490. John H. McManus, Cahoon's Hollow
491. J. A. Hatfield, Peaked Hill
492. James Drinan, Race Point
493. J. W. Campbell, 1885, S. Nauset
494. J. P. Wyman, Peaked Hill
495. Julia E. Whalen, Race Point
496. Br Sp, Jason, 1893, Peaked Hill
497. Job H. Jackson, Peaked Hill
498. Julia S. Bailey, Race Point
499. Nellie Lamper, 1897, Nauset
500. Marie O. Teel, 1894, Handkerchief
501. J. Arthur Lord, 1900, Coskata
502. James H. Hoyt, 1902, Great Point
503. John W. Hall, 1879, Tuckernuck
504. J. H. Carey, 1890, Shovelful
505. Jennie Phinny, 1890, Pollock Rip
506. John M. Ball, 1890, Wood End
507. Jane L. Newton, 1890, Monomoy
508. Jessie W. Starr, 1891, Shovelful
509. James H. Tripp, 1891, Provincetown
510. John P. Kelsey, 1891, Handkerchief
511. James M. Flanagan, 1893, Chatham
512. Jonathan Bourne, 1896, Pollock Rip
513. James A. Parsons, 1896, Handkerchief
514. Jordan L. Mott, 1898, Provincetown
515. Joseph Warren, 1899, Wood End
516. Jennie Greenbank, 1899, Chatham
517. Br Sc, John T. Culliman, 1901, Shovelfull
518. Br Sc, John S. Parker, 1901, Orleans
519. John F. Randall, 1902, Stone Horse
520. Jennie C. May, 1902, Peaked Hill
521. John C. Fitzpatrick, 1902, Shovelfull
522. Jennie E. Meservy, 1902, Monomoy
523. James B. Deputy, 1894, Handkerchief
524. John T. Williams, 1903, Orleans
525. James G. Blaine, 1903, Bearses Shoal
526. Joseph C. Baxter, Fishing Rocks
527. John Mooris, 1874, Dicken's Reef
528. John Mayo, 1879, Watch Hill Reef
529. Joseph Fitch, 1880, Sugar Reef
530. Julia Elizabeth, 1881, Catumb Reef
531. J. Kenneddy, 1883, Sugar Reef
532. J. Howell, 1883, Block Island
533. Julia A. Tate, 1884, Point Judith
534. John A. Matheson, 1885, Block Island
535. Josephine G. Colyer, 1885, N. Block Island

536. John Crookford, 1885, Mussel Bar
537. John Mann, 1886, W. Block Island
538. Josephine B. Knowles, 1886, Napatree Pt.
539. Jennie A. Cheyney, 1887, E. Fishers Island
540. John Strout, 1887, Seal Rock
541. John Teeney, 1888, New Shoreham
542. Josie Reeves, 1888, New Shoreham
543. Bg, John Welsh, 1888, Point Judith
544. John Proctor, 1891, Wicopesset Island
545. John Paul, 1893, Green Hill Point
546. James Ives, 1893, Sand Hill Cove
547. Jennie, 1894, Point Judith
548. John W. Smart, 1884, Catumb Reef
549. J. G. Pierson, 1894, New Shoreham
550. Jennie, 1895, Quonochontaug
551. Josie F., 1895, Napatree Point
552. Bg, John Harvey, 1898, Point Judith
553. Jonathan Cone, 1898, Mussel Bar
554. J. G. Fell, 1899, Mussel Bar
555. Bg, John J. Burlee, 1903, Watch Hill
556. Jennie R. DuBois, 1903, New Shoreham
556a. Bg, J. Palmer, 1838, Beavertail
557. Kate M. Hilton, Nauset
558. Kattie J. Burrett, 1890, Nauset
559. Br Bk, Kate Harding, 1892, Highland Light
560. Barge, Katahdin, 1898, Monomoy
561. Kate G. Robinson, 1900, Peaked Hill
562. Kate & Mary, 1902, Quonochontaug
563. Ella T. Little, 1898, Latimers Reef
564. Lady of the Ocean, 1898, Napatree Point
565. Lightning, 1887, Scituate
566. Lizzie W. Hannum, 1895, Buzzards Bay
567. Lizzie M. Center, 1901, Muskeget Channel
568. L. B. Snow, Off Highland Light
569. Leonessa, Peaked Hill
570. Levanter, Peaked Hill
571. Lanie Cobb, Chatham
572. Look Out, Pamet River
573. Br Sc, Lottie B., 1893, Nauset
574. Lexington, Chatham
575. L. F. Gould, Pleasant Bay
576. Laura Brown, Highland Light
577. Lottie S. Haskins, 1896, Orleans
578. Lavinia Bell, 1891
579. Lizzie Babcock, 1888, Beares Shoal
580. Lizzie Young, 1890, Handkerchief
581. Little Jennie, 1892, Race Point
582. Lady Leavitt, 1893, Provincetown
583. Laura E. Misser, 1894, Pollock Rip
584. Lettie H. Howard, 1894, Highland Light
585. Laura L. Sprague, 1894, Handkerchief
586. Lottie S. Haskins, 1895, Race Point
587. Lewis Jane, 1896, Chatham
588. Loderick Bell, 1897, Peaked Hill
589. L. J. Witmore, 1897, Shovelful
590. Lorna Doone, 1898, Chatham
591. Lucia Porter, 1898, Peaked Hill
592. Sl, Lila, 1898, Provincetown
593. Lester A. Lewis, 1898, Wood End
594. Letha May, 1898, Provincetown
595. Laura Robinson, 1900, Pollock Rip
596. Lizzie Smith, 1900, Monomoy
597. Br Sc, Lily, 1901, Mauset
598. Leonora, 1901, Nantucket Shoals
599. Liassa, 1901, Monomoy
600. Lizzie Griffin, 1901, Race Point
601. Lewis H. Giles, 1902, Wood End
602. Lyman M. Law, 1903, Pamet River
603. L. P. (?), 1892, Nauset
604. Laura Messer, 1895, Block Island
605. L. M. Lamond, 1897, Block Island
606. Lizzie Cochrane, 1882, Point Judith
607. Lavina Campbell, 1883, Block Island
608. Laura E. Gammage, 1884, Block Island
609. Laela Bell, 1884, Block Island
610. Lethe Linwood, 1885, Block Island
611. Lizzie B. Barker, 1885, Block Island
612. Laura Loon, 1886, Block Island
613. Lucy A. Blossom, 1886, Watch Hill Point
614. L. S. Livering, 1886, Block Island
615. Bk, Lady of the Lake, 1890, Block Island
616. Sp, Lydia Skolfield, 1891, Newport
617. Sl, Lizzie, 1894, New Shoreham
618. Leonessa, 1894, Watsons Pier
619. L. C. Foster, 1894, Block Island

620. Lady of the Lake, 1896, New Shoreham
621. L. T. Witmore, 1897, Catumb Rocks
622. Laurel, 1898, Catumb Rocks
623. St, Lewiston, 1898, Point Judith
624. Sl, Lorna, 1902, Quonachontaug
625. St, L. L. Fedensen, 1902, New Shoreham
626. Tug, Leyden, 1903, New Shoreham
627. Bg, Leomontin, 1853 or 4, Beaver Tail
628. Maggie Cummings, 1891, Napatree Point
629. Menumetrick, 1893, Watch Hill Point
630. Modeno, 1878, Cape Cod
631. Monmouth, 1887, Cape Cod
632. Mondego, 1900, Cape Cod
633. Monticello, 1902, Cuttyhunk
634. Bk, Mary Evans, Highland Light
635. Maggie A. Fisk, Cahoons Hollow
636. Miles Standish, Highland Light
637. Mary Cobb, Chatham
638. Marion Draper, Pleasant Bay
639. Marshall Parin, Pleasant Bay
640. J. M. Morales, Chatham
641. Mary Riley, Peaked Hill
642. St, May, Race Point
643. Mary Doane, 1885, Highland Light
644. Mary A. Hood, Race Point
645. Maggie & Lilly, Race Point
646. Maggie Mitchell, 1893, Pleasant Bay
647. Minnie C. Taylor, 1894, Coskata
648. Maggie Abbott, 1898, Watch Hill
649. Maud H. Dudley, 1897, Watch Hill
650. Masisett, 1900, Watch Hill
651. Mail, 1890, Handkerchief
652. Minnie F. Paine, 1888, Provincetown
653. Sl Yt, Myrtle F., 1890, Pollock Rip
654. Marie O. Teel, 1890, Pollock Rip
655. M. M. Merriman, 1891, Shoveful
656. Maggie J. Chadwick, 1892, Handkerchief
657. St, Minnie & Irwin, 1893, Provincetown
658. Moonbeam, 1893, Pollock Rip
659. Mary Adelaide Randall, 1894, Handkerchief
660. Maggie Sullivan, 1894, Handkerchief
661. Morning Star, 1895, Shovelful
662. Tpl Bkt, Monte Tabor, 1896, Peaked Hill
663. Maggie M. Keogh, 1897, Wood End
664. Mary A. Tyler, 1898, N. Brewster
665. Mary Cabral, 1898, Provincetown
666. Merridita, 1899, Pollock Rip
667. Myra B. Weaver, 1900, Handkerchief
668. Mount Hope, 1900, Pollock Rip
669. St, Mary C. Hartz, 1901, Race Point
670. Mark Pendlleton, 1901, Pollock Rip
671. Maud Briggs, 1901, Nauset
672. Manomet, 1902, Wood End
673. Marjory Brown, 1902, Wood End
674. Mary Farrow, 1902, Monomoy
675. Maggie Hatties, 1903, Rose & Crown Shoal
676. Matilda D. Berda, 1894, Great Point Rip
677. Melrose, 1902, Monomoy Point
678. Mary E. Link, 1893, Monomoy
679. Mary E. McHale, Quonachontaug
680. Bg, Meteor, 1869, Point Judith
681. Minnie Kinnie, 1875, Point Judith
682. Bg, Matilda S., 1876, Point Judith
683. Memento, 1879, Watch Hill Reef
684. Mary H. Stockham, 1881, Watch Hill Reef
685. Monmouth, 1882, Watch Hill Reef
686. Mary A. Fisher, 1882, Watch Hill
687. Barge, Manhattan, Watch Hill
688. Marcena, 1884, Beaver Tail
689. Mollie Porter, 1885, Catumb Reef
690. Mott Haven, 1885, Point Judith
691. St, Miranda, 1886, Point Judith
692. Mary Natt, 1886, Point Judith
693. Sp, Mary L. Cushing, 1887, Block Island
694. Mystery, 1887, New Shoreham
695. Maggie J. Smith, 1887, Narragansett Pier
696. Mary A. Dryoy, 1887, Point Judith
697. Meteor, 1888, W. Block Island
698. Maggie Cummings, 1891, Napatree Point
699. Tug, Mars, 1892, Point Judith
700. Deleted
701. Multnomah, 1893, New Shoreham
702. Sl, Mary, 1893, New Shoreham
703. Barge, Magella, 1894, Point Judith
704. Maria, 1894, New Shoreham

705. Maggie Abbot, 1896, Watch Hill
706. Sl, Murial, 1895, Watch Hill
707. Mary A. Brown, 1897, W. Block Island
708. Maria, 1897, Block Island
709. Mary Ellen, 1898, Point Judith
710. Maud H. Dudley, 1897, Wicopesset Island
711. Sl, Martha, 1900 Block Island
712. Mary Miller, 1898, Sand Hill Cove
713. Mary, 1864, Lions Head
714. Mail, 1900, Napatree Point
715. Sl, Motto, 1866, Beaver Tail
716. Mary Ann Eliza, 1871, Beaver Tail
717. Nautilus, 1898, Provincetown
718. Nimble, High Head
719. Nellie V. Rokes, 1889, Chatham
720. N. H. Skinner, 1900, Handkerchief
721. Nellie Lamper, 1893, Rogers Shoal
722. Br Sch, Nantasket, 1895, Bearses Shoal
723. Nellie M. Snow, 1896, Wood End
724. Nellie W. Snow, 1899, Provincetown
725. Nathaniel P. Doane, 1899, Race Point
726. Nellie Blanch, 1900, Race Point
727. Nightingale, 1901, Wood End
728. Nettie Franklin, 1902, Monomoy Point
729. Nellie S. Pickering, 1896, Long Shovel
730. Norman, 1903, Monomoy Point
731. Nelson Harvey, Whale Rock
732. Bg, Normany, 1864, Point Judith
733. Bg, Nellie, 1880, Fishers Island
734. Nellie D. Vaughn, 1898, Narragansett Beach
735. Nellie Eaton, 1888, Sturgeon Point
736. Bg, Nereus, 1892, Point Judith
737. Bg Nellie Pickup, 1893, New Shoreham
738. Sl, Nettje, 1894, New Shoreham
739. St, Maverick, 1896, Point Judith
740. North Star, 1900, Block Island
741. New York Pilot Boat, 1889, Lion's Head
742. Nellie Doe, 1867, North Beavertail
743. Oliver Ames, High Head
744. Oliver Scholfield, 1895, Chatham
745. Oliver Wendell Holmes, 1900, Monomoy
746. Opera, 1885, Nauset
747. St, Oceanus, Point Judith
748. Bg, Open Sea, 1879, Napatree Point
749. Ocean Spray, 1887, Block Island
750. Oakwood, 1888, Narragansett Pier
751. Oliver Chase, 1893, Point Judith Beach
752. Span St, Olinda, 1895, Fishers Island
753. Scow, Ocean View, 1897, Block Island
754. Sl, Opitsah, 1903, Quonochotaug
755. ———— Olds, 1887, Whale Rock
756. Pow Wow, Cahoon's Hollow
757. Bg, Persis Hinckley, Off Highland Light
758. Plymouth Rock, High Head
759. Pallas, 1882, Off Nauset Beach
760. Progress
761. Providence, 1883, Off Chatham
762. Phinias W. Sprague, 1889, Chatham
763. Paunchita, Off Peaked Hill
764. Panther, 1893, Provincetown
765. Perseverance, Race Point
766. Br Sc, Prudent, 1895, Handkerchief
767. Br Sc, Phoenix, 1896, Orleans
768. Philomena Manta, 1888, Provincetown
769. Sl Pointer, 1899, Race Point
770. St, Ponyer Quertier, 1899, Orleans
771. Paxinos, 1902, Wood End
772. Paxinos, 1902, Pollock Rip
773. Pochasset, 1897, Orleans
774. Propeller, Green Hill
775. Pinzi, Block Island
776. Paul & Thomas, 1880, Fishers Island
777. Paladium, 1881, S. W. Pt. Judith
778. St, Professor Morse, 1883, N. Block Island
779. Path Finder, 1887, New Shoreham
780. Plow Boy, 1888, Bartletts Reef
781. Pocahontas, 1890, Black Rock, B. I.
782. Sl, Parole, 1893, New Shoreham
783. Pontoons 1, 2, 3, 4, 1893, Narrangansett Pier
784. Promised Safety, 1895, Reef
785. Priscilla, 1893, Napatree
786. Pawtuckaway, 1896, Pt. Judith
787. Percy, 1897, Block Island
788. Bg, Plover, 1899, Sandy Pt.
789. Quoddy, 1888, Handkerchief

790. Richard K. Fox, Dec. 30, 1886, N. Chatham
791. Robert B. Smith, Peaked Hill
792. Rival, Race Point
793. Raymond T. Maull, Race Point
794. Ralph M. Eaton, Race Point
795. R. F. Hart, Race Point
796. Rebecca Bartlett, 1889, Shovelful
797. St, Rhode Island, The Bonnet
798. R. L. Tay, 1890, Chatham
799. Ring Dove, 1890, Chatham
800. Robert Bryon, 1890, Chatham
801. Race Horse, 1890, Pollock Rip
802. Richard Law, 1891, Monomoy
803. Rebecca J. Moulton, 1893, Pollock Rip
804. Rogers, 1893, Handkerchief
805. Rover, 1893, Provincetown
806. Richard F. C. Hartley, 1894, Stone Horse
807. Rebecca A. Toulane, 1894, Bearses Shoal
808. Rocky Glen, 1895, Shovelful
809. Robert Moore, 1895, Stone Horse
810. Richard Law, 1896, Nauset
811. Ranger, 1897, Chatham
812. Red Rover, 1898, Peaked Hill
813. Leaming, 1899, Orleans
814. Robert Byron, 1899, Race Point
815. Rose Cabral, 1901, Wood End
816. Roger Drury, 1902, Monomoy Point
817. Br Bg, Redwood, Point Judith
818. Robin, 1875, Whale Rock
819. Rachael Vaneman, 1878, Narraganset Pier
820. Rebecca W. Hudell, 1878, Block Island
821. Rose Brothers, 1887, New Shoreham
822. Tug, Robert Lockhart, 1890, Napatru Point
823. Rose Brothers, 1891, New Shoreham
824. Ranger, 1892, New Shoreham
825. Bg, Reliance, 1893, Block Island
826. Rapican, 1896, Narraganset Pier
827. Sl, Red Rover, 1894, Block Island
828. Sl, Rambler, 1896, New Shoreham
829. Regina, 1898, Block Island
830. Rhode Island, 1900, Brereton's Reef
831. Ringleader, 1901, Hyannis Harbor
832. John N. Sherwood, 1889, Watch Hill
833. Sparkling Wave, 1879, Shovelful Shoal
834. Smuggler, 1895, Cahoon's Hollow
835. Sea Lion, North of Orleans
836. Starry Flag, Peaked Hills
837. Sarah J. Fort, N. Highland Light
838. Susan R. Stone, 1890, Race Point
839. Sarah Godfrey, Cahoon's Hollow
840. Sarah C. Whorf, Race Point
841. Sophie Kranz, Race Point
842. Susan Stone, Orleans
843. Sylvester Whalen, 1898, Off Race Point
844. Samuel H. Walker, 1888, Chatham
845. Samuel Castner, 1857, Narragansett Pier
846. Shadow, 1891, Orleans
847. Searsville, 1891, Pollock Rip
848. Soolo, 1892, Pollock Rip
849. Storm King, 1892, Pollock Rip
850. Sarah D. Fell, 1894, Pollock Rip
851. Sea Fox, 1895, Billingsgate
852. Silver Dart, 1896, Highland Light
853. St. Nicholas, 1898, Monomoy Point
854. St, San Francisco, 1898, Peaked Hill Bar
855. Sea Bird, 1898, Nauset
856. School Girl, 1898, Provincetown
857. Standard Oil Co. #58, 1899, Race Point
858. Sl, Startle, 1899, Wood End
859. Silver Spray, 1899, Monomoy Point
860. Simon Flake, 1900, Monomoy
861. Silver Spray, 1901, Monomoy
862. Sarah C. Smith, 1901, Race Point
863. Sweepstakes, 1902, Shovelful
864. Sally E. Ludlam, 1902, Handkerchief
865. Br Sc, St. Bernard, 1902, Wood End
866. Sl, Sachem, 1902, Old Harbor
867. Sarah Potter, 1903, Handkerchief
868. S. F. Maker, 1903, Tiny Shoal
869. Sally B, 1895, Monomoy
870. St. Thomas, 1901, Muskeget Shoals
871. Seth M. Todd, 1903, Monomoy Point
872. Silas Might, Narragansett Pier
873. Sarah L., 1868, Near Light Pt. J.
874. Spray, 1869, Narragansett Pier

875. ...., Catumb Reef
876. Sandalphin, 1881, Sugar Reef
877. Sarah W. Blake, 1882, W. Pt. Jud.
878. ...., 1882, Watch Hill
879. Silver Slide, 1882, Point Judith
880. Snowy Daisy, 1883, Block Island
881. Sarah Babcock, 1883, Fishers Island
882. Scow, ..., 1883, Latimers Reef
883. S. C. Noyes, 1884, B. I.
884. Sarah Quinn, 1885, Fishers Island
885. Sl, ..., 1888, Watch Hill
886. Scow, ..., 1888, Pettasquamsett
887. Samuel C. Throp, 1890, S E. Block Island
888. Sl, Stranded, 1890, New Shoreham
889. Sunshine, 1891, Watch Hill
890. Sl, ..., 1891, Pettasquamsett
891. Tug, S. Thomas Brown, 1892, Watch Hill
892. Scow, No. 15 and 17, 1894, Narragansett Pier
893. Bg, Star of the East, 1896, E. Sand Hill Cove
894. Sl, S. L. Parker, 1896, New Shoreham
895. Sl, Sea Serpent, 1896, Block Island
896. Sl, Sharon, 1899, New Shoreham
897. S. S. Silvia, 1897, E. Block Island
898. Sl, Sunnyside, 1899, New Shoreham
899. Storm King, 1900, Block Island
900. Shamrock, 1900, Block Island
901. Swallow, 1900, Pt. Judith
902. Westport, 1900, Brentons Point
903. Sl, Swawa, Napareu Pt.
904. ...... Smith, 1882, Beaver Tail
905. ...., 1868, Kettle Bottom
906. ...., 1867, Shoemakers Place
907. ...., 1852, Shoemakers
908. ...., 1870, D. I. Light
909. ...., 1865, Brentons Reef
910. ...., 1870, Brentons Reef
911. ...., 1870, Brentons Reef
912. ...., 1878, Mackerel Cove
913. Sarah Graham, 1870, N. Beaver Tail
914. ...... Strickland, 1873, Brentons Reef
915. Thrasher, Handkerchief Shoal
916. Nautilus, 1896
917. T. W. Cooper, 1900, N. Coskata L. S. Sta.
918.
919. Barque, Tivoli, 1895, Pollock Rip
920. Thos. W. Hyde, 1893, Shovelful
921. T. B. Garland, 1893, Bearses Shoal
922. Thomas Brumidge, 1898, Race Point
923. Sl, Thomas B. Read, 1898, Provincetown
924. Thomas Brundage, 1899, Shovelful
925. Br Sc, Thos. Holder, 1899, Cahoons Hollow
926. Two Forty, 1901, Race Point
927. Br Sc, Theta, 1901, Peaked Hill
928. Sl, Triton, 1902, Nauset
929. Two Brothers, 1897, Nauset Bar
930. Tryall, Point Judith
931. Tillie E., 1881, Point Judith
932. Thomas R. Pillsbury, 1883, Point Judith
933. Bg, Toronto, 1886, Watch Hill Point
934. Ticker, 1873, Short Beaver Tail
935. Turget, 1860, Kettle Bottom
936. Thos. Borden, 1902, Hyannis Harbor
937. Minque, 1898, Provincetown
938. Venus, 1899, Plymouth
939. Viking, 1902, Monomoy
940. Vicksburg, 1890, Chatham
941. Br Sc, Viola, 1892, Handkerchief
942. St, Vigilant, 1898, Provincetown
943. Victoria, 1875, Pt. Judith
944. Venus, 1877, W. Point Judith
945. Vesta, 1883, Block Island
946. Vraie, 1885, Penguin Shoal
947. Vicksburg, 1886, Catumb Rocks
948. St Sch Yt, Vinita, 1888, Point Judith
949. Van Buren, 1890, New Shoreham
950. Vandalia, 1892, Watch Hill
951. Sl, Valkyrie, 1897, Block Island
952. Vamoose, 1898, Block Island
953. St, Yt, Vulcan, 1902, Quonochontaug
954. W. B. Daisley, Off Chatham
955. William E. Barnes, 1887, Nauset
956. William A. Maillin, Race Point
957. William Emerson, Peaked Hill
958. St, Wergeland, Nauset
959. William Boardman, 1891, Chatham

960. Welcome, Race Point
961. W. P. O'Hara, 1892, Peaked Hill
962. William Smith, Nauset
963. William Garrison
964. Wadena, 1902, Shovelful
965. William Slater, 1888, Chatham
966. W. O. Nettleton, 1898, Coskata
967. William Marshall, 1899, Coscata
968. Barge, Wasp, 1903, Off Clarks Point
969. William L. Burroughs, 1889, Handkerchief
970. William Gillum, 1890, Shovelful
971. Weybosset, 1890, Pollock Rip
972. Whistler, 1893, Provincetown
973. William M. Bird, 1893, Provincetown
974. Welcome R. Beebe, 1896, Cahoons Hollow
975. Br Sc, Walter Miller, 1897, Nauset
976. Willie H. Higgins, 1898, Peaked Hill
977. Wesley Abbott, 1898, Chatham
978. William A. Morse, 1898, Provincetown
979. Winnie Lawry, 1899, Chatham
980. William P. Hood, 1900, Orleans
981. Sl Yt, Wanda, 1900, Highland
982. William H. Oler, 1901, High Head
983. Winnegance, 1899, Muskegat
984. William E. McDonald, 1897, Great Point
985. Warrior, Sand Point
986. Tuice, Point Judith
987. Br Bg, Waywood, Point Judith
988. William S. Scull, 1877, Block Island
989. Wave Crest, 1889, Black Rock
990. Warren Gates, 1883, Point Judith
991. William E. Lee, 1883, S.W. Block Island
992. Wave, 1884, Watch Hill Point
993. William H. Oaks, 1885, Block Island
994. William DeWolf, 1885, Block Island
995. Wild Pigeon, 1886, Block Island
996. William H. Jordan, 1888, Block Island
997. Winnie Lang, 1890, Napatree Point
998. William G. R. Mowry, 1893, Block Island
999. Cat, West Wind, 1895, Spouting Rock Point
1000. Bg, Water Witch, 1896, Sachurst Point
1001. Warsteed, 1896, Quonochontaug
1002. William Rill, 1898, Sandy Point
1003. William Jones, 1871, Kettle Bottom
1004. Willie Perris, 1871-4, Conanicut Point
1004. Yankee Bride, 1891, New Shoreham
1005. Bk, Zulma, 1887, Off Nausett
1006. Zenobia, 1898, Orleans Beach
1007. Zephyr, 1901, Wood End
1008. Zephyr, 1896, N. Block Island
1009. Alma, 1888, Vineyard Haven
1010. Allen Oakes, 1891, Hyannis
1011. Andrew J. York, 1891, Nantucket Light
1012. Angola, 1898, Cross Rip
1013. Ardandhu, 1900, Robinsons Hole
1014. Asa H. Pervere, Monomoy
1015. Addie G. Bryant, 1895, Pollock Rip
1016. St Yt, Alva, 1892, Pollock, Rip
1017. Accasia, 1893, Chatham
1018. Bertha J. Fellows, 1885, Monomoy
1019. Benjamin Gurtside, 1889, Handkerchief
1020. Charles W. Morse, 1898, Newport
1021. Charlott Fish, 1892, Monomoy
1022. Davis Brothers, 1891, Dutch Island Bar
1023. E. C. Willard, 1898, Vinal Haven
1024. E. K. Hart, 1894, Tarpaulin Cove
1025. Barge, Excelsior, 1898, Hill Pond Bar
1026. Frank A. Magee, 1895, Pollock Rip
1027. Florence Nowell, 1893, Pollock Rip
1028. G. M. Farnsworth, 1858, Chatham Roads
1029. Hector, 1898, Vinal Haven
1030. Josiah Whitehouse, 1890, Gay Head
1031. Julia E. Pratt, 1884, Great Point Rip
1032. J. D. Ingraham, 1898, Vinal Haven
1033. Josiah R. Smith, 1895, Cuttyhunk
1034. J. B. Woodbury, 1878, Monomoy
1035. Katie Mitchell, 1893, Bass River
1036. Light of the East, 1894, Kill Pond Bar
1037. Lunet, 1898, Vineyard Haven
1038. Lucy Jones, 1892, Cross Rip
1039. Mary J. Castner, 1894, Pollock Rip

1040. Maria Adilaid, 1890, Cuttyhunk Shore
1041. Mary A. Heaton, 1895, Nauset
1042. Mary B. Smith, 1897, Vinal Haven
1043. Melinda Wood, 1894, Hyannis Bar
1044. Mary E. Oliver, 1891, Vinal Haven
1045. Barge, N. & W. No. 4, Sabines Point
1046. Nellie Doe, 1898, Vinal Haven
1047. O. D. Wetherill, 1894, Hill Pond Bar
1048. Barge, Oneonta, 1895, Pollock Rip
1049. Sl, Ocean Traveller, Shovelfull
1050. Quilp, Cuttyhunk
1051. Royal Arch, 1894, Monomoy
1052. Robert Moir, 1895, Hyannis Bar
1053. R. L. Dewis, 1897, Hedge Fence
1054. Bk, R. A. Allen, 1892, Handkerchief
1055. Stephen Raymond, 1893, Hyannis Harbor
1056. Barge, Shamokin, 1894, Pollock Rip
1057. S. S. Scranton, 1894, Buzzards Bay
1058. S. S. Bickmore, 1890, Hyannis
1059. Sarah L. Simmons, 1889, Pollock Rip
1060. Unknown, 1898, Great Pt.
1061. Unknown, 1895, Sow and Pigs
1062. Unknown, Bishops & Clerks
1063. Unknown, In Nautucket Harbor
1064. Unknown, In Edgartown Harbor
1065. Unknown, Shovelful
1066. White Foam, 1862, Bass River
1067. William Wilson, 1896, Monomoy Point
1068. St, Williamsport, 1902, Pollock Rip
1069. Belle, 1872, Peaked Hill
1070. German Bark, Francis, 1872, Peaked Hill
1071. Horatio Babson, 1876, Peaked Hill
1072. Lucinda Nickerson, 1876, Peaked Hill
1073. Massachusetts, 1877, Peaked Hill
1074. New Zealand, 1872, Pamet River
1075. Sp, Peruvian, 1872, Peaked Hill
1076. Walter Irving, 1878, Monomoy Point
1077. Juliette, 1893, Vineyard Haven
1078. R. H. Shannon, 1893, Vineyard Haven
1079. Nautilus, 1902, Chatham
1080. Unknown, Vineyard Haven
1081. Unknown, Vineyard Haven
1082. Unknown, Vineyard Haven
1083. Unknown, Vineyard Haven
1084. Mattie Atwood, 1887, Nantucket
1085. Alice Oakes, 1885, Nantucket
1086. Unknown, 1885, Nantucket
1087. Bg, Unknown
1088. Vesta R. Gates, 1884, Nantucket
1089. Martha Innis, 1883, Nantucket
1090. Mirrina, 1884, Great Point
1091. Warren Sawyer, 1884, Nantucket
1092. H. T. Townsend, 1885, Tuckernuck Flats
1093. Dolly Varden, 1885, Tuckernuck Flats
1094. Alva, 1885, Tuckernuck Flats
1095. Charles A. Ropes, 1885, Tuckernuck Flats
1096. Sammy Ford, 1885, Tuckernuck Flats
1097. Linden, 1885, Tuckernuck Flats
1098. French Vangilder, 1885, Tuckernuck
1099. Austin Locke, 1885, Nantucket
1100. T. B. Witherspoon, 1886, Nantucket
1101. James Watson, 1887, Nantucket
1102. George B. Ferguson, 1904, Nantucket
1103. Bg, Augola, 1887, Nantucket
1104. Lucy Jones, 1887, Great Point
1105. St, Cannonburg, 1888, Siasconsett
1106. Enola C., 1888, Great Point
1107. David Foss, 1888, Great Point
1108. Bk, Nostin Genetore, 1889, Great Point
1109. Eva B. Douglass, 1890, Nantucket
1110. Bk, Mentor, 1893, Rose and Crown
1111. Laura V. Rose, 1894, Handkerchief
1112. Elmiranda, 1895, Great Point
1113. Barkentine, Culdoon, 1898, Nantucket
1114. St. Elmo, 1898, Nantucket
1115. Vulcan, 1893, Nantucket
1116. Emma, 1899, Hawes Shoal
1117. G. Arthur Lord, 1900, Great Point
1118. M. J. Doley, Nantucket
1119. Richard S. Leaming, Muskegat Channel